P9-DLZ-116

WHAT
COLOR
IS YOUR
PARACHUTE?

"I DON'T HAVE A PARACHUTE OF ANY COLOR."

©ScienceCartoonsPlus.com

50TH ANNIVERSARY

WHAT COLOR IS YOUR PARACHUTE?

YOUR GUIDE TO A LIFETIME OF MEANINGFUL WORK AND CAREER SUCCESS

RICHARD N. BOLLES

WITH KATHARINE BROOKS

2021

TEN SPEED PRESS

California | New York

PUBLISHER'S NOTE

This publication is designed to provide accurate and authoritative information in regard to the subject matter covered. It is sold with the understanding that the publisher is not engaged in rendering professional career services. If expert assistance is required, the service of the appropriate professional should be sought.

Copyright © 2020, 2019, 2018, 2017, 2016, 2015, 2014, 2013, 2012, 2011, 2010, 2009, 2008, 2007, 2006, 2005, 2004, 2003, 2002, 2001, 2000, 1999, 1998, 1997, 1996, 1995, 1994, 1993, 1992, 1991, 1990, 1989, 1988, 1987, 1986, 1985, 1984, 1983, 1982, 1981, 1980, 1979, 1978, 1977, 1976, 1975, 1972, 1970 by the Marciana Bolles Revocable Trust

All rights reserved.
Published in the United States by Ten Speed Press, an imprint of Random House, a division of Penguin Random House LLC, New York.
www.crownpublishing.com
www.tenspeed.com

Ten Speed Press and the Ten Speed Press colophon are registered trademarks of Penguin Random House LLC.

The cartoon on page ii by S. Harris, treasure chest on page 16 by Zdenek Sasek, man with barbell on page 32 by makar, wheelbarrow on 35 by MaKars, the drawings on page 37 and 132 are by Steven M. Johnson, woman in sports clothes on page 69 and woman thinking on 95 is by Hein Nouwens, hand with pen on 113 is by alexblacksea, globe on page 129 by chronicler, hand with cell phone on page 137 by alex74, stack of coins on page 163 by Uncle Leo, musical note icon on page 177 by Muhammad Tajudin, lightbulb icon on page 177 by AB, heart icon on page 177 by il Capitano, leaf icon on page 177 by BlackActurus, book icon on page 177 by beth bolton, medical kit icon on page 177 by Hare Krishna, scale icon on page 177 by Mello, microphone icon on page 177 by andriwidodo, praying hands icon on page 177 by ester barbato, person on page 177 by Andrew Was, cartoon on page 238 by John Kovalic, typewriter on page 241 by AVA Bitter, woman hand with chess piece on page 277 by Maisei Raman, and woman handing man papers on page 291 by Morphart Creation.

Trade Paperback ISBN: 978-1-984-85786-6
Hardcover ISBN: 978-1-9848-5787-3
eBook ISBN: 978-1-9848-5788-0
ISSN: 8755-4658

Printed in the United States of America

Design by Debbie Berne

10 9 8 7 6 5 4 3 2 1

Revised Edition

The wonderful actress Anne Bancroft (1931–2005)
was once loosely quoted as saying about
her husband, Mel Brooks,

*My heart flutters whenever I hear his key
turning in the door, and I think to myself,
Oh goody, the party is about to begin.*

That is exactly how I feel about my wife,
Marci Garcia Mendoza Bolles, God's angel
from the Philippines, whom I fell deeply in love
with, and married on August 22, 2004. What an
enchanted marriage this turned out to be!

—*Richard N. Bolles*

• • •

For those who seek fulfilling and meaningful lives.
And for the career counselors and coaches who help guide them.

Deep appreciation and gratitude to Richard Bolles, who provided,
and continues to provide, the light and the guide.

—*Katharine Brooks*

CONTENTS

Introduction to the 2021 Edition

Why are you reading this book?

Maybe someone recommended it to you. Lots of people do that. While working on this latest edition, I lost count of the number of people who told me "my mother bought it for me" or "a friend used that book—and it worked!"

Maybe you're hoping to change your career, or you're seeking your first job, or you're returning to the workplace after some time away. Maybe recent changes in the economy have forced you to seek a new job—or even a new career field. Whatever your job or career challenge, the highly successful system in *What Color Is Your Parachute?* is your solution. And this new edition has much to offer:

- Updated career advice and information
- Specific guidance on changing careers, no matter your age
- Techniques for winning the mind game of the job search
- Employer-based advice for all aspects of the job search
- Advice for dealing with challenges you fear are holding you back
- Suggestions on how to connect with advocacy groups and others who can support you
- Special tips for job seekers who are introverts
- Updated social media advice, especially for job-search powerhouse LinkedIn
- Helpful rubrics to quickly analyze and improve your resume, cover letter, and LinkedIn profile
- Tips for creating powerful interview stories

- Internet-based job-search techniques and resources that actually work
- Salary and benefits negotiation guidance
- And, of course, the highly popular, successful, and classic Flower Exercise, which has been revised and updated

When *What Color Is Your Parachute?* was first published in 1970, it revolutionized the concept of job hunting. Unlike traditional guides to the job market, it helped job seekers understand themselves first, then find the jobs that fit, using a mix of good-humored advice and practical strategy. Richard N. Bolles also went against conventional wisdom to update the book annually, keeping it constantly relevant to new generations of job hunters facing changing times. By the time Richard passed away, it had become the bestselling job-hunting book in the world, with numerous awards and more than ten million copies published in twenty-two languages.

I have used his books throughout my own career; whether working in human resources at a department store, studying for my master's degree in rehabilitation counseling (where this book was required reading), or providing career counseling and coaching to a broad range of individuals through good and bad economic times. It was an honor to be asked to work on this edition and continue the important tradition of yearly revision.

Much of *What Color Is Your Parachute?* is written in the first person, so throughout this book you will see the word "I." Sometimes it will refer to Richard Bolles; sometimes to me. Most of the time it doesn't matter. Where the ownership of the statement is significant, you'll see (RB) after statements attributable to Richard Bolles and (KB) after statements attributable to Katharine Brooks.

What I love about the Parachute system is the level playing field it provides for all job seekers in every employment sector. In Richard's writings, you see his timeless advice and wisdom in action. His compassion and respect for all workers. His emphasis on the importance of choosing your career and not letting the job market choose it for you. His encouragement to take the time to do a thorough self-evaluation before hitting the job market. And his belief in the importance of all careers, from pipe fitters to harp builders to doctors. With his usual aplomb, he deconstructed the holy grail of every job seeker: a job that fits your passions and fulfills your life mission. And he was quite transparent, practical, and honest in his approach to that search.

On the top of my computer, I have a sticker that reads "This Isn't Career Development. This Is Rocket Fuel." Well, Richard and I don't have a rocket, but we do have a parachute to offer you. A way to land efficiently and happily in this crazy, messy landscape we call the job market. Safe and fulfilling journeys to you all.

—*Katharine "Kate" Brooks*

"Go and get your things," he said.
"Dreams mean work."

—PAULO COELHO

CHAPTER 1

WELCOME TO THE EVER-CHANGING WORLD OF THE JOB SEARCH

If you are trying to better understand yourself, and what you have to offer to the world, this book is for you.

If the recent turmoil created by the COVID-19 virus has impacted your work situation, this book is for you.

If you are out of work and want practical help, this book is for you.

If you are trying to understand how the world, and particularly the world of work, really works these days, this book is for you.

If you've been out of work a long time, and you think you're now permanently unemployable, this book is for you.

If you're on the edge of poverty these days, this book is for you.

If you're dealing with a disability, this book is for you.

If you're trying to figure out a new career or your first career, this book is for you.

If you are trying to figure out what you want to do next with your life, this book is for you.

If you're trying to find a better work/life balance, this book is for you.

If you're stuck in your role and need a way out, this book is for you.

If you're just graduating from college and have to live with your parents because you can't find any work, this book is for you.

If you're trying to start your own business, this book is for you.

If you're a returning vet, this book is for you.

If you're facing retirement and want to know what to do to support yourself, this book is for you.

A Quick Crash Course on the World of Work

Job markets are fickle. For some people, a lot of people, the past few years have been a great economic period with lots of opportunities. But recent developments related to COVID-19 changed the employment landscape for many industries. Even without the health-related impact, industries and jobs are changing rapidly. Depending on your career field, you may find lots of opportunities or very few. The process of finding a job seems overwhelming. Many a job seeker says, *"Out of work. Made up a resume. Sent it to all the places I'm supposed to. Went to all the internet 'job boards' and looked for vacancies in my field. Day after day. Week after week. Month after month. All of this worked the last time I went job hunting. But now? Strikeout! Nothing!"*

That's because writing a resume and using job boards isn't enough. Job-hunting methods change depending on what you're seeking, and the whole system has become more sophisticated. You need to look at the process through the eyes of the employer and adjust your strategy. While the general process of getting a job hasn't changed that much, the methods for searching have.

The good news is, no matter what the job market is doing, you are in charge. This is your search, and you get to control how it goes. Not everything, of course. But more than you think. That's what this book is all about. Here's what you need to keep in mind as you begin your search.

There Are Jobs Out There

Let's start with some good news: on average over the past few years, there have been between six and seven million vacancies available each month.[1] If you're currently out of work and looking for a job, this may seem unbelievable. You may feel you are up against overwhelming forces, that the situation you face is rather hopeless. Certainly the effect of COVID-19 has thrown any previous statistics about job vacancies out the window. The job market is likely to be volatile until the health crisis is resolved.

You may have struck out, again and again. It may feel like the opportunities aren't out there, but they are. You just need a better strategy for finding them.

How do we even know what the job market is doing? Basically, there are two government reports that tell us (and the media) how the job market looks. The Employment Situation Summary published by the Bureau of Labor Standards (www.bls.gov/cps) tells us the unemployment rate. This report, issued monthly, also tells you what the unemployment rate is in different sectors of the economy. A second government report, the Job Openings and Labor Turnover Survey (JOLTS; www.bls.gov/jlt), tells you how many jobs are open in any given month. You can always use these website addresses to find the latest numbers.

Of course, the question for us when we're out of work is, "If there are jobs available each month, why can't I get one of them?" That's the subject of the rest of this book.

Many Jobs Are Being Reimagined

Have you heard the term "disruption"? It's everywhere, thanks to the internet and the technology boom of robotics, artificial intelligence (AI), issues related to the pandemic, and so on. Virtually no workplace has been unaffected by changes wrought by technology and current events which have positive but also negative effects on the job seeker. The long-term effects of COVID-19 on the workplace remain to be seen, but the increase in working-from-home opportunities may signal a greater increase in virtual workplaces. There are also cultural changes brought on by the increasing diversity of the workplace, and economic changes from the increased emphasis on the bottom line and profit, even in non-profit areas. Many doctors, lawyers, and even college professors lament that their professions are more like businesses these days. With the rise in artificial intelligence and computers that can perform jobs previously held by humans, we each need to look at our own industry and position to determine how at-risk we are for a "disruption."

Many industries have already felt the impact of AI and robotics. Certain jobs—such as cashiers, bank tellers, telemarketers, receptionists, and assembly line workers—have been replaced by machines, robots, and online technology. The transportation industry has been visibly disrupted, with commercial taxis and shuttles being replaced by Ubers and Lyfts. And there will likely be disruption for Uber and Lyft drivers, not to mention truck drivers, when driverless vehicles become commonplace.

At the same time, many aspects of the workplace will remain the same, and not every job will be replaced by robots and artificial intelligence. A Pew Research Center report on robotics offers hope in that technology often creates new jobs while reducing old jobs. And technology can reduce the drudgery of many jobs, opening the opportunity for more interesting and innovative jobs.[2]

Robots and related technology will not eliminate all jobs; rather, they will tackle certain tasks within jobs. This means that most jobs are going to become a partnership between people and machines. Large segments of the world of work will not see or feel this reimagination until some years down the road; other parts are already seeing it, or will see it soon. We must begin—now—to reimagine our own lives in the world of work and get comfortable with the idea of future jobs as a partnership between people and machines.

It's Always *Your* Job Search

You are not powerless during the job hunt, regardless of whether the job market is strong or weak. Of course, employers have significant power in the process. But that doesn't mean they hold all the power. You have the ability to compete in the job market and, armed with the techniques in this book, to approach the job search in a powerful and professional manner, no matter what occupational field you're in or what job you are seeking. You have control over the quality of your job search materials, the research you conduct, the interviews and networking you do, and virtually every other step in the process. You also get to define what "success" is for you. For some people it's a title, prestige, or money. For others it's serving a purpose or finding meaning. Sometimes it's all of those factors. However you define career success (and we will examine that later), the good news is you control a lot of this process. Knowing that the employer has the ability to say yes or no can make you feel powerless, but that's all the more reason to take charge of your search.

A comprehensive research study[3] found that you can at least double your chances of success in your job search by doing six things:

- Mastering job search skills
- Improving the way you present yourself in interviews and elsewhere
- Being more aware of and confident about your skills
- Taking action
- Setting goals
- Getting help when needed

In other words, the mere act of reading this book and completing the exercises has the potential to more than double your odds of success in the job search!

As you go along in this process, the key word you're looking for is employability. *Am I employable? And how can I make myself more employable?* That's the purpose of this book: to make yourself as strong— and employable—a candidate as possible for the industries you're interested in.

Employers and Job Hunters View the Job Search Differently

So we know there are jobs out there, but here's where the challenge begins. Job hunters and employers don't approach the search in the same way. The rules of engagement for each side are different, and in some ways employers and job seekers speak different languages. We think we have contacted an employer correctly with an email and attached resume; what we didn't know was that employer accepts resumes only through a website and won't open emails. We "follow the rules": write resumes, create cover letters, use employment agencies, and/or respond to online job postings and websites.

But employers don't always reach for resumes first. They prefer to hire people they know or have a strong connection to, so when an opportunity opens up they are more likely to look within their company or seek a recommendation from someone within their company. An unsolicited resume from a stranger isn't going to be as appealing. The chart on the facing page provides a great summary of the difference between how employers prefer to seek new employees and how most job hunters look for jobs.

We also have different expectations of each other. Here are some ways that employers and job seekers differ:

- **You want the job market to be a hiring game, but the employer regards it as an elimination game—until the very last phase.** Larger companies or organizations are looking at that huge stack of resumes on their desk, with a view—first of all—to finding out who they can eliminate. On average, a job posting receives hundreds of responses or resumes. But employers want to interview only a few candidates. Getting that stack of resumes down to a manageable number is the employer's first preoccupation.

- **You want the employer to take the initiative to find you.** And when they are desperate they will (*especially if you have applied math and technical skills!*). Some HR departments will spend hours and days combing the internet looking for the right person. But generally speaking, the employer prefers that it be you who takes the initiative to find them.

Many If Not Most Employers Hunt for Job Hunters in the Exact Opposite Way from How Most Job Hunters Hunt for Them

THE WAY A TYPICAL EMPLOYER PREFERS TO FILL A VACANCY

1 **6**

From Within

Promotion of a full-time employee, or promotion of a present part-time employee, or hiring a former consultant for in-house or contract work, or hiring a former "temp" full-time. Employer's thoughts: "*I want to hire someone whose work I have already seen.*" (A low-risk strategy for the employer.)

Implication for Job Hunters: See if you can get hired as a temp, contract worker, or consultant at an organization you have chosen—aiming at a full-time position only later (or not at all).

2 **5**

Using Proof

Hiring an unknown job hunter who brings proof of what he or she can do in terms of the skills needed.

Implication for Job Hunters: If you are a programmer, bring a program you have done—with its code; if you are a photographer, bring photos; if you are a counselor, bring a case study with you; and so on.

3 **4**

Using a Best Friend or Business Colleague

Hiring someone whose work a trusted friend of yours has seen (perhaps they worked for him or her).

Implication for Job Hunters: Find someone who knows the person-who-has-the-power-to-hire at your target organization, who also knows your work and will introduce you two.

4 **3**

Using an Agency They Trust

This may be a recruiter or search firm the employer has hired or a private employment agency—both of which have checked you out, on behalf of the employer.

5 **2**

Using an Ad They Have Placed

(Online or in newspapers and the like.)

6 **1**

Using a Resume

Even if the resume was unsolicited (if the employer is desperate).

THE WAY A TYPICAL JOB HUNTER PREFERS TO FILL A VACANCY

- **In being considered for a job, you want your solid past performance (summarized on your written resume) to be all that gets weighed.** However, the employer weighs your whole presentation, including your social media profile(s) and what they assess from your interview or other interactions with you.

- **You want the employer to acknowledge receipt of your resume—particularly if you post it right on their website**—but employers generally are too swamped with other things to have time to do that, so very few do. Most employers, for legal and other reasons, do not. Now that you know this, don't take it personally.

Why are these strategies so contrary to each other? Values. Job hunters and employers have completely different values during their search.

Employers' main value/concern is **risk**.

Job hunters' main value/concern is **time**.

Let me explain.

We job hunters want strategies that will enable us to cover as much of the job market as possible, in the least amount of time. So our value is **time**. Our chosen vehicle is a resume. We want to write it, or have it written for us, then be able to spread it across a vast landscape, with a click of the mouse.

The employer's chief value, on the other hand, concerns **risk**. The employer wants to hire the person who is the lowest possible risk. I mean *the risk that this hire won't work out*. And hiring the wrong worker can be costly to an organization. The cost isn't only financial. A bad hire can hurt employee morale, threaten teamwork and productivity, and even damage an organization's reputation.[4]

This information should help you understand why it's imperative that you adjust your job-hunting technique to fit the employer's needs. Again, this book will help you do just that.

It's Hard to Predict How Long the Job Hunt Will Take

An old formula used to say that for every $10,000 in salary, expect to spend one month looking for the position. This means if you hope to earn $50,000 you can expect to take five months to find a job. This isn't accurate anymore, but there is an interesting correlation between time on the search and the compensation for the position. Many minimum-wage jobs can be found rather quickly, even in a poor economy. But the higher the compensation and the more competition comes into play, the longer the search will take. That is, unless the skill set needed for the position is rare.

You really have no idea what might be going on behind the scenes in an organization's selection process. Often searches take longer than the employer expects as well. Sometimes the funding for a position is withdrawn. Or there's a decision to postpone hiring due to internal issues. Vacations, holidays, and so on can play havoc with interview scheduling. The bottom line is that there are factors influencing the length of time for a job search—many of which you'll never know.

Recent reports from the Department of Labor indicate that for about 30 percent of job seekers, the length of the job search is one to three months. For 14 percent of job seekers, it can take three to six months, and 21 percent indicated their search took over six months.[5]

Keep in mind when you see unemployment rates that not everyone taken into account wants to be in the labor force, for the time being. Some people are either discouraged about the job market (that's 453,000 people) or may be outside the labor force for other reasons (1,225,000 people), such as school or family responsibilities, ill health, or transportation problems.[6]

Long-term unemployment (more than one year) is a more complex situation. There are often other factors that go into someone's unemployment lasting over a year. Even if you've been out of work by choice, getting back into the workplace has its special challenges and can be discouraging unless you have honed your job-hunting skills. It's imperative to make sure your skills are current and appropriate for the economic times. If you've been job-seeking for more than a year without success, that's a clear sign that whatever you are doing isn't working. It's time for a course correction. This book will help you correct your course and find new energy and hope.

You Will Likely Not Stay in One Job for a Long Time

You may have parents or grandparents who stayed with one job or one company for many years. But the time spent in one job has been decreasing over the past few decades. Of jobs that workers found between ages eighteen and twenty-four, 69 percent lasted less than a year and 93 percent lasted less than five years. *Ah, youth,* we think to ourselves. No, it's not a matter of youth; even at jobs that workers found between the time they were thirty-five and forty-four, 36 percent lasted less than a year, and 75 percent lasted less than five years.[7]

Many factors go into the likelihood you'll stay with same job for many years, from personal decisions (family to support or care for; children who don't want to move) to field of employment (tenure for teachers; union membership) to the monetary value and desirability of your skill set. Some fields require that you move around to move up or gain a better salary. When you change jobs by choice, you often can obtain a much higher salary than you would if you remained in the lockstep salary plans of your present employer.

A 2018 Pew Research analysis of census data found that more than a third of the workforce is now made up of millennials, and they are changing the career landscape.[8] As a group, they are much more likely to seek a better work culture, and they are willing to move to find that culture.

In general, full-time jobs (usually defined as working more than thirty-five hours a week) are getting harder and harder to find. This is frustrating for many workers who would like to work full-time. The number of people with part-time jobs who really want to work full-time currently numbers 5,060,000.[9]

As a result, a lot of job hunters have redefined what they're looking for. Some *seek* shorter-term jobs, often just for the length of a project, or whatever the parameter may be, to increase their flexibility.

The number of temp or part-time jobs continues to rise as more employers hire workers for short-term projects or specific tasks. An entire sector of the job market includes people who really only want short-term jobs, such as independent contractors, consultants, freelancers, and contract workers. This trend was first made famous by Daniel Pink in his 2001 book, *Free Agent Nation*.[10] Currently, part-time workers in the US total 27,551,000 (that's 17.2 percent of all those employed, right now). By all accounts, the number and percentage of freelance workers is expected to grow every year. The increase in freelance work and work-from-home opportunities created by COVID-19 is likely to continue long beyond the pandemic, as employers and workers discover the advantages of working remotely.

The reason for this increase in temporary hiring, as you've probably guessed, is employers' desire to keep their costs down. In the face of the global economy and online competition, employers across the country (and, indeed, across the world) have developed a budget-friendly strategy, hiring only when they need help, and letting the employee go as soon as they don't need that help.[11] Not to mention that part-timers don't have to be paid any benefits or granted paid vacation time. Indeed, 20 to 30 percent of those employed by the Fortune 100 now have short-term jobs, either as independent contractors or as temp workers, and this figure is predicted to rise to 50 percent during the next six years. Employers in the IT industry, in particular, are increasingly hiring someone for the time it takes to complete a project, rather than permanently hiring that person. Even in industries where people are hired allegedly for longer periods, employers are much more ready to cut the size of their workforce just as soon as things even begin to look bad. You thought you were being hired for a number of years—they said that, they meant that—but then fortunes change, and suddenly you're back out on the street, job hunting once again.

You Are Always Job Hunting

Given that jobs don't last as long as they used to, we may be job hunting again, sooner than we think. How often? In a study released August 24, 2017, by the US Department of Labor, it was revealed that the average person in the US born between 1957 and 1964 held 11.9 jobs between the ages of eighteen and fifty.[12] A recent blog post in *The Muse* indicated that 58 percent of its millennial user-base planned to change jobs in 2019. Job seekers are increasingly willing to move to find better opportunities.[13] Job hunting is no longer an optional exercise. It is a survival skill. This means the one thing in our life that we must get really skilled at, and become masters of, is the *new* job hunt.

Job Hunting Is Increasingly Online
(But You Still Need People Skills)

As ever-larger portions of the job search can be done online, your computer is your best ally in the process, so take full advantage of its power. Whether you use a word processor to create a targeted resume and upload that resume to a job board or website, use email to communicate with potential employers or your network, or develop your social media profile on LinkedIn, your computer can help you every step of the way. As social media and other sites have become ingrained into our daily lives—LinkedIn, Facebook, Twitter, Instagram, Pinterest, WhatsApp, Zoom, YouTube, and the like—job hunters and employers have figured out how to use them in the job hunt. In fact, you can use free project management software such as Trello (https://trello.com) to organize and set up all the steps of your search. And, of course, you aren't limited to your computer. Your smartphone and "wearables" such as watches all can help you with your search. Many employers now text job candidates instead of using email.

Note: Some readers may not be all that comfortable with the latest online and smartphone technology. Consider asking (or hiring) a computer-savvy family member or friend to help. Your local library can be particularly helpful: most libraries have public computers you can use and often offer classes related to computers. Taking the time to learn about and be more comfortable with a wide range of computer skills can help immeasurably in your search and on the job.

The internet is an invaluable source of information for your job search. Job seekers often lament that they would like to do something else but don't know what's out there. Well, the internet pretty much answers that question. One of the best ways to determine what jobs are posted these days is to search the key job boards, websites, and social media sites. Many employers now post openings on Facebook, Twitter, and Instagram and elsewhere—or at least they post the announcement of the posting, which you can then find on their website. You may or may not end up applying for positions from these sites, but if nothing else they will help you learn more about job descriptions and better understand the type of work that might interest you. You will also quickly learn the language of that workplace: the terminology in the job listing will help you formulate a better application. So try it out. This topic will be covered in depth later, but for the moment, think about an industry of interest, a job title you're considering, or even a geographic area you'd like to move to. Search these sites and see what you learn:

- **Indeed.com** is a mega job board that finds thousands of openings in every field or industry across the country.

- **Proven.com**, a site for employers, provides a list of the best job boards for job seekers at this address: https://blog.proven.com /100-best-job-boards-to-find-niche-talent.

- **Niche job boards** can help you find job vacancies in particular fields or industries. For instance, if you're interested in media-related jobs, Mashable.com is worth a look (https://jobs.mashable.com/). For a listing of a variety of opportunities from health care to finance to bilingual, visit www.good.co/blog/list-of-100-niche-job-boards.

- **Company job boards** on their website can be a terrific resource, particularly if you know what companies you are interested in. Always wanted to work at Walt Disney World? Their casting center is almost always hiring (https://parksjobs.disneycareers.com/walt-disney-world-resort). Just go to any company's website and look for a link to "careers," "jobs," or "opportunities." If you can't find anything, look for their human resources page. Just know that what is posted might be the tip of the iceberg (more on that later).

- **Age-related job boards** are another option if you fall into a specific category such as teenager or over fifty. If you're a teenager, check out http://readyjob.org/companies-hire-teens. Or if you are an experienced worker over fifty: check out AARP's job board at https://jobs.aarp.org/.

One word of warning as you investigate job search boards: don't get scammed. The job search process is fraught with misstatements, lies, and outright fraud. Be especially careful of job opportunities advertised on general websites where anyone can place an ad, such as Craigslist or Reddit. While these sites contain lots of legitimate opportunities, scammers do get through sometimes. Do not pursue any job opportunity where you are asked to cash/deposit a check, wire money to anyone, or otherwise engage in unusual monetary transactions. Be suspicious of "training fees" or charges to do a background search. Do not complete online applications requiring your address, social security number, and other private information until you are 100 percent sure it is a legitimate opportunity.

This is just a start to give you an idea of all the opportunities in your area of interest. Just remember that despite our increasing reliance on computers for much of the job search, you will still need to meet people and develop your communication skills throughout the job search process.

What You Need to Succeed in the Job Search

There's plenty of research on what makes a successful career search, but what we have learned might surprise you. A previously mentioned research study identified several key elements for a successful job search, including the ability to set goals, take action, develop confidence, and improve your self-presentation. But some research points to another important factor for success in the search: self-compassion. It's easy to get down on yourself for being less than perfect, or to compare yourself to others and find yourself lacking. It's important to take care of yourself throughout this process. Set up rewards for taking action, regardless of the outcome. Seek support when you need it. Silence the inner critic and focus on gratitude and what went well each day.

You know that the world of work is constantly changing and you will need to keep up with what's changing in the job search. In today's world, the person who gets hired is not necessarily the one who can do that job best; rather, it's the one who knows the most about how to get hired.

So, we are going to have to learn new skills to survive in this reimagined world. We must begin by knowing ourselves better. Imagine you are hiking in a wilderness and find a strong running stream suddenly swirling around your feet; your first instinct would be to find something solid to stand on, before you get swept off your feet. In the midst of all this reimagining that is swirling around you, taking an inventory of yourself will give you that "something solid to stand on." A good self-inventory form can be found in this book, in chapters 5 and 6. Knowing who you are, what you like and do best, what kindles your brain, and what enables you to do your best work has never been more important than in this reimagined workplace that is already here. Don't ignore this step in your job search.

Then we must ask ourselves, *How will I fit in, in this disrupted world where jobs are increasingly becoming partnerships between people and machines?* For some of you, these are exciting times. You love technology and can't wait for the latest development. For others, you will have to reimagine your attitude toward artificial intelligence, and start thinking of machines (including robots) as friends come to help us with certain tasks, not as enemies come to steal our jobs away. By the end of this book, you will have a strong grasp of where you will fit best and how to get there most efficiently and effectively.

If you learn new advanced job-hunting skills, you can not only survive, but thrive. The rest of this book is devoted to showing you exactly how to do that.

I am not lucky. You know what I am?
I am smart, I am talented, I take advantage
of the opportunities that come my way, and
I work really, really hard. Don't call me lucky.
Call me a badass.

—SHONDA RHIMES

CHAPTER 2

THE JOB SEARCH IS A MIND GAME: HERE ARE TEN WAYS TO WIN

The job search is hard work. You may be out of work right now. You might have been laid off or fired. Maybe you're stuck or unhappy in your current job. Unemployment or feeling disconnected from your work can take a terrible toll on your spirit. In a study of over six thousand job hunters, interviewed every week for up to twenty-four weeks, it was found that the longer someone is unemployed, the more their life satisfaction declines, and their levels of anxiety and sadness rise.[14]

I (RB) know this from my own experience. I have been fired twice in my life. I remember how it felt each time I got the lousy news. I walked out of the building dazed, as though I had just emerged from a really bad train wreck. The sun was shining brightly, not a cloud in the sky; and, since it was lunch hour, as it happened, the streets were filled with laughing, happy people who apparently had not a care in the world.

I remember thinking, *The world has just caved in—my world, at least. How can all these people act as though nothing has happened?*

And I remember the feelings. The overwhelming feelings, which only intensified in the weeks after that. Describe my state however you want— feeling sad, being in a funk, feeling despair, feeling hopeless, feeling like things "will always be this way," or feeling depressed—it doesn't matter. I was terribly unhappy. Unemployment was rocking my soul to its foundations. I needed to know what to do about my feelings.

I have since learned that my experience was not in the least unusual. Many of us, if not most of us, when we are out of work for a long time feel weary and depressed. Our greatest desire is to get rid of these depressed feelings. And fortunately there are ways to do this.

Ten Ways to Stay Resilient in the Job Search

I saw a bumper sticker the other day that said, "Don't Believe Everything You Think." What a wonderful reminder that our thoughts aren't always our friends. We tend to trust what we're thinking, and most of the time we can. But not always. We often have an over-sharer in our head that would like to remind us of every mistake we have made, or when we were less than perfect, or why we won't be perfect in the future. Just because you think something doesn't make it true. So when your thoughts are working against you, remember they are just thoughts. You can change them. You can focus on more positive thoughts instead.

The more you know about how you are thinking, the more you can challenge negative thoughts that are holding you back and shift your focus to more positive thoughts that will propel you forward. You will develop what psychologists call "resilience": the ability to cope with discouraging situations and challenges in our lives. By taking on the challenges of a job search, you are demonstrating your resiliency and ability to cope with challenges.

At a workshop I (KB) was running for individuals who had recently been laid off from the tech industry, I asked the participants to complete a mind-map exercise examining their lives. A woman on crutches approached me in tears. She told me that not only had she recently been laid off, but her husband had left her and she'd broken her ankle when she tripped off a curb. She simply couldn't see anything positive in her situation. On one level she's correct: she has experienced a lot of negative events. But I looked at her and said, "And yet, here you are. You could have used every legitimate excuse in the book not to come to this job-search program today. You could have stayed on your couch watching TV, and no one would have blamed you. Instead, you chose to be here. I'd like you to look at the map you just created and think about other times in your life where you have overcome obstacles." She started smiling and went back to her seat, where she wrote furiously about her life from a new perspective. You can do the same.

We can shift our focus and change the way we think about our situation. Here are ten ways to do this (with suggested resources). Keep in mind that different suggestions will appeal at different times, so try one that fits for now and come back later to try a different one.

1. Take care of your body and mind by getting adequate sleep.

Do this even if it means taking naps during the day because your attempts to sleep at nighttime are, at the moment, a disaster. We tend to feel depressed if we are short on our sleep, or our body is otherwise run-down.

There are two states that can be easily confused: The world never looks bright or happy to us when we are very short on sleep. And the world never looks bright or happy to us when we are feeling depressed.

It is easy to confuse these two feeling-states. Over the years, I have seen many job hunters who thought they were depressed over their situation only to later discover they were depressed just because they were so tired. Or a bit of both. Anyway, sleep or nap, we often turn into happier, more upbeat people, just by catching up on our sleep. This can make us feel better—sometimes much better.

2. Keep yourself physically fit and healthy.

Job hunters have told me they found it important to get regular exercise, even if it's just a daily walk. Seeing green trees, sunlight, mountains, flowers, and other people and their pets can all do wonders for your mood. You should also see your doctor as needed, and keep up with annual physicals and medical tests. Eat healthy meals, and treat yourself with a favorite food item when you can. Be sure to drink plenty of water each day, because dehydration can affect your mood. Try cutting back or eliminating as much sugar as possible from your diet.

3. Treat yourself kindly.

For many years, job search research focused on the importance of self-esteem and confidence (also called self-efficacy) as the key factors in a successful search. But another finding has recently emerged: the importance of self-compassion. How do you talk to yourself when you're in this process? I'll bet you say things to yourself you would never say to a friend. Self-compassion involves telling yourself some key phrases focusing on your safety, your health, your happiness, and your peace of mind. When you are feeling anxious, for example, instead of berating yourself or fighting your feelings of anxiety, try a suggestion from Dr. Chris Germer (https://chrisgermer.com/mindful-path-self-compassion/). Tell yourself, "Just afraid." Maybe shrug your shoulders when you say this, to emphasize, "No big deal." Because that's what anxiety is: fear. By soothing yourself, normalizing your feelings (everyone feels afraid at times, and the job search can be scary), and giving yourself permission to feel without judgment, you become your own support system. Building a strong support network is another way to show self-compassion.

Here's a fun way to treat yourself kindly: Go on fun mini-adventures. Look for inexpensive places like parks. Often there are portions of our surroundings that we have never explored, but a tourist would hit on the very first day they were there. I (RB) lived in New York City for a long time; never once went up in the Empire State Building. I lived in San Francisco for years; never once went out to the zoo. You get the point. If I lived in either of these cities today and was unemployed for any length of time, I would set out to visit places I'd never seen. Seek out supportive friends to take along on these adventures or to boost your mood when you most need it. We can stop obsessing about how much we lost from our past and turn our face toward the future. There are new worlds to conquer, after all.

4. Believe that your behavior matters.

What you do makes a difference. Many people who have given up simply believe that they can't do it. They feel helpless and have lost hope for their own future. Feeling overwhelmed by the changes in your industry or workplace can increase feelings of helplessness. You might be interested to learn about the work of Dr. Martin Seligman, an expert on "learned helplessness." He studied how people (and animals) become helpless in certain situations, particularly when they feel they have no control of the circumstances or the outcome. After years of studying this, Dr. Seligman suddenly turned his research around and started studying "learned optimism"; that is, how we can learn to be optimistic in the same way we learned to be helpless. And we can. Dr. Seligman's book *Learned Optimism* can teach you how to think differently. He also offers a free optimism assessment (you just have to register). Go to https://www.authentichappiness.sas.upenn.edu/ and find the Optimism Test under "Questionnaires."

So feeling helpless is a state of mind that you can change. It starts by recognizing that if anyone has the power to make changes in your life, it is you. Because it is your life. You start by recognizing the challenges you are facing and then take action to overcome them. What you choose to do matters, and you need to believe that. It will make a difference in your life. Simply asking yourself, *What actions would I take if my behavior counted?* can start you on a new path.

5. Develop a flexible mindset by reframing your situation.

Change your perception of reality by selecting what you focus on. This is not wishful thinking or the power of attraction. You don't think of a new job and magically it appears. Rather, you combine hard work with the belief that you can be successful. There's a system of thinking called "appreciative inquiry" that operates on several key principles.

The first is that we create our reality. This doesn't mean denying what is going on in your life, but rather pointing out that you can choose what aspects of your life to focus on. Another principle states that since we can choose what to focus on, choose the positive aspects. Finally, a third principle tells us to ask ourselves better questions to get better answers. So instead of asking yourself, *Why is this job search so hard?* or *Why can't I get more done?* try asking yourself, *What would I like to see more of in my life now?* or *What would I like to focus on today to move my job search forward?*

Where have you succeeded in the past? If you currently have a job or have held a job in the past, you must have done something right to get that job. What other times have you set goals and achieved them? I know this might sound a little silly, but it's important to remind yourself. We tend to forget all that we have accomplished and focus on what we didn't get done.

Do you have a tendency to feel anxious about the job search? Are you anxious in interviews or when approaching a possible network connection? What if you reframe your anxiety as *energy*? You do feel more jazzed up when you're anxious, right? What if instead of worrying about your anxiety, you focused on how much energy you have to do this particular task? Energy is a good thing to convey to a potential employer.

If you tend to focus on what's not working, consider making a gratitude list. Write down two to three things you're grateful for today, and then do it again tomorrow, and the next day. Make it a mental game to see how many things you notice during the day that you can be grateful for. Just don't create a lot of rules around this list. The latest research tells us that gratitude lists lose their effect (which is powerful, by the way) if we turn them into a chore by requiring ourselves to write them every day. Try making a list for a week and then stop. Continue it only when you want to.

Focus on other people instead of yourself. If your unemployment or job search is dragging on and on, and you're starting to have a lot of time on your hands, find someplace in town that is serving people worse off than you are, and go volunteer there. I'm talking food banks, hospitals, housing aid—that sort of thing. You can do a search on Google, put in the name of your town or city plus the name of the problem you want to help with, and see what turns up. If you determine to help someone else in need while you're unemployed, you won't feel so discarded by society.

6. Let your mind wander and envision a new future.

Another principle of appreciative inquiry is that *images inspire action*. When we envision a positive future, we are more likely to move toward it. Take some time to meditate and think about what an ideal future would look like to you. Focus on the opportunity you have to advance your career, to find a new career path, to learn something new about yourself. To make your vision clearer, try making a list. In several of her books, author Julia Cameron recommends that you create a list of twenty-five things you like. She then uses her list to help her make decisions about her life. If you are picturing gloom and doom in your future, keep this in mind: *you are not a fortune-teller*. In complex situations, such as job-seeking, it is hard to predict future outcomes. You might meet someone tomorrow who will lead you to your next job. So focus on positive possibilities: what might happen. And then work and do everything in your power to make that positive dream real.

Consider making a vision board or put up pictures of the success you're seeking. Clip pictures from magazines or the internet that visually express what you're hoping to achieve. Find words or quotes that empower you. There's nothing magical here; making a vision board isn't going to magically produce the job. But what it will do, if you look at it every day, is remind yourself of what's meaningful and important to you. You can then decide what steps you will take that day to bring yourself closer to your goal.

7. Harness the power of goal setting.

One way to focus on a positive reality and future is to set meaningful goals. Think of steps you could take (even baby steps) that would improve your situation. Can you set some goals that are relatively easy to accomplish? Be sure to write them down and then cross them off as you complete them. There is no feeling like the satisfaction of crossing items off your to-do list—wouldn't you agree? I like to give myself a little edge in the process by jotting down a task I just completed before I started writing my list. Then I can cross that off right away. Just knowing that I have already done something toward my goals for the day gives me a boost as I look at the other tasks yet to be accomplished. If you're setting goals for your job search, maybe write "Purchase copy of *What Color Is Your Parachute?*" You've already done that, so you get to cross it off. Maybe even set another goal of "Start reading *What Color Is Your Parachute?*" Guess what? Cross that off, too. Don't you feel better already? This may sound silly, but it's based in research, so give it a try.

One goal to set is to complete the Flower Exercise in this book (see page 111). This exercise alone will help you feel more empowered and focused and will help you find the meaning in what you're doing. Completing each step of the flower puts you one step closer to your dream job and gives you more self-awareness and confidence.

Focus on the units of your search, not the whole task at once. That's why books have chapters. You don't have to read and do everything in one sitting. You can set smaller goals of a chapter at a time—even an exercise at a time. Be reasonable with your to-do list. Some experts even suggest a "to-don't" list: items that you hope to do soon but that just aren't reasonable to do today. This can help with feeling overwhelmed when you look at your list. Keep it focused on the one or two or three things you *can* do today—not all the things you need to do eventually.

8. Avoid procrastination.

If you find yourself procrastinating, here's a great word to learn: resistance. Resistance is at the heart of our procrastination. It seems illogical: you want a job, so you should do all you can to get that job. Right? Well, the problem is that the more important something is to us, the more likely we are to resist it. Because we want it to be perfect. We're afraid we will fail. We're afraid of rejection. So we resist. Writers can be champion resisters: there's nothing worse than that blank page or computer screen. Several excellent books have been written about resistance, and I encourage you to read one if this is an issue for you. One favorite is *Do the Work* by Stephen Pressfield. Mr. Pressfield is a former Marine who has struggled with resistance for much of his writing life. He has excellent suggestions for getting past it, including a wonderful phrase: "turning pro." He says that creating the mindset of "turning pro" (becoming professional) will help us overcome our natural reticence. He compares a "pro" to an "amateur." A professional will take themself and their work seriously. An amateur won't. A professional will do the work that is needed to get the job done well. An amateur won't.

Think about it: how could you "turn pro" in your job search? How can you show yourself at your best throughout the process? How can you take yourself and your job search seriously? Every section of this book will help you do that if you follow the suggestions. Take note and perhaps write down any triggers that might pull you off the job-search path. What distracts you from your progress? What could you do to lessen those distractions?

9. Expand your mental horizons and learn something new.
Read up on subjects that have always interested you, but you've never had enough time to explore. Visit your local public library for books, CDs, DVDs, and online resources. If your library card isn't current, get a new one. You'd be amazed at the wealth of resources libraries offer these days beyond traditional books.

If you can't think of any subject, there's always self-improvement and the human mind. Your mind, afer all, is working hard to figure out what to do next. The more we understand it, the better we can heal. If you're looking for suggestions, I'd read anything by Martin Seligman. I've already recommended *Learned Optimism*, which, as one reviewer commented, "vaulted me out of my funk." It has excellent chapters on dealing with depression. Or there's Seligman's 2012 book *Flourish*. Psychologist David Burns's excellent book *Feeling Good* has been clinically proven to improve both depression and anxiety. Many self-help authors have lots of videos on YouTube if you'd prefer to listen rather than read.

Speaking of videos, there are millions of *free* videos, podcasts, webinars, and so on online, where you can learn just about anything. You can type the format you prefer, plus the subjects that interest you, into your favorite search engine, such as Google, and then pick through whatever turns up. There are also, of course, books. From online bookstores, there are tons of ebooks available, running around ten bucks, or a little more. You can also enroll in low-cost online classes through Udemy (www.udemy.com) or other online vendors.

10. Find positive ways to channel your frustrations or anger.

Exercising to the point of exhaustion can be a great way to burn off the excess energy and anxiety you're feeling. Go for a run. Walk the dog. Jump rope. Some people find it helpful to punch a pillow or a punching bag to get the angry energy out. It's astonishing how many of the unemployed have told me (RB) this actually helps them get rid of some of their anger. And this helps lift our depression as well. Sometimes feeling *down* and feeling *angry* seem almost to be two different sides of the same coin. If you don't have a gym in your life, you can build one at home, simply by putting a pile of pillows on top of your bed, and then pounding the pillows repeatedly, as hard as you can—without breaking anything in your hands, wrists, or arms. This often really helps. We are strange creatures.

If none of these suggestions are helpful and the job search is dragging you down mentally and emotionally, consider enlisting the help of a professional psychologist, counselor, or coach.

When to Seek Outside Help

Sometimes in a job search you may feel you're hitting too many road-blocks or losing momentum. If this happens to you, here are a few questions to consider.

- Do I feel in control and not overwhelmed?
- Have I set goals for my search?
- Am I keeping up with those goals?

If not, you may need some help. But this doesn't mean you need to hire someone. You might be able to enlist the support of a friend or relative to discuss your challenges with. Perhaps they can help you set goals and serve as an accountability partner in the process. You can also check in your community for job-search groups. Sometimes libraries, state employment agencies, or other groups offer free or low-cost support groups and training sessions. Take advantage of what is already free in your community.

Let me share an interesting research study that might help.[15] The study focused on how people perceived the steepness of a hill. The researchers learned that we are more likely to perceive a hill as steeper if we are alone. If we have the support of a friend, the hill seems less steep. And get this: even if we just *imagine* we have a friend with us, we perceive the hill as less steep. Having a supportive friend (or even being your own best friend) can be one of the best ways to perceive your job search as less difficult.

The next chapter is designed to help you deal with the emotional and other challenges of the job search, so keep reading. But if further reading doesn't help, and you are overwhelmed and unmotivated, you would be wise to seek professional help. Keep the following five points in mind.

1. If you need help with your emotions or mood, consider speaking with your doctor or hiring a licensed psychologist or counselor. They will be able to best assess how much your emotional state might be influencing your ability to find work. You can check with your state licensing agency to get a list of names and then look them up online to learn more about their scope of practice. You can also check out *Psychology Today*'s list of therapists (https://www.psychologytoday.com/us/therapists) and note which ones list "career" as an area of practice.

2. If you seek the help of a career coach, keep in mind that anyone can call him/herself a career coach. There are currently no required standards for that title. So tread carefully and do your homework before paying for services. There are several certifying agencies that will ensure the individual has received at least some level of training. Check out the coach's credentials through BCC (https://www .cce-global.org/BCC) or the ICF (https://coachfederation.org/).

3. Certifications and licensure are a great way to start investigating, but do your due diligence. Check with the Better Business Bureau to ensure that no complaints have been filed. Ask for referrals from your friends. Review the practitioner's website thoroughly, knowing that, again, websites are not monitored; they present what the practitioner wants to say. Not everyone will be a good match for you, even if they have the appropriate credentials. Find out whether you can have an initial consultation for free (maybe by phone) before you sign up for any services.

4. When you contact the coach/counselor, ask them what services they provide, and how they provide them. What education/training qualifies them for this role? You can ask their success rate, although

this seldom can be verified. Ask about their fees and if you can see a copy of their client contract (some will post these online). If anyone promises you a job or guarantees employment, walk away. Fast.

5. Finally, no matter who you enlist to help you, they won't do your search for you. You will still end up doing a lot of the work. You will still have to create a compelling resume, interview, and all the rest of it. So why not try this book first? Give it a chance, and call in the professionals only when you can't go further on your own, for whatever reason.

As you can see, a successful job search relies on the thoughts and attitudes you take into that search. Finding ways to support and motivate yourself in the process, maintaining self-compassion and acting in ways that promote your well-being will ensure that your search, however challenging, won't take a personal toll on your happiness.

The next chapter addresses another area of concern in the job search: challenges that you suspect might keep you from getting that dream job. We'll explore those challenges and ways to resolve them.

Opportunities to find deeper powers
within ourselves come when life seems
most challenging.

—JOSEPH CAMPBELL

CHAPTER 3

HOW TO DEAL WITH ANY CHALLENGES YOU HAVE IN THE JOB SEARCH

In the last chapter we discussed how to change your thinking about the job search and view everything from a more positive and resilient perspective. But I know what you're thinking. If you've had a job interview (or interviews) and got turned down, you're thinking that there is some issue (*hidden or obvious*) that is keeping you from getting hired. Something you can't just *think* your way out of.

Maybe you were thinking this even before you went in for that interview. (*You turned to this chapter straightaway, didn't you?*)

You're thinking, *I'm getting turned down* (or *I will be turned down*) because:

I have a physical disability *or*
I have a cognitive disability *or*
I have a neurodevelopmental disability *or*
I never graduated from high school *or*
I never graduated from college *or*
I am just graduating *or*
I graduated two years ago and am still unemployed *or*
I graduated way too long ago *or*
I am too beautiful or handsome *or*
I am too unattractive *or*
I am too overweight *or*
I am too underweight *or*
I am too old *or*
I am too young *or*
I am too near retirement *or*
I have only had one employer in my life *or*
I have hopped from job to job all my life *or*
I have been out of the job market too long *or*
I have been in the job market far too long *or*
I am too inexperienced *or*
I have a prison record *or*
I have a psychiatric history *or*
I have not had enough education and am underqualified *or*
I have too much education and am overqualified *or*
I am LGBTQ+ *or*
I am Latinx *or*

I am Black *or*

I am Asian *or*

I am not diverse enough *or*

My English is not very good *or*

I speak heavily accented English *or*

I am too much of a specialist *or*

I am too much of a generalist *or*

I am ex-clergy *or*

I am ex-military *or*

I am too assertive *or*

I am too shy *or*

I have only worked for volunteer organizations *or*

I have only worked for small organizations *or*

I have only worked for large organizations *or*

I have only worked for the government *or*

I come from a very different culture or background *or*

I come from another industry *or*

I come from another planet.

The challenge is that everyone could potentially have an "issue" when it comes to finding employment. So let's get one thing straight from the beginning: you can't possibly have an issue that will keep *all* employers from hiring you. You can only have an issue that will keep *some* employers from hiring you. No matter what issue you have, or think you have, it cannot possibly keep you from getting hired anywhere in the world. It can only keep you from getting hired *at some places.*

There are millions of separate, distinct, unrelated employers out there with very different requirements for hiring. If you know what your unique *talents and skills* are, I guarantee some employer is looking for *you.* You have to keep going. Some employers out there *do* want you, no matter what the others think. Your job is to find *them.* Every employer wants to hire people with the skills they need. To make your search successful, keep your focus on what you *can* do, and remove your attention from what you *can't*. The good news is that many employers are actively seeking a diverse workforce and have begun creating strong new diversity programs. Check the websites for any employers you are considering working for and look for any statements on diversity. Does their human resources office have special programs to encourage diversity in their workplace? Are there special hiring initiatives, or are they attending job fairs focusing on diversity? These are clues that the organization is more likely to be welcoming to all.

The biggest challenges individuals with disabilities and other issues face is overcoming stigma or misunderstandings about their issues. And overcoming stigma or misunderstandings is something you can proactively do in the job search through your interview, presentation of your skills in social media and on your resume, and through networking with people who want to help you.

The Legal Stuff

Let's pause a moment to discuss the legal aspects of your challenges. Although you may suspect a particular issue is keeping you from being hired, you may not be correct.

Employers by law are not permitted to discriminate in their hiring process on the basis of the following:

- Race
- Color
- Religion
- Sex (including pregnancy, sexual orientation, or gender identity)
- National origin
- Age (forty or older)
- Disability
- Genetic information (including family medical history)

Unfortunately, you won't always know if the employer is discriminating against you in one of these protected areas. Discrimination (like prejudice or bias) can be subtle, unconscious, and hidden. But if you believe you are a victim of illegal discrimination, know your rights.

Depending on your experience of discrimination, your first step should be to consult a lawyer. Many lawyers will offer a short free consultation to determine if you have enough proof to proceed with a legal case. Lawyers will often caution you, though, of potential risks to filing a lawsuit, based on your situation. They might be able to provide other options for you, such as filing a complaint or proceeding with your concerns in other ways.

Some of the laws that protect job seekers from discrimination include:

- Title 7 of the Civil Rights Act of 1964
- The Equal Pay Act
- The Fair Labor Standards Act
- The Age Discrimination in Employment Act
- The Americans with Disabilities Act (ADA), the ADA Amendments Act of 2008
- Section 503 of the Rehabilitation Act of 1973

There are many legal statutes both federal and state that protect your rights. Various federal agencies have a role in enforcing and investigating claims, including:

- The US Equal Employment Opportunity Commission (EEOC)
- The US Department of Transportation
- The Federal Communications Commission
- The US Department of Justice (DOJ)
- The US Department of Education (ED)
- The US Department of Health and Human Services (HHS)

The US Civil Rights Center within the Department of Labor also regulates workforce and labor practices.

One of the best ways to learn about your rights in a discrimination situation is through advocacy groups and organizations established to support individuals in their quest for nondiscrimination. The box below provides a starting guide.

Supportive Organizations for Discrimination Concerns

This list is not comprehensive but will get you started in your search to learn about your legal rights and determine whether you have a case for discrimination. (If you are a member of a union, you can also check with your union representative.) Here are some websites to check out.

AARP (http://www.aarp.org/)
AARP provides invaluable information if you believe you have been discriminated against due to your age.

Americans with Disabilities Act (http://www.usdoj.gov/crt/ada/adahom1.htm)
If you believe you have been discriminated against due to a disability, medical condition, or genetic condition, this site will provide you with the information you need.

Human Rights Campaign Foundation (http://www.hrc.org/)
The HRC advocates for LGBTQ+ workers. If you believe you have been discriminated against due to your sexual orientation, be aware that a recent Supreme Court decision has increased your legal rights against discrimination.

Legal Momentum: Advancing Women's Rights (http://www.legalmomentum .org/) and the National Women's Law Center (http://www.nwlc.org/)
If you believe you have been discriminated against due to your female gender, these organizations can help you understand your legal rights.

National Employment Lawyers Association (http://www.nela.org)
This organization can help you find a local attorney who specializes in employment law.

National Workrights Institute (http://www.workrights.org/index.html)
This nonprofit organization seeks to keep workers informed of their rights in the workplace.

Office of Civil Rights (http://www.ed.gov/about/offices/list/ocr/ aboutocr.html)
This federal office handles discrimination cases particularly in cases involving agencies, schools, or organizations that receive federal funding.

The US Equal Employment Opportunity Commission (http://www.eeoc.gov/)
Established by the Civil Rights Act of 1964, this overarching agency is responsible for enforcing the federal statutes prohibiting employment discrimination.

Workplace Fairness Issues (http://www.workplacefairness.org)
This organization provides information about ways to proceed if you believe you have been discriminated against.

Accommodating Disabilities

Many companies are coming to understand the value of hiring individuals with disabilities and are starting special recruiting programs (often under general diversity hiring initiatives) to locate and recruit talented employees with disabilities. For example, some companies have now recognized the value of hiring neurodiverse workers (individuals with such diagnoses as ADD, autism, learning disabilities, obsessive-compulsive disorders, and so on). They have found that autistic workers are particularly valuable in positions that require focus, repetition, and attention to detail, such as accountant, computer programmer, bank teller, statistician, and mechanic. Individuals with ADD often make great entrepreneurs, emergency room staff, graphic artists, product designers, and surgeons. Every person has their own strengths and aptitudes, and a particular disability label does not imply that they would be good in a particular career. When possible, get a professional evaluation of your strengths and challenges to find the best job fit. Work with your state vocational rehabilitation office to receive job evaluation and guidance. In some cases, particularly if you have been injured in an accident, insurance companies will hire vocational specialists who can help you find new employment if necessary.

What if you have a disability that seems to block your dreams? Perhaps there is something you've always dreamed of doing, but your disability makes it seem impossible.

Well, first of all, make sure you have received the best medical advice and treatments possible. Since your initial diagnosis, someone may have invented a technology, treatment, or strategy that could make your life easier.

You probably already know how to accommodate your disability if you've had it for a while, but if it's a relatively new issue, you might not be aware of accommodations that might help you. For example, let's say that you are wrestling with decreased vision. Some three million US adults over the age of forty are. Search for "low vision" or "visually impaired" and you will turn up techniques and technology for dealing with this disability. (For example, https://lowvisionfocus.org from the Hadley School for the Blind has free audios and videos that cover such themes as how to use the iPhone and iPad to enhance your vision.)

An excellent online resource for both employers and individuals with disabilities is the Job Accommodation Network (https://askjan.org/info-by-role.cfm#for-individuals), which provides detailed charts of recommended accommodations for a wide variety of disabilities, from Addison's disease to fragrance sensitivity to mental health issues to vertigo.

Look particularly for any professional associations that deal with your disability. Contact them and ask them what information they have. There may be support groups or systems you haven't discovered yet. Finding support is key. It is tiring and isolating to do everything alone. Support groups can provide a safe place to share your feelings and frustrations— and can even be a potential source of job leads. Be sure you join support groups that focus on positive ways to move forward despite challenges.

An alternative way to accommodate your disability is to search for jobs *similar* to the one you want to do, but can't.

Example: One career counselor was working with a young adult who had always dreamed of being a commercial airplane pilot. The killer: His eyesight was too poor to be a pilot. Well, there was a clue as to where to go from there. It was the way our would-be pilot talked about planes. He loved planes.

So the counselor sent him out to the large airport nearby, and told him to list every kind of occupation that he saw or heard about, there at the airport—besides pilot. The next day he showed his list to his counselor. It was very long. When asked if he'd come across any occupation that interested him, he said, "Yes. I love the idea of making the seats that they put inside new airplanes." So that's the job he pursued. He ended up in the airline industry, even though he couldn't be a pilot.

To ensure that your disability isn't a factor in your ability to do a job, start by reviewing the job description, paying particular attention to the job functions. Note if there are any activities that you are unable to do. If so, determine if this is something that can be reasonably accommodated by the employer. Consider how they would accommodate your situation and be prepared to make suggestions to the employer when you interview. Research typical accommodations for your disability so that you are prepared to discuss them with a potential employer. Sometimes job functions listed on a job description aren't imperative to the position, so don't eliminate yourself from consideration for a position that might not be a perfect fit.

You get to choose when (or if) you reveal your disability to an employer. If your disability is hidden (learning disability, ADD, or epilepsy, for example) you may choose not to reveal anything, particularly if you don't anticipate it being a factor in your ability to do the work. Once you are hired, you can discuss your disability, if accommodations are needed. If your disability is more apparent (physical/mobility issue, blindness, or deafness, for example) you should consider when to reveal the information. Certainly if you are invited to an interview at the company site and will need accommodations (automatic door openers, ramps, and so on) it's best to mention this after your interview is scheduled. When you arrive at the interview, if you have not already done so, it's perfectly appropriate (though not legally required) to discuss your condition and how it can best be accommodated. For example, if you have hearing loss, you can indicate that you use hearing aids that help but that you might also request a relatively quiet work setting free from lots of distracting conversations. This would be a reasonable accommodation. Many employers are making genuine concerted efforts to hire people with disabilities, so use this to your advantage. Explain how your disability has helped you (perhaps made you more sensitive to others or more aware of your own strengths and skills) and how you will bring a diverse viewpoint to the setting. And the more comfortable you are with explaining your disability and how you have overcome it where possible, the more comfortable an employer will be with you—and more likely to hire you. Employers generally like people who have shown resilience through challenges, and you may have a perfect story about this.

Other Potential Employer Judgments or Biases

We've looked at key issues where federal laws exist to prevent outright discrimination in the workplace, but employers are human and will make judgments about candidates based on many other factors not covered by standard discrimination laws. As a job seeker, part of your role is to be aware of potential negative judgments or biases and address them as needed. Focus on your strengths and skills throughout the process. If an employer turns you down, don't allow that experience to discourage you. It's just one employer. There are more out there, and someone will see you for your strengths and talents.

Here are some suggestions for overcoming potential employer biases that could become barriers to your employment:

Out of Work Too Long

Some employers have this bias and others don't. If you've been out of work for a year or more, you will find employers who won't hire you because of this. Too bad! Just keep going until you find employers who don't have that prejudice. It helps to prepare a story that describes your time out of work in a positive light. Focus on the learning, knowledge, or skills you acquired, the volunteer activities you did, the family responsibilities you managed, and so on. For a list of employers who have promised to hire even the long-term unemployed, see http://big.assets.huffingtonpost.com /est_practices_recruiting_longterm_unemployed.pdf.

Work-related Barriers

These can take the form of changing fields of employment, looking for a job in a distant location, moving from a small employer to a large employer or vice versa, changing jobs too quickly, staying at your previous job too long, and so on. You can see the challenge. Virtually everything you might have experienced in your job history is subject to review. Your best plan of action is to know what the employer's resistance might be and be prepared to explain your history. Stay positive and focus on what you did well. If you left jobs quickly, discuss your desire to find a long-term opportunity. If you are doing a long-distance search, express your willingness to do Skype or Zoom interviews and travel to the new location if needed. You get the idea. Focus on what was good about your past behavior and what you have learned or hope to accomplish now in this new role.

Age

Generation bias seems to be the rage these days, with insults directed at "those millennials" or the dismissive phrase "OK, boomer." So age discrimination can work both ways.

Some employers can be skeptical about hiring workers who are "too young." They are concerned that younger workers might not have the same work ethic as older workers, or that they might not stay with the job for long. They might be concerned about the amount of training a young person will require. So if you are young, keep these concerns in mind and be sure to let the employer know that you are eager to learn and hope to stay in this position and/or with this company for a while.

And if you're one of the millions of baby boomers (the 76 million people born between 1946 and 1964) who are entering the so-called retirement years, you may find it particularly hard to find a job. You might not have a generous pension waiting for you when you hit sixty or sixty-five; you may have to keep working long after you ever thought you would have to. If you are over forty, you are legally protected from age discrimination, but that doesn't mean you won't encounter it. After age forty it becomes important to consider why such a bias might exist and what you can do to reduce a potential employer's concerns.

The first concern is usually about energy and flexibility. Employers might be concerned that you won't have the same energy or ambition as a younger worker, but fortunately this is an issue you can address in your interview. You can provide examples of your continued commitment to your profession or your eagerness to start again in a new field. You can discuss your interest in ongoing learning and the new skills you have developed in the past few years.

But another concern in hiring an older worker is money. Given all their years of experience, many who are job hunting over forty (and particularly, over fifty) expect a salary befitting all their years of experience and wisdom, only to discover that some employers aren't willing to pay that much—because they could hire two less experienced workers in their twenties for what it would cost them to hire just one (albeit with greater value).

And yet, despite this prejudice, there are still employers out there who *will* hire you, regardless of how old you are, if you come with a positive attitude about your aging and **you convey energy and enthusiasm.**

Job-hunting success, regardless of your age, often requires this kind of persistence: keeping at it, keeping at it, keeping at it, working at your job hunt far longer and far harder than the average job hunter would ever dream of doing, because you know you will be valuable to any organization that is able to see you clearly, without prejudice.

Education

Employers may have two biases here: they may consider you undereducated—that is, *lacking* in knowledge or skills needed for the position—or overeducated—that is, having *too much* knowledge, skills, or experience.

In the latter case, they are likely concerned that you will be bored, expect a larger salary than they are prepared to pay, or want to be promoted too quickly. They might assume that you are seeking a particular position simply as a way to get into the organization, and you will become dissatisfied if you have to stay in it for any length of time. If this is the case, you need to offer a clear explanation of why you are seeking this position. Perhaps you rose to a position that required more of you in terms of hours or responsibilities. It's not unusual for great line workers to be promoted to management roles only to learn they miss the work they used to do, or they don't like their new management duties. In that case, you have an excellent story to tell.

On the other hand, if they consider you undereducated, this could be a literal fact (such as lacking a required degree or licensure) or a bias ("We only hire people with college degrees"). This is an increasingly common issue: many employers list a college degree as a basic requirement regardless of the position. It can exclude individuals who worked their way up in an organization that acknowledged their skills, not their degree. To overcome this bias, you must be very clear about the skills you possess for this position and provide proof that you can perform them as well as someone with a degree. Having a portfolio or other demonstration of your skills can be particularly helpful here. You should express a desire to learn and to build skills as needed. You might also inquire whether the employer sponsors on-the-job training or pays for additional education. You might be surprised to learn that is part of the benefits package. But regardless of future learning opportunities, you must strongly demonstrate your ability to perform the duties of the position and your ability to hit the ground running when you are employed.

Returning Veterans

Many veterans feel their military skills and training are not appreciated or respected by employers. And certainly, some employers *are* biased against hiring returning vets. They've seen one too many headlines about PTSD, even though four out of five returning vets do *not* have post-traumatic stress disorder. Fortunately, there are other employers who know this, who actually prefer to hire returning vets. Veterans enjoy an advantage with many employers, including federal, state, and local governments, where military service can give you extra points in your application, placing you ahead of civilian candidates. If you are a veteran, check with your VA office to learn about any employment assistance programs they may offer. You might be able to find a local support group that would give you the opportunity to meet with fellow veterans facing the same challenges you are in the job-search process. As a veteran you can increase your likelihood of success in the job market by making sure your resume doesn't contain too much military lingo. In your interviews, try to avoid using too many military acronyms or terms civilians won't understand. You will need to translate your military experience so that employers better understand what you did in the service. Focus on your overall leadership skills, ability to follow directions and set goals, and the hard work you are capable of handling. Virtually all employers are seeking those traits in employees.

Ex-offenders

Ex-offenders face particular challenges in the hiring process due to the increasing use of background and credit checks. It is extremely important that you use as many connections, networks, or agencies as possible to assist you in this process. Keep in mind that many states are starting to change their laws around requiring disclosure of past criminal convictions. Check the rules in your state or city.

There are a number of helpful resources. For example, Mark Drevno has written a book for ex-offenders called *Jails to Jobs*. Mark will send readers of *Parachute* an electronic version of his book *for free*, if they email him at info@jailstojobs.org requesting it, and mention that they are a reader of *Parachute*. He also runs a public charity called Jails to Jobs, with a website called (you guessed it) www.jailstojobs.org, that gives step-by-step help with finding employment. The site includes a Tattoo Removal Directory, which is helpful for anyone who feels their tattoos are keeping them from getting a job and wants them removed. Mark also has a new book, *Tattoo Removal*. There are already 282 such programs in 43 states. Anyone who wants to start a community program can secure a free electronic version of this book; just email Mark and mention you saw this mentioned in *Parachute*.

There is also a free sixty-seven-page workbook you can print out from your computer. The *STEP AHEAD Workbook* was produced with funding from the Minnesota Department of Corrections. Currently it is sponsored by Minnesota State Colleges and Universities: https://careerwise .minnstate.edu/exoffenders/workbook.html.

The Department of Labor's CareerOneStop site offers guidance and support for ex-offenders, including videos and a downloadable PDF of state resources, including where to find training and job listings: www.careeronestop.org/ExOffender/default.aspx.

HelpforFelons.org offers state-by-state information about jobs, financial support including food stamps and housing, temp agencies, and so on: https://helpforfelons.org/reentry-programs-ex-offenders-state.

The National Conference of State Legislatures also offers information for employers and former offenders at their site: www.ncsl.org/research /civil-and-criminal-justice/ex-offender-employment-opportunities43.aspx.

Everyone Else

Unfortunately, employer bias exists in almost every work setting, and you may never know why you didn't receive an offer. But we are living in changing times, and the anti-racism movement may be just what is needed to improve hiring policies and the work environment. Employers often seek candidates who "fit" their workplace, not always realizing that "fit" can be a code for only hiring people who look and act like them. One way to challenge "fit" is to focus on "add." What do you add to the work environment? Yes, you might be different or have unique characteristics from the people who currently work in a particular setting, and that's actually a benefit. How can you help an employer see the benefit in hiring you, with all your individual traits and skills? Here is a letter that I got from a successful job hunter recently:

> Before I read this book, I was depressed and lost in the futile job hunt using want ads only. I did not receive even one phone call from any ad I answered, over a total of four months. I felt that I was the most useless person on Earth. I am female, with a two-and-a-half-year-old daughter, a former professor in China, with no working experience at all in the US. We came here seven months ago because my husband had a job offer here.
>
> Then, on June 11 of last year, I saw your book in a local bookstore. Subsequently, I spent three weeks, ten hours a day except Sunday, reading every single word of your book and doing all of the flower petals in the Flower Exercise. After getting to know myself much better, I felt I was ready to try the job hunt again. I used *Parachute* throughout as my guide, from the very beginning to the very end—namely, salary negotiation.
>
> In just two weeks I secured (you guessed it) two job offers, one of which I am taking, as it is an excellent job, with very good pay. It is (you guessed it again) a small company, with twenty or so employees. It is also a career change: I was a professor of English; now I am to be a controller!

I am so glad I believed your advice: there are jobs out there, and there are two types of employers out there, and truly there are! I hope you will be happy to hear my story.

As we went along in the interview, some of the things the employer told me were, "I'm very flexible with schedules. I want to put people in activities that I know they'll be the best in, but that means that some weeks you're scheduled for three evening shifts. If that's ever a problem, I really want you to tell me, because I can fix it. I'm also a firm believer that you need to be at your absolute best before you can pour into people here. That means, if you get really stressed out, I want you to tell me. Just yesterday one of our employees came to me and said, 'I'm so overwhelmed right now!' So I sat down with her and we moved some stuff around. Now, that also means that we are extremely team-oriented. If someone cannot take a shift because something is going on at home, everyone needs to be willing to take that up sometimes. But, you always know that everyone here is willing to do the same for you. Also, when we're stressed we seem to resort to silliness."

I knew immediately that this was the place for me. . . .

A Common Issue for Job Seekers: Shyness

During the whole job hunt, what personal traits are likely to work against you? Well, shyness is near the top of the list. Shyness in this context is a catchall term for other difficulties with social interaction; it could also be labeled social anxiety or introversion. These are different conditions, and there are medical treatments for social anxiety, for example, but they all can have an impact in how you approach the job-search process. Each person has their own unique issue around communication: you might be fine writing resumes and cover letters but dread calling someone. You might get sweaty palms at even the thought of an interview. You may cringe at the thought of having to create a LinkedIn profile, because it's so public. Maybe you're fine with a one-on-one interview but nervous about meeting with a group of people. Sometimes low self-esteem, as well as anxiety, can cause issues in the job search. But the bottom line here is that the job-search process requires most people to "extrovert" themselves—to be more social and public-facing—than they would normally be. At some point we will have to go face-to-face with people. And this can be a particularly threatening part of the process. If you believe that your "shyness" might be interfering with your ability to communicate in the job-search process, consider speaking with your doctor, a psychologist, or a counselor who can help you better identify whether medical or therapeutic treatment might be helpful.

You are not alone. Surveys have found that as many as 75 percent of us have been painfully shy at some point in our lives. Many of us still are. (This always comes as a great surprise to my European friends, because they picture Americans as assertive, aggressive, and other similar qualities. And sure, some of us are, but that's not who most of us are, especially when we're out of work and have to sit across the desk from employers, face to face. I myself have been painfully shy for much of my life. But no one ever guesses.)

So what to do if you are overwhelmed or having difficulty with all the social interaction we're going to have to do during our job hunt? Here are ten suggestions:

1. First, don't apologize for being who you are. Work with it—find your strengths and get to know them so well that you focus on them in interviews. (To learn more about the value of introversion, read books like *Quiet* by Susan Cain or *The Introvert Advantage* by Marti Olsen Laney.) It's okay to mention that you tend to have an understated style. In fact, that can be a great response to the typical "What is your weakness?" interview question. You can say something like "I tend to have an understated style, and people don't always know what I'm thinking. So I have learned to make

sure I give my feedback explicitly when needed, and I encourage people to ask me if I haven't been clear. For instance, if you have any questions for me or if I haven't answered something clearly, I hope you will ask me to clarify it." You could also mention that you don't tend to talk too much, and you make a point of listening to all opinions before you make a decision.

2. You may never be comfortable in certain settings like interviews, but you can learn to function well in them, and then you can go home, where you are comfortable. A small amount of discomfort and "faking it" can go a long way.

3. Practice self-compassion (as discussed in chapter 2). Introverts and shy people can be particularly hard on themselves: analyzing every moment, being too sensitive to "mistakes" they might have made. You feel self-conscious when on public display—and many times in the job search you will feel like you *are* on public display. In his excellent book *Feeling Good*, Dr. David Burns cautions against being a "mind-reader" or a "fortune-teller"—guessing what people are thinking and/or presuming we know how something will turn out. Remember, when you live inside your head, your head is the only information you're getting—and it can be wrong. As Dr. Burns says, just because you feel something doesn't make it true.

4. After an interview, networking event, or any other extroverted activity, don't be too hard on yourself. Don't overanalyze your situation and dwell on those moments that make you cringe.

5. Focus on your successes. What have you done well? What are the three strengths you want an employer to know about you? How can you craft those strengths into a story that an interviewer might want to hear? I know many introverts who tell wonderful, clever stories.

It's that anxiety about speaking to an audience that keeps you from telling them. The more you know about your strengths, the less you'll be tempted to focus on your challenges.

6. Rehearse. In front of a mirror, with a friend, using your computer's webcam or cell phone. The more you do something, the less foreign and the less nerve-racking it is. If you tell your interview stories to the mirror, then to the webcam, then to a friend, you are not only rehearsing and improving the story but also decreasing your stress level.

7. Practice mindfulness meditation. The world can be particularly stressful for shy people and introverts, and you need to detox in a healthy way. It's not unusual for introverts to experience anxiety, and mindfulness meditation has been shown to be one of the best ways to handle stress. A few minutes of mindful breathing before the interview can be a big help.

8. Keep in mind that most introverts do well in a one-on-one interactions, and that is how most job interviews are conducted. Keep reminding yourself that this interview is really just a conversation. Focus on the interviewer and ask them questions. Use your natural curiosity to overcome your anxiety.

9. Medium-size groups can be challenging, so if you're facing a group interview, try focusing on one person at a time. Pay attention to the person asking the question (try not to be distracted by what someone else might be doing) and make sure you answer their question while making eye contact with everyone in the room. Resist a tendency to always look at the primary person while ignoring other people. Find the friendly face—there's usually at least one in the interview.

10. Always follow up the interview with a thank-you note. It's not unusual to realize after an interview that you should have told the interviewer something you forgot, so use the note as your chance to bring this up. But don't bring it up by writing "I misspoke" or "I may not have explained this"; instead, write something like "I'd like to add a point to my response about . . ." Choose your comments wisely. Don't restate or correct everything you said in the interview! Just pick one thing (two at most) that you want to clarify. Otherwise, spend the note reiterating the connection between you and the position, what you learned, and how you're looking forward to the opportunity to work for their company. (See page 205 for more on thank-you notes.)

11. Prepare for networking events by planning ahead. You're probably not that comfortable with the small talk at these events. Start by finding a comfortable setting—like the small tables often set up around the room. You can always talk about the food with whomever is at the table. Many introverts have strong passions and can talk about them when they're with like-minded people. So when you meet someone, make it an experiment to find out what you have in common. Focus on likely commonalities like TV shows, movies, or music. Read a newspaper earlier on the day of the event. Check the headlines for interesting events people might want to talk about. Have some conversation starters ready; entertainment is always a good start—concerts, festivals, sporting events.

12. Play to your strengths. If you're better online than in person, take advantage of online networking opportunities like LinkedIn, Facebook, and any internet-based gatherings of professionals in your field. Many valuable relationships have been formed and many jobs have been acquired solely through online networking.

Finally, while introversion, shyness, or social anxiety may be an innate trait, anyone can learn social skills and appropriate networking and interviewing behavior. If the guidance in this book isn't enough, find a psychologist, counselor, friend, or coach who will help you practice for your interviews and for networking situations.

So, what to do if we are shy and feel utterly unequipped to deal with all the social interaction we're going to have to do during our job search?

There is an answer, and a method that works. But first, a bit of history.

John Crystal, whose groundbreaking work as a career counselor provided much of the basis for the Parachute Approach, often encountered this challenge. He suggested that the way anyone cures themself of shyness is through enthusiasm. If you're talking with someone, for example, and you are enthusiastic about the topic under discussion, in your excitement you will forget that you are shy. Everything depends on what you're talking about and how you feel about that topic.

So, he said, if you're shy, go after only those jobs you feel really enthusiastic about. Seek information only about those mysteries and puzzles and gaps in your knowledge that you feel enthusiastic about resolving.

John followed this up by inventing a practical three-stage plan of action to cure job hunters of shyness. Those who have followed John's advice in this regard have had a success rate of 86 percent in overcoming their shyness and fears and finding a job.

Daniel Porot, a job expert from Switzerland, subsequently took John's system and organized it. He observed that John was really recommending three types of interviews, as I note in chapter 9:

- Practice interviewing—which, among other things, is a warm-up for
- Informational interviewing—which, among other things, is a warm-up for
- Employment interviews

Each type of interview prepares you for the next, and there you have it: a three-stage plan for overcoming shyness.

Daniel, who has been Europe's premier job-hunting expert for decades, organized this into an attractive, well-thought-out chart and gave it its now-famous name: the PIE method. It has helped thousands of job hunters and career changers all around the world with their shyness and with their job hunt.[16]

Why is it called "**PIE**"?

P is for the warm-up phase. John Crystal named this warm-up "The Practice Field Survey." Daniel Porot calls it P for pleasure.

I is for informational interviewing.

E is for the employment interview with the person who has the power to hire you.

How do you use this P for practice (or pleasure) to get comfortable about going out and talking to people one-on-one? By choosing a topic—any topic, however silly or trivial—that is a pleasure for you to talk about with your friends or family. To avoid anxiety, choose something unconnected to any present or future careers that you are considering. The kinds of topics that work best for this exercise are:

- A hobby you love, such as skiing, board games, exercise, technology
- Any leisure-time enthusiasm, such as a movie you just saw that you liked a lot
- A longtime curiosity, such as how they predict the weather, or what astronauts do
- An aspect of the town or city you live in, such as a newly revamped historic district
- An issue you feel strongly about, such as unhoused people, racial justice issues, climate change, peace, health, returning veterans

There is just the one criterion for choosing a topic: it should be something you love to talk about with other people. It's preferable to choose a subject you know nothing about but feel a great deal of enthusiasm for than something you know an awful lot about but it puts you to sleep.

Having identified your enthusiasm, you then need to go talk to someone who is as enthusiastic about this thing as you are. For best results with your later job hunt, this person should be someone you don't already know. Ask around among your friends and family: *Who do you know who loves to talk about this?* It's relatively easy to find the kind of person you're looking for.

You love to talk about skiing? Try a ski-equipment store clerk or a skiing instructor. You love to talk about writing? Try a professor who teaches English at a nearby college. You love to talk about physical exercise? Try a trainer, or someone who does physical therapy.

Once you've identified someone you think shares your enthusiasm, you then go talk with them.

When you are face to face with your fellow enthusiast, the first thing you must do is relieve their understandable anxiety. We've all had someone visit us who has stayed too long, who has worn out their welcome. If your fellow enthusiast is worried about your staying too long, they'll be so preoccupied with this fear that they won't hear a word you are saying.

So, when you first arrange to meet them, let them know you want only ten minutes of their time, full stop. Exclamation point! And watch your time like a hawk, using your watch or smartphone timer.

Okay, you're there. What to talk about? Well, each topic invites its own particular set of questions. For example, I love movies and TV, so if I met someone who shared this interest, my first question would be, "What movies or shows have you seen lately?" Or "What do you think of *Game of Thrones?*" Or "Who's your favorite actress?" And so on.

If it's a topic you love and often talk about, you'll know what kinds of questions you'll begin with. But if no questions come to mind, try one of the following, which have proved to be good conversation starters for thousands of job hunters and career changers before you, no matter what their topic or interest.

Ask the person you're practice interviewing:

- How did you get involved with/become interested in this [hobby, curiosity, aspect, issue, or enthusiasm that you are so interested in]?
- What do you like the most about it?
- What do you like the least about it?
- Who else would you suggest I talk to who shares this interest?
- Can I use your name?
- May I tell them it was you who recommended that I talk with them?

Then, choosing one person from the list of several names they may have given you, say, "Well, I think I will begin by going to talk to this person. Would you be willing to call or email ahead for me, so they will know who I am when I reach out?"

Incidentally, it's perfectly okay for you to take someone with you during this practice interviewing—preferably someone who is more outgoing than you feel you are. And on the first few interviews, let them take the lead in the conversation, while you watch to see how they do it.

Once it is *your turn* to conduct these practice interviews, it will usually be easy for you to figure out what to talk about.

Alone or with someone, keep at this practice interviewing until you feel very much at ease in talking with people and asking them questions about things you are curious about.

In all of this, as you're trying to conquer shyness, *fun* is the key. If you're having fun, you're doing it right. That depends, of course, on how enthusiastic you are about what you're exploring.

If you're not having fun, you need to keep at it until you are. It may take seeing four people. It may take ten. Or twenty. You'll know. Once you're comfortable with practice interviewing, you'll be ready to move on to the next step, informational interviewing.

	PLEASURE P	INFORMATION I	EMPLOYMENT E
Kind of interview	Practice field survey	Informational interviewing or research	Employment interview or hiring interview
Purpose	To get used to talking with people for enjoyment; to "penetrate networks"	To find out if you'd like a job, before you go trying to get it	To get hired for the work you have decided you would most like to do
How you go to the interview	You can take somebody with you	By yourself, or you can take somebody with you	By yourself
Who you talk to	Anyone who shares your enthusiasm about a (for you) non-job-related subject	A worker who is doing the actual work you are thinking about doing	An employer who has the power to hire you for the job you have decided you most would like to do
How long a time you ask for	Ten minutes (and *don't* run over—asking to see them at 11:45 a.m. may help keep you honest, since most employers have lunch appointments at noon)	Ditto	Ditto (or nineteen minutes; but notice the time, and keep your word)
What you ask them	Any curiosity you have about your shared interest or enthusiasm If nothing occurs to you, ask: • How did you start, with this hobby, interest, etc.? • What excites or interests you the most about it? • What do you find is the thing you like least about it? • Who else do you know who shares this interest, hobby, or enthusiasm, or could tell me more about my curiosity?	Any questions you have about this job or this kind of work If nothing occurs to you, ask: • How did you get interested in this work and how did you get hired? • What excites or interests you the most about it? • What do you find is the thing you like the least about it? • What kinds of challenges or problems do you have to deal with in this job?	You tell them what it is you like about their organization and what kind of work you are looking for You tell them: The kinds of challenges you like to deal with. What skills you have to deal with those challenges. What experience you have had in dealing with those challenges in the past.

	PLEASURE **P**	INFORMATION **I**	EMPLOYMENT **E**
What you ask them (continued)	• Can I go and see them? • May I mention that it was you who suggested I see them? • May I say that you recommended them? Get their name and address.	• What skills do you need in order to meet those challenges or problems? • Who else do you know of who does this kind of work, or similar work but with this difference_____? Get their name and address.	
Afterward: that same night	Send a thank-you note.	Send a thank-you note.	Send a thank-you note.

Copyright © 1986 by D. Porot. Used by special permission. Not to be reproduced without permission in writing from D. Porot.

One Final Consideration: Self-Esteem Versus Egotism

This ending seems a little ironic, since we just spent some time on the challenges of being too shy or introverted. But the other end of the personality spectrum can be just as challenging. As most of us know, the proper attitude toward ourselves is called "good self-esteem." But self-esteem is an art. An art of *balance*. A balance between thinking too little of ourselves and thinking too much of ourselves.

The term for thinking too much of ourselves is "egotism" or "narcissism." We have all run into it, at some point in our lives, so we know what it looks like. There are a lot of new books about narcissism. We are warned about the increasing narcissism in our society, from politicians to celebrities. We even have mythologies warning us against it; the story of Narcissus comes to mind. Poor guy! (If you are unfamiliar with the myth, https://en.wikipedia.org/wiki/Narcissus_(mythology) is a good starting point for popular and academic sources.)

Unfortunately, to avoid sounding self-centered, a lot of us go to the other direction. We shrink from declaring our strengths and talents. We fail to mention our special gifts. And in so doing, we can look ungrateful. We can act like we don't appreciate our gifts—and maybe are even embarrassed by them.

So how do we adopt the proper attitude toward our gifts—speaking of them honestly, humbly, gratefully, without sounding egotistical and narcissistic?

Here's how: the more you see your own gifts clearly, the more you must pay attention to the gifts that others have.

The more sensitive you become to how unique you are, the more you must become sensitive to how unique those around you are.

The more you pay attention to yourself, the more you must pay attention to others.

If you are careful to consider the impact you are having on those around you, whether in a job-search situation or not, you will be less likely to fall into the narcissism trap. Take time to ask the employer interviewing you how their day is going. Be interested and pleasant when greeting any staff at the organization where you are interviewing. Take the time to write a thank-you note or email after your interview. Put yourself in the reader's mind when you write your resume and cover letters.

The more you ponder the mystery of *you*, the more you must ponder the mystery of all those you encounter: every loved one, every friend, every acquaintance, every stranger.

People from other cultures will tell you about "the tall poppy" theory of life, with its implication that you shouldn't stand taller than others in your field. That has a lot of truth to it. But you make yourself equal to others not by lowering yourself, but by raising them.

Pay attention to others. What are the favorite skills of your best friend or mate? Do you know? Are you sure? Have you asked them what *they* think they are? Have you complimented them on these skills, say, during the past week? Start now!

Just remember, it's okay to praise yourself, as long as that heightens your awareness of what there is to praise in others.

Here's a quick way to check in about your skills.

Focus on What You *Can* Do, Not What You *Can't*

To get your mind off what you *can't* do and onto what you *can*, take a blank sheet, online or off, and divide it into two columns:

I have these skills	My favorite skills

Here is a list of action verbs that represent skills. (It's rather comprehensive, but you should feel free to add other ideas.) Using this as a starting point, write down the main skills you have. Use additional sheets, if needed.

When you are done with the first column, pick out your favorite *five* things that you *can* do, and *love* to do, and fill in the second column. Write out some examples of how you actually did *that*, sometime in your past. Your *recent* past, if possible.

A List of 248 Skills as Verbs

achieving	dancing	fixing	judging
acting	deciding	following	keeping
adapting	defining	formulating	leading
addressing	delivering	founding	learning
administering	designing	gathering	lecturing
advising	detailing	generating	lifting
analyzing	detecting	getting	listening
anticipating	determining	giving	logging
arbitrating	developing	guiding	maintaining
arranging	devising	handling	making
ascertaining	diagnosing	having	managing
assembling	digging	responsibility	manipulating
assessing	directing	heading	mediating
attaining	discovering	helping	meeting
auditing	dispensing	hypothesizing	memorizing
budgeting	displaying	identifying	mentoring
building	disproving	illustrating	modeling
calculating	dissecting	imagining	monitoring
charting	distributing	implementing	motivating
checking	diverting	improving	navigating
classifying	dramatizing	improvising	negotiating
coaching	drawing	increasing	observing
collecting	driving	influencing	obtaining
communicating	editing	informing	offering
compiling	eliminating	initiating	operating
completing	empathizing	innovating	ordering
composing	enforcing	inspecting	organizing
computing	establishing	inspiring	originating
conceptualizing	estimating	installing	overseeing
conducting	evaluating	instituting	painting
conserving	examining	instructing	perceiving
consolidating	expanding	integrating	performing
constructing	experimenting	interpreting	persuading
controlling	explaining	interviewing	photographing
coordinating	expressing	intuiting	piloting
coping	extracting	inventing	planning
counseling	filing	inventorying	playing
creating	financing	investigating	predicting

preparing	recruiting	sewing	transcribing
prescribing	reducing	shaping	translating
presenting	referring	sharing	traveling
printing	rehabilitating	showing	treating
problem solving	relating	singing	troubleshooting
processing	remembering	sketching	tutoring
producing	rendering	solving	typing
programming	repairing	sorting	umpiring
projecting	reporting	speaking	understanding
promoting	representing	studying	understudying
proofreading	researching	summarizing	undertaking
protecting	resolving	supervising	unifying
providing	responding	supplying	uniting
proving	restoring	symbolizing	upgrading
publicizing	retrieving	synergizing	using
purchasing	reviewing	synthesizing	utilizing
questioning	risking	systematizing	verbalizing
raising	scheduling	taking instructions	washing
reading	selecting	talking	weighing
realizing	selling	teaching	winning
reasoning	sensing	team-building	working
receiving	separating	telling	writing
recommending	serving	tending	
reconciling	setting	testing	
recording	setting up	training	

Everyone Has Issues—So Focus on Strengths

How do your unique skills and traits add to the workplace? How will you perform the job in a way that is different and better? How will you be more inclusive and connect with everyone? We all have issues that might make an employer less likely to hire us. But if you keep the focus on your skills and strengths, as well as your interests and values, you will find the best place for your talents. Remember, you are hired for your skills. Keep in mind that while discrimination still exists, many organizations are actively trying to hire a more diverse workforce, and your background and skills might be exactly what they need.

Keep your focus on what you do well and seek employment opportunities that would benefit from your skills. You always have a choice about what you will focus on when you are job seeking. Try not to focus on your areas of concern or those issues that might not be as appealing to an employer. Keep your focus on what you *can* do, not what you *can't*. Always keep a learning mindset: what can you learn on this job, or what can you learn that will make you a better candidate? Keep your focus on all the reasons why an employer might hire you, and why they would be lucky to have you. Bottom line: you must offer yourself as a skilled and helpful resource for this employer. Skills always overcome challenges. Find the skills, and you find the job. In the next section of this book you will have a chance to focus on all the skills you have acquired so that you'll be prepared to tell a potential employer what you have to offer.

Unless—*unless*—you are so focused on the idea that you are held back by this issue, and so obsessed with what you *can't* do, that you have forgotten all the things you *can* do.

Unless you're thinking of all the reasons why an employer might not hire you, instead of all the reasons why an employer would be lucky to get you.

Bottom line: you must offer yourself as *a skilled and helpful resource* for this employer. Skills always overcome challenges. Find the skills, and you find the job.

In the next section of this book you will have a chance to focus on all the skills you have acquired so that you'll be prepared to tell a potential employer what you have to offer.

I was told many years ago by my grandmother who raised me: If somebody puts you on a road and you don't feel comfortable on it and you look ahead and you don't like the destination, and you look behind and you don't want to return to that place, step off the road.

—MAYA ANGELOU

CHAPTER 4

CHOOSE A CAREER, CHANGE A CAREER, OR FIND A JOB: WHAT WORKS

You're reading this book because you're either planning your career, switching to a new career, or looking for a job. In this chapter we'll map out the most efficient and effective ways to move forward. I know you don't want to waste time in this process, so you will learn what works—and what doesn't. There are a lot of myths out there about how to proceed with the job search. I'll clear those up and point you in the right direction.

In one sense, the overall process for changing your career or finding a job is relatively simple: You determine what you want to do; you identify the key employers who might hire you; and you contact those employers until one of them hires you. Simple, right? It's not. The job search involves a lot of work and a lot of time. In this chapter we'll examine the basics; the subsequent chapters will sharpen your job-seeking practices.

Choosing or Changing Your Career

Let's start with the big picture first: Are you choosing a career for the first time? Or have you been in one career field and now want to change it? In either case, you're in luck, because the next section of this book provides one of the best—and most thoroughly time-tested—ways to choose or change your career. The Flower Exercise, as we call it, is a great way to break down all the key "know yourself" elements needed to consider your new or next career. The more you know about yourself—your likes/dislikes, strengths/weaknesses, interests, and career needs—the better choices you will be able to make immediately and well into the future.

But first let's take a look at what ideal career planning looks like:

As you can see from this illustration, good career planning often involves starting with a narrow idea or two, expanding those ideas into 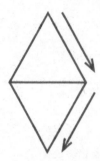 a much broader spectrum, and then narrowing down again to find the best fit. Good career planning postpones the narrowing down until you have first broadened your horizons and expanded the number of options you are thinking about. Say, for example, you're a journalist, but maybe you have thought of teaching, or drawing, or doing fashion. You first expand your mental horizons, to see all the possibilities, and only then do you start to narrow them down to the particular two or three that interest you the most. As you think about your career change, here are some suggestions to consider.

Explore Broadly

Look into *any* career that seems fascinating or even interesting to you. But *first* talk to people who are already doing that work, to find out if the career or job is as great as it seems from the outside. Ask them: *What do you like best about this work? What do you like least about this work? And, how did you get into this work?* This last question can give you important clues about how you could get into this line of work or career yourself. Ask them how they perceive their career: what are its component parts? Every person may see their vocation in a different light. Don't assume that the way the person you are interviewing defines it is the way you must, also. Beneath any job title, there is often lots of room for you to maneuver and define that job in a way that uniquely suits you, your gifts, and your creativity.

Preserve Stability

In moving from one career to another, make sure that you preserve constancy in your life as well as change during the transition. In other words, don't change *everything*. When you are moving your life around, you need a firm place to stand, and that place is provided by the things that stay constant about you: your character, your faith, your values, your gifts or immutable skills.

Start with *You*, Not the Job Market

If you can, you'll do better to start with yourself and what *you* want, rather than with the job market and what's "hot." The difference is *enthusiasm* and *passion*. Yours. You're much more attractive to employers when you're *on fire*. Maybe times are just too tough for you right now to risk starting with your vision of what you want to do with your life, but *try*. And maybe you can find the passion in what you do by focusing on the benefits of having a job, any job.

Some people try to game the job search by focusing not on what they want but on projections about the coming needs and wishes of the job market. These projections are also called "hot" jobs, though I'd take that with a grain of salt. They are often guesses. A projection from Glassdoor.com, reported on CNBC (https://www.cnbc.com/2019/01/22/glassdoor-the-20-best-jobs-in-america-in-2019.html), listed these top ten hot jobs for 2019:

1. Data Scientist
2. Nursing Manager
3. Marketing Manager
4. Occupational Therapist
5. Product Manager
6. Development & Operations (DevOps) Engineer
7. Program Manager
8. Data Engineer
9. Human Resources (HR) Manager
10. Software Engineer

So how many of those jobs sound interesting to you? How many use the skills that you have? If something fits you, then by all means investigate it. But if the jobs don't look interesting to you, then this is just another useless list. Hot job lists, while interesting, seldom help anyone make a career decision.

The US government gets into this projections game—though on a more sophisticated level—with its *Occupational Outlook Handbook 2018–2019*, online at www.bls.gov/ooh. Here you can browse careers and occupations by occupational group, number of new jobs projected to be available, faster-than-average job growth projected, level of education or training required, median pay, and so on. Oh, and it has a lovely feature called "similar occupations." That's great if for any reason you don't qualify for some job that otherwise really fascinates you. Bottom line: while picking a hot career can sound like a smart decision, it can backfire on you later.

Because the best career search always starts with *you*, the Flower Exercise in chapter 5 is one of the most invaluable steps you can take in this process.

Focus on What You Enjoy

The best *work*, the best career, for you, the one that will make you happiest and most fulfilled, is going to be one that uses your *favorite* transferable skills; in your *favorite* subjects, fields, or special knowledges; in a job that offers you your *preferred* people environments, your *preferred* working conditions, with your *preferred* salary or other rewards, working toward your *preferred* goals and values. This requires a thorough inventory of who you are. Doing the Flower Exercise in the next section of this book will help.

Take Your Time

It takes longer to do most job-hunting activities than you might expect. Many people think a resume is a quick document they can write in an hour or two. But to do a resume well will take more time. And you don't want to rush it. The more time and thought you can give to the choosing of a new career, the better your choice is going to be. There is often a penalty for seeking quick and dirty fixes. Take your time, knowing it's okay to make mistakes. Most of us will have at least five to seven *careers* during our lifetime, and ten or more *jobs*.

Keep It Fun

Choosing and then finding employment in a new career you really fancy should feel like a fun task, as much as possible. The more fun you're having, the more this points to the likelihood that you're doing it right. To make it more fun, take a large piece of white paper and then, with some colored pencils or pens, draw a picture of your ideal life: where you live, who's with you, what you do, what your dwelling looks like, what your ideal vacation looks like, all of it. Don't let *reality* get in the way. Pretend a magic wand has been waved over your life, and it gives you everything you think your ideal life would be. Now, *of course* you're going to tell me you can't draw. Okay, then make symbols for things, or create little "doodads" with labels—whatever works so that you can *see* all together on one page your vision of your ideal life, however primitively expressed.

You could also make a vision board by cutting pictures and quotes out of magazines (or from the internet) and gluing them onto a piece of paper. The power of this exercise sometimes amazes me. Reason? By avoiding words and using pictures or symbols as much as possible, it bypasses your logical mind and focuses on your creative mind, whose job is to engineer change. Do fun things like this, as you're exploring a new life for yourself.

Study What You Enjoy in School

If you're just graduating from high school, don't go get a college degree in some career field just because you think that this will guarantee you a job! It will not. Or even if it does, this approach makes sense only if you want and like the job.

I wish you could see my emails, filled with bitter letters from people who believed this myth, went and got a degree in a field that looked just great, thought it would be a snap to find a job, but are still unemployed two years later. Good times or bad. They are bitter (often), angry (always), and disappointed in a society that they feel lied to them. Law graduates in particular have been in the news in recent years, suing their law schools for falsifying employment figures for graduates.

To avoid this costly mistake, what you must do is take the choosing of a career into your own hands, with the help of this book, and then explore the career you've chosen down to the last inch, find out if you love it, and *then* go get your degree. Not because it guarantees you a job, but because you feel passion, enthusiasm, and energy with this choice. If you follow the suggestions in this book for social media, resume writing, and so on, you will be able to explain your education to an employer in their language. You will feel you have found the kind of life that other people only dream of.

Use Career Tests Sparingly

You will find career tests everywhere: in books, on the internet, in the offices of guidance counselors, vocational psychologists, and career coaches. And *sometimes* this turns out to be exactly the kind of guidance, the kind of insight, the kind of direction, that career choosers or changers are looking for. But tests can show only a limited view of your personality traits and interests. They don't usually measure specific skills.

Many tests can be deliberately skewed in the direction you want, so if you want to be a lawyer you can adjust your answers to fit what lawyers might say. People who are undecided about careers often end up looking undecided on their test results. So why take tests at all? Well, they do provide some helpful nuggets of information. For instance, a test that looks at your strengths might give you your top five strengths, which you could then turn into stories for an interview. A test that tells you your personality traits might help you think about careers that fit those traits. The information isn't necessarily bad—it's just often incomplete. So in taking a test, you should just be looking for clues, hunches, or suggestions, rather than for a definitive answer that says "this is what you must choose to do with your life."

Interest-based career tests can only reflect what you know about yourself at the time you take the test; they can't predict what skills or talents you might have or want to use. They are meant to be interpreted broadly, yet people almost always interpret their results literally. One psychology professor who has had an outstanding career in research, writing, and teaching took a career test in college that pointed him toward accounting. He looked at the accounting curriculum but found it dry and boring. He later realized that the test was probably reflecting the fact that he liked math and his father was an accountant. Accounting was simply a field he was familiar with, not really a career interest. Creative types often get results like "florist" on career tests even if they have no interest in plants; one computer-based test became notorious for recommending that social types who "like people" become funeral directors, much to the dismay of some. If the test isn't interpreted carefully by a skilled counselor, you are likely to be led astray. A career test can be ultimately helpful in shaping your ideas, but do not expect it will tell you what to do. Tests won't give you all the answers. But they can provide some insight, so take them if you want. Just keep your expectations low.

If you like tests, help yourself. There are lots of them on the internet. Counselors can also give them to you, for a fee; if you want one of these, shop around. If you want to know where to start, you might try these tests, the ones I personally like the best:

Dr. Martin Seligman's assessment website, Authentic Happiness.
This site provides a variety of assessments related to work, including the Values in Action (VIA) Survey of Character Strengths and the Work-Life Questionnaire, at https://www.authentichappiness.sas
.upenn.edu/testcenter. They are all free, but you need to create a password.

The University of Missouri's Career Interests Game can be found at https://career.missouri.edu/career-interest-game. This is based on a shortened version of John Holland's Self-Directed Search (SDS), the "Party Exercise." It's well redesigned here.

If you want further suggestions, you can search "career tests" or "personality tests" online and see what turns up. You'll find lots and lots of stuff. Just be careful that you aren't charged for the tests unless you are willing.

Let's Break Down the Career Change Process

A great way to think about how to choose or change your career is illustrated in the diagram below, which shows the systematic breakdown and building up to define a career that fits you.

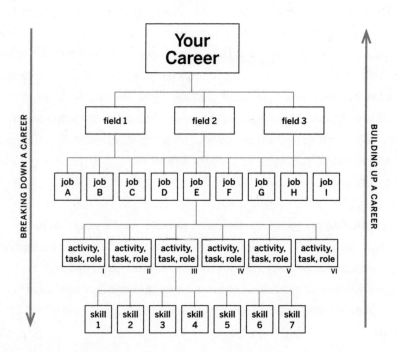

You can approach this diagram in two ways:

You can start at the bottom by listing your most important skills: the ones you are particularly good at and the ones you enjoy doing. You then break these skills into specific tasks or job duties related to them. For instance, you might have a skill as a writer. You could then think about using that in a job setting by choosing what you would write: news articles, grants, project designs, and so on. You would then identify the jobs that incorporate those duties, ultimately determining broad fields worth exploring as your career choice.

You could also start at the top. Perhaps you already have a career idea you'd like to transition to or start. Maybe it's marketing. So you start with "Marketing Career" at the top and then you break it down to two or three fields, such as advertising, sales, or public relations. From there you find job postings related to those fields, and you note the activities and duties described in those postings. Finally, you analyze the skills needed—and ultimately compare yourself with these opportunities to determine the best fit.

Changing a Career in Two Steps

This is not so much a way to identify a new career as a way to move into that career once you have figured out where you want to go next. This plan has worked very well for many career changers: changing careers in two steps, not one.

And how exactly do you do that?

Well, let's start with a definition: a job is *a job title* in a *field*.

That means a job has two parts: *title* and *field*. *Title* really stands for *what you do*. *Field* is *where you do it*, or *what you do it with*.

A dramatic career change typically involves trying to change both at the same time. That's the *Difficult Path* in the diagram on page 80. The problem with trying to take this difficult path is that you can't claim any prior experience. But if you do it in two steps, ah! That's different.

Three Types of Career Change, Visualized

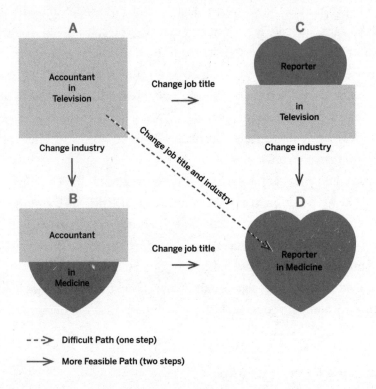

Let's say you are presently an accountant working for a television network, and you want to make a career change. You want to become a reporter on new medical developments.

If you try the Difficult Path above, and you go out into the job market as A—accountant in the television industry—and you try to jump to a new career as D—reporter in medicine—well, that's a pretty large jump. Of course, sometimes you can pull that off, with a bit of luck and a carefully crafted social media profile that highlights your knowledge and skills related to the new field. But what if?

What if that doesn't work? Then you're likely to run into the following scenario:

Interviewer: "So, I see you want to be a reporter. Were you ever a reporter before?" Your answer: "No."

Interviewer: "And I see you want to be in the medical field. Were you ever in the medical field before?" Your answer: "No."

End of story. You are toast.

On the other hand, if you were to change only one of these *at a time*—field or job title—you could always claim prior experience.

In the diagram on the facing page, let's say you move in two steps, from A to B and from B to D, over a period of three years.

Interviewer during your first move (a change just in your field): "Were you ever in this kind of work before?" Your answer: "Yes, I've been an accountant for x years."

Interviewer during your second move (now a change in your job title): "Were you ever in this kind of work before?" Your answer: "Yes, I've been in medicine for x years."

Another example: Let's say you make a different set of two moves over a period of three years: you move from A to C and from C to D.

Interviewer during your first move (a change just in your job title): "Were you ever in this kind of work before?" Your answer: "Yes, I've been in television for x years."

Interviewer during your second move (a change just in your field): "Have you ever done this kind of work before?" Your answer: "Yes, I've been a reporter for x years."

By doing career change in two steps, each time you make a move you can legitimately claim that you've had prior *experience*.

Needless to say, your likelihood of getting hired each time has just increased tremendously.

Career change looks different for everyone. For some it can be an easy switch; for others it is a slow process requiring additional education or training. It is not unusual to have to accept less pay to move into your new field. It's important to move forward in small increments if necessary. Avoid comparing yourself with others. You may feel like you're behind your cohorts when you do a career switch. After all, you have some catching up to do in your new field. But if the field is something that will ultimately make you happier, then it will be worth it.

Let's look at an interesting real-life example of a career change:

In college, Tricia Rose Burt had focused on "practical" courses: a major in communications and a minor in business. This seemed logical; since everyone in her family worked in business, it was assumed she would follow along. And she succeeded. After college she worked in public relations for about ten years, including a stint as a corporate communications director. *But* . . . she was extremely unhappy. She worked with a career counselor who helped her see that an artistic side of her personality was not being expressed. She enrolled in art classes at the School of the Museum of Fine Arts in Boston.

She soon discovered that while her corporate job paid her bills, it also drained her soul. Making art gave her energy and purpose. At age thirty-four she quit her lucrative corporate career, sold her car, cashed out her retirement savings, and moved to Ireland to become an artist.

Four years later she returned to the United States and worked as a visual artist for the next ten years, supplementing her income through teaching, arts administration positions, and the like. She had opportunities to return to consulting but turned them down.

And then the 2008 recession hit.

People stopped buying her artwork. And corporations were not lining up to hire consultants. So, she said, with her usual wry humor: "I decided to create a one-woman show that had been in my head for about thirteen years—because performance is such a lucrative career path!"

She developed a one-woman show, "How to Draw a Nekkid Man" (https://www.triciaroseburt.com), which led her to The Moth, an internationally acclaimed storytelling organization based in New York City. She is a frequent guest storyteller with The Moth, and is also part of MothWorks, their corporate arm that teaches business executives the art and craft of storytelling.

Working with her own clients as well, she travels around the country as a speaker and storytelling consultant and still has time to write, make art, and develop one-woman shows.

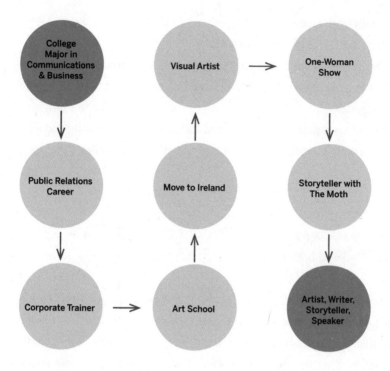

This diagram illustrates Tricia's career path. Her story is interesting on several levels. She learned that her definition of career success changed over the years. Initially success meant security, stability, and a good income. She still knows that income is important (she recommends that all artists have a firm grounding in business), but she has learned to adjust her life to fit her income. She also knows that it's important to work around people who are creative, challenge her intellectually, and share her curiosity. She now realizes that there's been a constant theme through all her careers: storytelling. Every position she has had involved some sort of storytelling, even with a corporation.

So what is her advice for others who decide to change careers?

- Just because your family and friends go in one direction doesn't mean you have to go with them.
- Being different from everyone else is a fantastic way to be.

- Trust your gut.
- The path will not be linear.
- Whatever experiences you have are never wasted.
- Change is not nearly as hard as you think it is. Not changing can be deadly.
- Being secure is wildly overrated. (Although she recommends investing in your retirement starting right after college.)

The Two Completely Different Strategies for Finding a Job

There are two different ways you can go about the job hunt or a career change. There's the way everyone tells us we should hunt for work. Because that's the way we've always done it. Because that's the only way we know. This strategy has a name: the traditional approach. Most of us know how to do this, or we can quickly learn. It doesn't demand much time. You begin with the so-called job market. You look at the ad postings by employers, online and off. You approach those companies that look the least bit interesting to you. Wait to see if you get any responses. At the same time, you slap together a resume. Post it. Or send out bushel baskets of resumes to mailing lists. If that doesn't turn up any job offer, send out another ton of resumes. Post your resume everywhere.

If this all works for you, great! (But then, if it did, you probably wouldn't be reading this chapter, would you?)

But if it doesn't work (for you), the good news is there is a radically different second way to hunt for work or a career change: the Parachute Approach.

Here you begin not with the job market but with yourself. You figure out who you are, and among all your gifts, which ones you most love to use. Then (and only then) you go looking for organizations that match *you*. And you do not wait until they announce they have a vacancy. You approach them anyway, not through a resume but through a person, specifically a bridge person—someone who knows you and also knows them, and therefore is a bridge between you two.

If you've been using the traditional approach, and it's not working, stop. You need to switch approaches. Try using the Parachute Approach—as outlined in the right-hand column of the chart below. Take a look at the Traditional Approach column, and see how many of those actions you've been taking. Then look at the Parachute Approach column and note what actions you should take instead.

Sure, it's harder to use this approach.

Sure, it requires more of you. It's more work.

Sure, it asks you to do some hard thinking and reflect on who you are and where you're going with your life.

But that is precisely its value. Remember the statement in the first chapter that it's your job search and you're in charge? Well, this is part of taking charge and owning your search. It's not just about jobs. It forces you to first step back and think about your whole life. And what you want out of life. It begins with Who (are you?) before considering What (shall I do?).

Who precedes What.

These, then, are the two basic job-hunting or career-changing strategies that are at your command. Each strategy can be broken down further, into twelve elements as illustrated in this chart:

	THE TRADITIONAL APPROACH	THE PARACHUTE APPROACH
What you are looking for	A job.	An ideal job: one that uses your favorite skills and favorite fields or knowledges.
How you see yourself	As not in control. You will be lucky to get a job.	As a resource who controls the search process. They will be lucky to get you.
Your basic plan	Look at job boards for what is available.	Determine, before you start looking, what job would interest and motivate you.

continued ▶

	THE TRADITIONAL APPROACH	THE PARACHUTE APPROACH
Your preparation	Do research to find out what the job market wants and what the "hot jobs" are. Your best weapon is your ability to "fit in."	Do homework on yourself, to figure out what you do best, *and* most love to do. Your best weapon is your enthusiasm!
How you figure out which employers to approach	You wait for them to identify they have a vacancy.	Doing informational interviews, you figure out which organizations most interest you—in light of your homework—even if they do not have an advertised vacancy at the time.
How you contact them	Through your resume.	Through a bridge person—a connection you have made through LinkedIn or other research.
The purpose of your resume	To sell them on why you should be hired there.	To get a first interview with them.
Your main goal if you get an interview	To sell them on why you should be hired there.	You have a great conversation that gets you another interview there.
What you talk about in the interview	Yourself, your assets, your experience.	Their interests and needs. Fifty percent of the time you let them ask the questions. Fifty percent of the time you ask them the things *you* want to know about the place, and the job there, and how you can help.
What you're trying to find out	Do they want me?	Do I want them? (As well as "Do they want me?") Can I do the work I most love to do, here, and at the same time help them?
How you end the final interview there	You ask them: "When may I hope to hear from you?" (You are leaving things hanging.)	Determine the best way to convey your enthusiasm and ask about the hiring process. Could an offer be made that day? (You are seeking closure.)
What you do after getting the job but before you start	Send a thank-you note. Then, "it's over." Rest, relax, and savor the successful end to your job hunt.	Send a thank-you note. Then, keep on quietly looking. (Their offer may still fall through before you start, due to unforeseen developments there.)

Traditional Job-Search Techniques That Can Work

Now, not everything about the traditional approach is bad. In fact, some of the traditional techniques still work, particularly if you approach them with a new frame of mind—that is, you have done your homework and know your top skills and the employment setting you would most enjoy. Before we move on to the Parachute Approach, here are some traditional techniques still worth pursuing.

1. **Looking for employers' job-postings on the internet.** This one seems logical, right? You need a job, so you go online to find job listings. You send in your resume and you wait. And hope. But the odds are generally against you, simply because of the sheer numbers of other people who are doing the same. On the other hand, you will hear success stories occasionally, which is why this method can't be discounted.

    Examples:
    A job seeker—a systems administrator in Taos, New Mexico, who wanted to move to San Francisco—posted his resume on a San Francisco online site at 10 p.m. on a Monday night. By Wednesday morning he had over seventy responses from employers.
    A marketing professional developed her resume following guidance she found on the internet and posted it to two advertised positions she found there. Within seventy-two hours of posting her electronic resume, both firms had contacted her, and she is now working for one of them.
    A college administrator sees an online job posting for a housing manager at a nearby college. She sends a resume, gets an interview, and accepts the offer.

Are these stories just flukes, or is this a universal experience? Mostly it has to do with the career field the person is seeking and the law of supply and demand. If you are in a field like engineering, finance, or health care, where the demand is greater than the supply, the traditional approach is more likely to be successful, at least in terms of getting a response from the employer. But if you're in a field where the supply of applicants is greater than the demand, you will likely not hear anything from employers. They simply don't need to use this method to find applicants. This is where the Parachute Approach of finding a human connection will be much more effective.

2. **Going to private employment agencies or search firms for help.** These firms, also known as staffing agencies, talent agencies, and recruiting firms, used to place just office workers; now it's hard to think of a category of jobs they don't try to place, especially in large metropolitan areas. You can find these firms by Googling "employment agencies" with your location or employment field, such as "employment agencies in Austin, TX" or "employment agencies marketing careers." These agencies vary greatly in their staffing (ranging from *extremely competent* on down to *inept*, or *running a scam*), so do your research before signing on. You can always check the agency through the Better Business Bureau (www.bbb.org) to see if any complaints have been filed. And *never pay a fee to an agency*. Their fees should be paid by the employer who hires you. If they charge a fee, walk away.

3. **Answering ads in professional or trade journals, appropriate to your field.** This means looking at professional organizations in your profession or field and answering any ads that intrigue you. Some job boards will be limited to members only, but the websites often contain articles about the job search for the profession. A directory of these associations and their journals can be found at www.directoryofassociations.com.

4. **Joining job-search support groups.** These groups can be found in virtually every community. While their job-hunting success rate *varies*, they can be valuable in providing emotional support and reducing your feelings of isolation.

   Most support groups meet only once a week, and then for only one, two, or three hours, at best. Even so, they provide a community for the otherwise lonely job hunter. This is a great gift. *No one should ever have to job hunt all by themselves if they can possibly avoid it.* We all need encouragement and support, along the way. Check with your local library or use Meetup.com to find potential groups.

5. **Going to the state or federal employment office.** Your local federal/state unemployment service office (www.dol.gov/dol/location.htm) or their nationwide CareerOneStop business centers (www.careeronestop.org) provide guidance on how to better job hunt and find job leads. They can be a great resource for jobs in government: local, state, and federal. A quick way to locate state job sites is to simply Google the name of your state with "human resources." Virtually every state has its own human resources or employment site you can use to discover job openings and even apply online. A great website for federal job opportunities is usajobs.gov (https://www.usajobs.gov/). This is the official site for all federal job openings and is free to use. Be careful about sites that promise links to government jobs but have the domain extension ".com," because they might charge you a fee to find and apply for opportunities you could apply for without charge elsewhere. Research any job placement or application site carefully before you pay any fees.

6. **Going to places where employers pick up workers.** If you're a union member, particularly in the trades or construction, and you have access to a union hiring hall, this method will find you work.

What they may not tell you, however, is how long it may take to get a job at the hall, and how short-lived such a job may be. In the trades, it's often just a few days. Moreover, this job-hunting method is closed to a large percentage of job hunters.

If you've got manual labor skills but are not a union member, there's something similar to union halls: employers may pick up workers (called "day laborers") early in the morning on established street corners in your town or city (ask around). It's called "pickup work," and it's usually short term, yard work or other physical labor, usually with a cash payment to you *that day*. It's definitely *temp* work, but if you're not finding full-time work, as yet, this may be a stopgap approach that at least can bring in a little money.

7. **Participating in the gig economy/freelance work.** The modern-day version of pickup work is the "gig economy," also called the "sharing economy" or "access economy." If you have a particular talent that others would value, check out sites like FlexJobs, Freelancer, Freelance Writing, Guru.com, LinkedIn ProFinder, Sologig (for IT and engineering work), Upwork, and Fiver. You can explore using your *home* (airbnb.com) or your *car* (either uber.com or lyft.com) to make some extra money. Other sites for offering services and goods include DogVacay, for pet sitters and dog walkers (dogvacay.com); TaskRabbit, for tasks and deliveries (taskrabbit.com); Zaarly, for home service providers in a few select cities (zaarly.com); Poshmark, for fashion (poshmark.com); and Etsy, for "handcrafted, vintage, custom, or unique" goods (etsy.com). If you want to explore this kind of work, try putting "sharing economy jobs" in your search engine to find the latest opportunities. While these opportunities represent short-term, stopgap ideas, it's always possible you'll meet someone who can help you find a better opportunity.

8. **Asking for job leads.** It never hurts to ask family members, friends, and people you know in the community (or on LinkedIn) if they know of any place where someone with your talents and background is being sought. It is a simple question: "Do you know of any job vacancies at the place where you work—or elsewhere?" Also ask, "Do you know anyone who might be aware of job openings?" Believe it or not, *using this method will give you better results than just sending out unsolicited resumes online.*

9. **Knocking on the door of any employer, office, or manufacturing plant.** This method works best with *small* employers (twenty-five or fewer employees), as you might have guessed. Sometimes you blunder into a place where a vacancy has just opened up. One job hunter knocked on the door of an architectural office at 11 a.m. His predecessor (for he did get hired there) had just quit at 10 a.m. that morning. If you try this method and nothing turns up, you broaden your definition of *small employer* to those with fifty or fewer employees.

Well, that's it. That's the Traditional Approach. These job-hunting methods were not created equal. Some methods, as we have seen, have a pretty good track record, and therefore will repay you for time spent pursuing them. But other methods have a really terrible track record and are a waste of your time and energy. Remember, while each of these methods can be useful, generally, on their own, they just don't produce strong outcomes. They must be integrated into a larger process. So if you limit yourself to only a few methods, you are not as likely to be successful. It's all about *conservation of energy*. And wisdom would say conserve your energy. Invest it well.

In the next chapters we will turn to the other approach to job hunting or career-changing: the Parachute Approach. It begins not with examining the job market, but with examining yourself.

The Parachute Approach and Using the Flower Exercise

This pathway to choosing or changing your career is not as popular as, say, relying on the internet, because it requires a lot more time of you and a lot more work. As I describe in chapters 5 and 6, it is a careful, thorough, step-by-step process for ensuring that you are choosing a career that fits you like a glove: a dream career, or dream job; your mission in life, as it is often called. It is not for the faint-hearted or the lazy. But if the other ways to change careers don't turn up any careers that look interesting to you, you may end up being very grateful that there is this way. I get letters like this all the time:

"I have already benefited greatly from the Flower Exercise. I found hope in having a second alternative after doing the homework . . ."

"The series of life-changing activities in this book has definitely helped me to better understand who I am, to further appreciate my talents, and to utilize the resources I have readily available."

As you'll find in chapters 5 and 6, here are the steps involved in this way of choosing a new career:

1. You do the Flower Exercise (chapters 5 and 6), which establishes the basic aspects of who you are (represented by petals), so you can match a career to you.

2. Then you put together on one piece of paper your five favorite transferable skills and your three favorite fields of knowledge, and you start informational interviewing to find the names of careers that fit your aspects.

3. Along the way, you see if you can figure out how to combine your three favorite fields of knowledge into one career, to make yourself unique.

4. Try on the jobs to see if they fit you, by talking to actual workers in the kind of career or careers you have tentatively picked out.

5. Then you find out what kinds of organizations have such jobs in the geographical area that interests you (where you are already?).

6. Then you find out the names of actual organizations that interest you, where you could do your most effective work.

7. And finally, you learn about those places before you walk in, or secure an appointment to talk to them about working there, whether or not they have a known vacancy at that moment.

In essence, what you're doing here is looking at your past, breaking that experience down into its most basic components (namely, skills), then building a new career for the future from your favorite components, retracing your steps from the bottom up, in the exact opposite direction. This is illustrated in the model on page 78.

Five Final Tips for Choosing/Changing Careers

Whenever you have to choose or change a career, here are five things to keep in mind. (Many of these you're already aware of, I'm sure; this is just a reminder.)

1. Go for *any* career that seems fascinating or even interesting to you. But *first* talk to people who are already doing that work, to find out if the career or job is as great as it seems at first impression. Ask them: *What do you like best about this work? What do you like least about this work? And how did you get into this work?* This last

question can give you important clues about how you could get into this line of work or career yourself. Ask them how they perceive their career: what are its component parts? **Every person may see their vocation in a different light. Don't assume that the way the person you are interviewing defines it is the way you must, also. Beneath any job title there is often lots of room for you to maneuver and define that job in a way that uniquely suits you, your gifts, and your creativity.** One architect, for example, may perceive his or her vocation in a different way from another architect. When Frei Otto received the Pritzker Prize for Architecture posthumously in March 2015, it was said that he "embraced a definition of architect to include researcher, inventor, form-finder, engineer, builder, teacher, collaborator, environmentalist, humanist, and creator of memorable . . . spaces." Otto was inspired by "natural phenomena— from birds' skulls to soap bubbles and spiders' webs."[17]

2. In moving from one career to another, make sure that you preserve constancy in your life as well as change, during the transition. In other words, don't change *everything*. To paraphrase Archimedes's observation about his mythical long lever: *Give me a fulcrum and a place to stand, and with a lever I will move the Earth.* When you are moving your life around you, you need a firm place to stand, and that place is provided by the things that stay constant about you: your character, your faith, your values, your gifts or immutable skills.

3. If you can, you'll do better to start with yourself and what *you* want, rather than with the job market and what's "hot." The difference is enthusiasm and passion. Yours. You're much more attractive to employers when you're *on fire*. Maybe where you are times are just too tough for you to start with your vision of what you want to do with your life—for now, anyway—but *try*.

4. The best *work*, the best career, for you—the one that makes you happiest and most fulfilled—is going to be one that uses your *favorite* transferable skills, in your *favorite* subjects, fields, or special knowledges, in a job that offers you your *preferred* people environments, your *preferred* working conditions, with your *preferred* salary or other rewards, working toward your *preferred* goals and values. This requires a thorough inventory of who you are. Detailed instructions can be found in chapters 5 and 6.

5. Be patient. This is a process of discovery: about yourself and the workplace. Insight into what works best for you will come in time. If you are young, or relatively young, it's okay to make a mistake in your choice. You'll have time to correct a bad decision. Most of us will have at least five to seven *careers* during our lifetime, and ten or more *jobs*.

A final note: **Job hunting is, or should be, a full-time job.** If your job hunt isn't working, you must increase the amount of time you're devoting to your job hunt. If you want to devote as little time to your job hunt as possible, then fine; try it. But if that doesn't lead to a job, then you are going to have to devote more time to it.

Where you have to realistically, I think,
understand that the days are getting shorter.
And you can't put things off,
thinking you'll get to them someday.
If you really want to do them,
you better do them. . . .
So I'm very much a believer in knowing
what it is that you love doing
so that you can do a great deal of it.

—NORA EPHRON

CHAPTER 5

THE FLOWER EXERCISE: SELF-INVENTORY, PART 1

Make no mistake. What follows in this section of the book is the most powerful self-inventory and job-hunting method you can use. You will develop a deeper knowledge of who you are and what you need in your job. This method, faithfully followed, step by step, works *for a majority of job seekers*. If you use this approach you will have a much greater chance of finding work than if you just send out your resume. Not just work, but work you really want to do. What we sometimes refer to as our "dream job."

Heads up: It will take some time to complete this section of the book, so you might be tempted to skip it. Don't. Let's examine why.

Why a SELF-Inventory?

Why does an inventory of who you are work so well in helping you find work, after traditional job-hunting methods have failed? That's important to know, because the answer will keep you motivated to finish this inventory when otherwise you might say OMG, *this is just too much work!* And just give up.

Okay, following are eight reasons why this works so well.

1. By doing this homework on yourself, you learn to describe your-self in at least six different ways, so you can approach multiple job markets. With an inventory of who you are, you stop identifying yourself by only one job title. Now you can think of yourself as not just a "computer tech" or "construction worker" or "accountant" or "engineer" or "teacher" or "ex-military" or whatever. You are a person who has these *multiple* skills and experiences. If, say, teaching and writing and growing things are your favorite skills, then you can approach either the job market of teaching, or that of writing, or that of gardening. Multiple job markets open up to you, not just one (as with retraining a worker for a new field).

2. Doing this exercise will bring mindfulness to the process, which has been shown to improve decision making. Take this time to focus on yourself and what is most important in your life now. You will make smarter choices and keep yourself open to possibilities.

3. By doing this homework on yourself, you can describe in detail exactly what you are looking for. This greatly enables your friends, LinkedIn contacts, and family to better help you. You approach them not with "Uh, I'm out of work; let me know if you hear of anything," but with a much more exact description of what kind of "anything," and in what work setting. You will have a story to tell them. About your skills. About your traits. About the job you're seeking. This helps them to focus, and to look for something very specific, thus increasing their helpfulness to you, and your ability to find jobs you would otherwise never find.

4. By ending up with a picture of a job that would really excite you, and not just any old job, you will inevitably pour much more time, energy, and determination into your job search. *This is really worth looking for.* So you will redouble your efforts, your dedication, and

your determination when otherwise you might try but soon give up. Persistence is the essence of a successful job hunt, and persistence becomes your middle name, once you've identified a prize worth fighting for.

5. By doing this homework, you will no longer have to wait to approach companies until they say they have a vacancy. Armed with the knowledge you've gained, you can choose places that match who you are. And then you can approach them (through a contact, or what I like to call a "bridge person" because they know both you and them, and thus serve as a bridge between you)—knowing confidently that you will be an asset there, whether they have a job opening or decide to create one for you.

    Wait—create one for me? No, I'm not kidding. This happens more often than you would ever think, to the prepared job hunter or career changer. One job hunter wrote to me recently:

    > In my mind I knew where I wanted to work: a company I had had a couple of meetings with about an imperfect job about two years ago and fell in love with. I found the CEO on LinkedIn and asked him if he remembered me and would he be up for a short meeting if I promised it would be fun. He said he would love to meet, and I pitched the idea of setting up a training academy for them. About a month later, I had an email to say they definitely want to go ahead with providing training as I had pitched it. The job did not exist, they had not conceived of the job, and it meets all my criteria because I thought of it. [From] *Parachute* to dream job in six months is not bad, is it?

6. When you are facing, let us say, nineteen (or ninety) other competitors for the job you want—equally experienced, equally skilled—you will stand out above them all, because you can

accurately describe to employers exactly what is unique about you and what you bring to the table that the others do not. You will have compelling stories to back up your statements.

7. If you are contemplating a career change, maybe—after you inventory yourself—you will see definitely what new career or direction you want for your life. Often you can put together a new career just using what you already know and what you already can do—with much less training or retraining than you thought you would have to do. It may turn out that the knowledge you need to pick up can be found in a vocational/technical school, in a one- or two-year college, or even online through a certificate or short-term training program. But first, before you spend money on additional education or training, please, please, inventory who you are and what you love to do.

    And sometimes, *sometimes*, that dream job can be found simply by doing enough *informational interviewing*. Example: A job hunter named Bill had worked for a number of years in retail; now he was debating a career change to working in the oil industry. He knew virtually nothing about that industry, so he went from person to person who worked at companies in that industry, just informally seeking information about the industry. The more of these informational interviews he conducted, the more he knew. In fact, coming down the home stretch, just before he got hired in the place of his dreams, he found he now knew more than the people he was visiting did about their competitors and some aspects of the industry.

    In other words, with certain kinds of career change, there is more than one way to pick up the knowledge you need.

8. Unemployment is an interruption in most of our lives. If you are unemployed, you have the opportunity (desired or not) to pause, to think, to assess where you really want to go with your life. Martin Luther King Jr. had something to say about this:

The major problem of life is learning how to handle the costly interruptions. The door that slams shut, the plan that got side-tracked, the marriage that failed. Or that lovely poem that didn't get written because someone knocked on the door.

A self-inventory is just the type of thinking and assessing that Dr. King refers to. The Parachute Approach, with its demand that you complete an inventory of who you are and what you love to do before you set out on your search for (meaningful) work, helps you take advantage of the opportunity that this interruption presents.

So there you have it: the eight reasons why this inventory of who you are works so much better as a method of job hunting than all other methods.

Being out of work, or thinking about a new career, should speak to your heart. It should say something like this:

Use this opportunity. Make this not only a hunt for a job, but also a hunt for a life. A deeper life, a victorious life, a life you're more proud of.

The world currently is filled with workers whose weeklong cry is, "When is the weekend going to be here?" And, then, "Thank God it's Friday!" There's a reason one of the most popular insurance ads on TV features a camel announcing gleefully "It's hump day!" For too many people, their work puts bread on the table but . . . they are bored out of their minds. They've never taken the time to think out what they uniquely can do, and what they uniquely have to offer to the world. The world doesn't need any more bored workers. *Dream a little. Dream a lot.*

One of the saddest pieces of advice in the world is "Oh come now—be realistic." The best parts of this world were not fashioned by those who were "realistic." They were fashioned by those who dared to look hard at their wishes and then gave them horses to ride.

How to Do Your SELF-Inventory

The Flower Diagram describes who you are in *seven* ways, summarized on one page, in one graphic. After all, you are not just one of these things; you are *all* of these things. The Flower Diagram is a complete picture of *you*. All of you. In the language of the workplace.

And believe me, you want the complete picture. I'll tell you why. Let's say there is some job out there that matches just one petal, one aspect of yourself, one way of defining who you are; for example, let's say this job lets you use your favorite knowledges that you already have. But that's it.

That job doesn't let you use your favorite skills, nor does it have you working with the kinds of people you most want to, nor does it give you the surroundings where you can do your best work.

What would you call such a job? At the very least: *boring*. You would barely be able to wait for *Thank God it's Friday!* Some of us have already sung that song. A lot.

But now let us suppose you could instead find another kind of work that matches seven different sides of you, or seven petals. What would you call *that* work? Well, that's *your dream job*.

So, your complete Flower Diagram is a picture of who *you* most fully are. *And,* at the same time it is a picture of a job that would most completely match and fulfill all that you are. Where you would shine, because it uses the best of you.

Make it your goal to completely fill in your Flower in the next chapter. *And try to feel it as a joy rather than a duty.* Determine from the beginning that this is going to be fun. Because it sure can be. And should be. Are you ready to get started on finding your dream career? Here's what you will need.

Where Can I Find the Flower Exercise?

Readers have asked for a list of all the places, or forms, where they can find this Flower. Here are the three main forms:

In the next chapter. Of course. A paper version, here in the book on pages 186–187. Free, since you already have the book.

In a workbook. The *What Color Is Your Parachute? Job Hunter's Workbook* has larger pages: 8 by 10 inches.

Online. In response to many requests, a few years ago we produced an online video course, walking you through the Flower Exercise step by step, with me as your guide throughout. You'll need a computer and a printer to print out the worksheets. (The course was put together on Udemy's platform by the principals at eParachute—myself as content and onscreen host, Marci Bolles as executive producer, Gary Bolles as producer, and Eric Barnett as technical consultant.) It can be used by individual readers or by a whole workshop. It is available at a discounted price for readers of this book; order at www.eParachute.com/para20. You can also access the course directly at www.udemy.com. Occasionally, like all Udemy courses, it will be on sale.

And, since you asked, there are other online resources on topics related to the Flower Exercise and this book. You'll find dozens of videos at www.youtube.com /user/TheParachuteGuy, and a bunch of articles at www.jobhuntersbible.com. One word of caution: don't spend a lot of time on these side roads. Stay focused on your one main task: completing your Flower, in whatever form you choose. You can go roaming later.

Mental Preparation

Start the Flower Exercise with a beginner's mind. It's tempting to immediately think about everything you already know about yourself. But to get the most out of this exercise, start by forgetting. Begin by forgetting any past job titles. When you ask yourself *Who am I?* you must drop the vocational answer that first springs to mind. Like: I'm an accountant, or

I am a truck driver, or a lawyer, or a construction worker, or salesperson, or designer, or writer, or account executive. That kind of an answer locks you into the past. You must think instead: "*I am a person . . .*"

"*I am a person who* . . . has had these experiences . . ."
"*I am a person who* . . . is skilled at . . ."
"*I am a person who* . . . knows a lot about . . ."
"*I am a person who* . . . is unique in this way or that . . ."

Yes, this is how a useful self-inventory begins. You are a person, not a job. Be curious. Open. Looking forward to what you will learn.

A Timeline for Completing the Exercise

The Flower Exercise is pretty amazing in its scope. You aren't just developing a list or two about your skills or interests; you are doing a deep dive into yourself and your future career plans. For this reason, you want to devote a reasonable amount of time. What's reasonable, you ask? Well, that depends. You will have the option of doing some of the exercises online, and that can make the process go more quickly. You will be asked to write some short essays, and it may take a while to come up with ideas. Or maybe you're a bundle of energy and you knock out all those essays in one sitting. This is really about you, your energy, and your style. Look over the whole section and see the different petals. Decide how you want to proceed.

Set a completion goal and then create a flexible plan. Divide your exercises into units of time or completion of a segment. Maybe that means you take one day to do each petal; maybe you set a goal of working for sixty minutes and stop when the time is up. Or you set aside a weekend to work on the whole thing. Or a few evenings. Just take a look at your calendar and estimate the time you'll need. You might be pleasantly surprised to learn it all goes much more quickly than you thought it would. Or you might find that you need to stop and think about some of the petals, and it takes a little longer. Just stay loose: it's okay if it takes longer than you anticipated. You're probably getting more information about yourself than you ever expected.

Find a great location to work on your flower. For some, it will be the local coffee shop. Nothing like some caffeine to boost your energy and ambient noise in the background to help you focus. That said, maybe you prefer a completely quiet setting. Maybe you can work at home in the evenings, or maybe there's too much activity or distractions. Know yourself. And be creative in finding a location to get the work done. Don't let your surroundings be an excuse for not working on this.

Consider completing your flower with a friend or fellow job seeker. If you want, create a group to work on it together. (Meetup.com is a great site for establishing a short-term group that could meet to work on this.) The point is, if you are better motivated by others participating, then find someone to collaborate with.

Lots of Paper (Digital or Physical)

Study after study in the field of neuroscience shows that writing things down is one of the most effective ways to clarify thinking. We remember better and are more likely to succeed with our plans and goals when we write them down. So it just makes sense to take some time to write down what is important about our career choices. And the Flower Exercise is designed to help you do that. You will start by using a lot of paper and writing a lot of ideas, but ultimately you will narrow everything down to the final product, the one piece of paper, called "The Flower." Not a journal, or a bunch of Post-it Notes, or several pieces of paper. Just one page. (Write small.)

To get started, you will need a number of disposable blank pieces of paper—I call them *worksheets*—to do a particular exercise (or two) that I will show you, for each flower petal. I emphasize *disposable*. You will ultimately be copying the final results from these worksheets onto your Flower Diagram, after which you can recycle these worksheets if you want.

Some Kind of a Graphic or Picture

Again, brain researchers have discovered that when making a decision about your life, it helps immensely if you don't just put a flood of *words* on that one piece of paper but also add some kind of a graphic, picture, or diagram. Particularly when you're dealing with a lot of information (known as *cognitive load* in psychology), graphic organizers can help you more easily remember, understand, and address the information you're working with. Researchers have discovered that this encourages the right side of your brain to spring into action—the part of your brain that can look at a whole bunch of apparently unrelated data and exclaim, *Aha! I see what it all means.* Some like to call this your intuitive side, the opposite of your logical side.

In the workshops that I taught from 1970 to 2012, I encouraged my students to choose any graphic they wished. We needed a picture with seven parts to it, corresponding to the seven parts of you that are important in finding matching work. Well, the favorite graphic turned out to be a picture or diagram of yourself as a flower, with seven petals. Hence the title of our self-inventory: the Flower Diagram (or Flower Exercise).

A Prioritizing Instrument or Grid

It is easy to imagine that the purpose of a self-inventory is to gather a series of personal *lists*, to which you then try to match possible jobs or careers. For example, *Here's a list of all the things I want in my place of work.* Or *This is a list of all the skills I want to be able to use at my next job, or career.* But over the past forty years or so, we have discovered that lists are useless, unless and until the items on each list are put into order of priority or importance for you: *this item is most important to me, this is next most important, and the next, and the next, and so on.*

Why is this? Well, we live in an imperfect world, and—at least initially—you may not be able to find a match for all the items on your lists. You may be able to find a match for only *some* of the items. There will be only a partial overlap between "dream job" and "actual job," in which case it is important that the overlap be the items you care the most about, not the least. And how will you know that, unless you put the items on each list in order of importance to you? In some cases, you can just "eyeball" it. Certain priorities will just "pop" when you look at the list. If this describes your lists, then you can highlight or put a star next to the items that reflect your priorities. Simple. Done.

On the other hand, sometimes the things that "pop" are just the items that are most familiar or comfortable to you, and you're just repeating old patterns that might keep you in a rut. For that reason, a grid that can help you prioritize your thoughts can be extremely helpful. I know it looks a little complicated, but once you get the hang of it, it's actually pretty easy to do. And it will work on a variety of your upcoming petals, as you will see.

Here is the problem visually summarized:

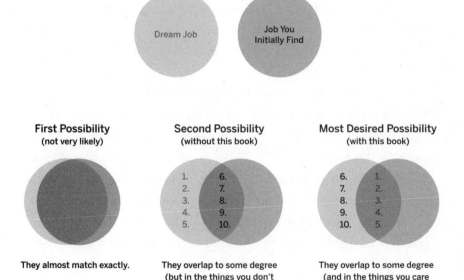

Okay, so prioritizing is essential. How do you go about this? Having compiled a list of, say, ten items on one of the petals in your Flower Diagram, how will you decide which of the ten is absolutely the most important to you, which of the ten is next most important, and so on? At first sight it seems a bewildering challenge. Actually, it's easier than you think, *if . . .*

. . . **you compare just two items at a time**, until you've compared all the possible pairs in that list of ten items. With all the pairs displayed in one diagram, this works out to be a grid. And the most popular form of that grid turns out to be my Prioritizing Grid, which I invented back in 1976. It can be used for any number of items you choose, but the most common and simplest form of it is for ten items.

You can find blank copies of this Prioritizing Grid in three main places:

In this book. A ten-item paper version appears throughout the next chapter (see page 123). You have my permission to copy or reproduce that Grid as many times as you wish, *for your own private use* (not for inclusion in an ebook or another published work).

In a workbook. *What Color Is Your Parachute? Job-Hunter's Workbook* is available online or at bookstores; the workbook pages are larger than this book's—8 by 10 inches.

Online. I have given my friend Beverly Ryle permission to produce a simple online version of my Prioritizing Grid that is automated and interactive. It is free at www.beverlyryle.com/prioritizing-grid. You can use my ten-item grid there or customize a grid for any number (of items) you choose. Needless to say, you can use her website as many times as you wish, and print out the results each time for your own keeping. I'll provide instructions for filling out the grid later.

Before you go on to fill in the petals in the Flower Exercise, it is sometimes helpful to ask yourself: *Which petals—which parts of a job—do I instinctively feel will be most important to me—at least for now—and in what order?* The petals are set up in a flow, so to speak, in that one item leads to the next:

1. The people you work with
2. The look and feel of your workplace
3. The degree to which it lets you use your favorite skills, abilities, or talents
4. The degree to which this job lands you in your favorite field or fields of knowledge and interest
5. The salary
6. The geographical location
7. The degree to which it gives you a sense of purpose for your life, or fits in with the purpose you want your life to serve

You don't have to follow this order if you have a pressing need to explore one area first. And don't waste time pondering which petal to start with. If you don't have a strong preference, then do them in the order in which they are presented.

Are you curious which petals other people have most often picked as their first priority in the past? The answer varies. If they're just trying to survive, their first choice is usually Petal Five, the Salary petal. If they're on in years, it's Petal Seven, the Purpose petal. If they're anywhere in between, it's Petal Three, the petal dealing with abilities, talents, skills. But all seven petals are important to you; don't leave any of them out.

Just start. Wherever you want. And have fun. You're exploring a new world of possibilities. Let's go . . .

Where flowers bloom, so does hope.

—LADY BIRD JOHNSON

CHAPTER 6

THE FLOWER EXERCISE: SELF-INVENTORY, PART 2

Are you ready to start? Let's take a look at the petals you will be encountering in this exercise. This self-inventory is a flower with *seven* petals. That's because there are seven sides to you, or seven ways of thinking about yourself, or seven ways of describing who you are—*using the language of the workplace*:

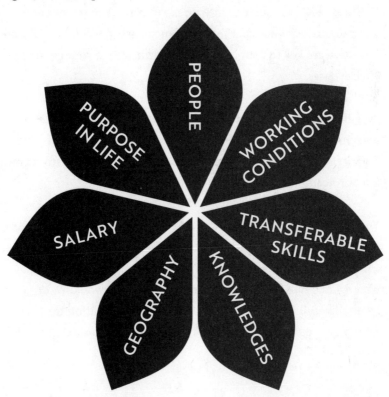

If you prefer a different metaphor, you are like a diamond, with seven facets to you, as we hold you up to the light.

1. **You and People.** You can describe *who you are* in terms of the kinds of people you most prefer to *work with or help*—age span, problems, needs, physical or mental disabilities, education level, geographical location, etc.

2. **You and a Workplace.** Or you can describe *who you are* in terms of your favorite workplace, or working conditions—indoors/outdoors, small organization/large organization, windows/no windows, etc.— because they enable you to work at your top form, and greatest effectiveness.

3. **You and Skills.** Or you can describe *who you are* in terms of what you can do, and what your *favorite* functional/transferable skills are. For these are key to your being in top form, and at your greatest effectiveness.

4. **You and the Knowledges You Already Have.** Or you can describe *who you are* in terms of what you already know—and what your *favorite* knowledges or interests are among all that stuff stored away in your head.

5. **You and Geography.** Or you can describe *who you are* in terms of your preferred surroundings—here or abroad, warm/cold, north/ south, east/west, mountains/coast, urban/suburban/rural/rustic— where you'd be happiest, do your best work, and would most love to live, all year long, or part of the year, or vacation time, or sabbatical—either now, five years from now, or at retirement.

6. **You and Salary/Responsibility.** Or you can describe *who you are* in terms of your preferred salary and level of responsibility—working by yourself, or as a member of a team, or supervising others, or running the show—that you feel most fitted for, by experience, temperament, and appetite.

7. **You and Your Purpose in Life.** Or you can describe *who you are* in terms of your goals or sense of mission and purpose for your life. Alternatively, or in addition, you can get even more particular and describe the goals or mission you want *the organization* to have, where you decide to work.

PETAL ONE

PEOPLE

I Am a Person Who . . . Has These Favorite Kinds of People

My Preferred Kinds of People to Work Beside or Serve

Goal in Filling Out This Petal: To identify the types of people who can either make the job delightful or ruin your day, your week, your year.

What You Are Looking For: (1) Coworkers and colleagues: a better picture in your mind of what kind of people surrounding you at work will enable you to operate at your highest and most effective level. (2) Clients or customers: a better picture in your mind of what kind of people you would most like to serve or help: defined by age, problems, geography, and so forth.

Form of the Entries on Your Petal: They can be adjectives describing different kinds of people ("kind," "patient") or they can be types of people, as in the Holland Code or Myers-Briggs typologies (see pages 115–118).

Example of a Helpful Petal: (1) People who are creative, smart, fun, and hardworking. (2) People who are engaged in their work and seeking a way to sell or market their product.

Holland Code: IAS. (1) Kind, generous, understanding, fun, smart. (2) The unemployed, people struggling with their faith, worldwide, all ages.

PETAL ONE, WORKSHEET #1

A HEXAGON: THE PARTY GAME EXERCISE

One of the most helpful classifications for determining the type of people you enjoy and the work environment that might best suit you is the Holland Code developed by Dr. John Holland. Every job or career has a characteristic **people environment**. Tell us what **career** or job interests you, and we can tell you, in general terms, what kind of people you would prefer to work with (from among six possibilities). Or start at the other end: tell us what kinds of people you prefer to work with—in terms of those same six factors—and we can tell you what careers will give you *that*. Surveying the whole workplace, Dr. Holland said there are basically six people environments that jobs can give you. Let's tick them off:

1. The **Realistic** People Environment: Filled with people who prefer activities involving the explicit, ordered, or systematic manipulation of objects, tools, machines, and animals.

    I summarize this as: **R** = *people who like nature, or plants, or animals, or athletics, or tools and machinery, or being outdoors.*

2. The **Investigative** People Environment: Filled with people who prefer using their brain, specifically the observation and symbolic, systematic, creative investigation of physical, biological, or cultural phenomena.

    I summarize this as: **I** = *people who are very curious and like to investigate or analyze things, people, data, or ideas.*

3. The **Artistic** People Environment: Filled with people who prefer activities involving less organized, ambiguous, free activities and competencies to create art forms or products.

    I summarize this as: **A** = *people who are very creative, artistic, imaginative, and innovative, and don't like time clocks.*

4. The **Social** People Environment: Filled with people who prefer activities involving working with others to inform, train, develop, cure, or enlighten.

   I summarize this as: **S** = *people who want to help, teach, or serve people.*

5. The **Enterprising** People Environment: Filled with people who prefer activities involving influencing others to attain organizational or self-interest goals.

   I summarize this as: **E** = *people who like to start up projects or organizations, or sell things, or influence, persuade, or lead people.*

6. The **Conventional** People Environment: Filled with people who prefer activities involving the explicit, ordered, systematic manipulation of data, such as keeping records, filing materials, reproducing materials, organizing written and numerical data according to a prescribed plan, operating business and data-processing machines. "Conventional," incidentally, refers to the "values" that people in this environment usually hold—representing the historic mainstream of our culture.

   I summarize this as: **C** = *people who like detailed, organized work, and like to complete tasks or projects.*

According to Holland's theory, every one of us *could become skilled in all six,* if we were given enough time. Instead, in the limited time we have from childhood to adulthood, we tend to develop preferences and survival skills in just **three** of these people environments, and this is determined by who we grew up with, who we admired, and what time we gave to practicing expertise in these three people environments, as we wended our way into adulthood. From among the six letters—RIASEC— you name your three preferred people environments, and this gives you what is called your Holland Code; for example, SIA. Your question is, *Which three?*

Generally, most people can just "guess" at their type. (I was friends with John for many years, and back in 1975 I invented a quick and easy way for you to find out your code, based on John's Self-Directed Search [SDS]. It turned out that it agrees with the results you would get from John's SDS 92 percent of the time—this made John laugh.) But if you want a more certain answer, and one of the best ways to learn your code, you can take the free O*NET Interest Profiler online, which will give you your three-letter code (www.mynextmove.org/explore/ip). You can also take Dr. Holland's official SDS ($9.95 at www.self-directed-search.com).

But if you're in a hurry, this is close. And doesn't require access to the internet. I call it "The Party Exercise." Here is how the exercise goes:

This hexagon diagram is an aerial view of a room in which a party is taking place. At this party, people who share the same interests have (for some reason) gathered in one of the six corners.

R for "Realistic"
People who have athletic or mechanical ability, prefer to work with objects, machines, tools, plants, or animals, or to be outdoors.

I for "Investigative"
People who like to observe, learn, investigate, analyze, evaluate, or solve problems.

C for "Conventional"
People who like to work with data, have clerical or numerical ability, carrying things out in detail, or following through on others' instructions.

A for "Artistic"
People who have artistic, innovative, or intuitional abilities, and like to work in unstructured situations, using their imagination or creativity.

E for "Enterprising"
People who like to work with people—influencing, persuading, performing, leading, or managing for organizational goals or for economic gain.

S for "Social"
People who like to work with people—to inform, enlighten, help, train, develop, or cure them, or are skilled with words.

1. Which corner of the room would you instinctively be drawn to, as the group of people you would most enjoy being with for the longest time? (Leave aside any question of shyness, or whether you would have to actually talk to them; you could just listen.)

   Write the letter for that corner here: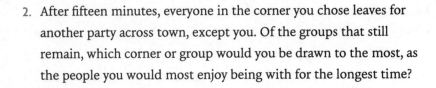

2. After fifteen minutes, everyone in the corner you chose leaves for another party across town, except you. Of the groups that still remain, which corner or group would you be drawn to the most, as the people you would most enjoy being with for the longest time?

   Write the letter for that corner here: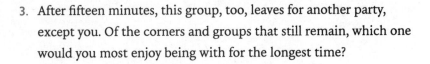

3. After fifteen minutes, this group, too, leaves for another party, except you. Of the corners and groups that still remain, which one would you most enjoy being with for the longest time?

   Write the letter for that corner here:

   The three letters you just chose are your Holland Code.
   Put that code here:
   Now, copy that code onto Petal One, My Preferred Kinds of People to Work With, found on pages 119–124. So far, so good.

PETAL ONE, WORKSHEET #2

MY FAVORITE PEOPLE

Why do *the people you prefer* to be around matter at all, in the larger scheme of things? Because the people we work with are either energy drainers or energy creators. They either drag us down and keep us from being our most effective, or they lift us up and help us to be at our best and perform at our greatest effectiveness.

Here is an exercise to help you identify which is which, for you. Copy this table onto a larger piece of paper—8½ by 11 inches—before you start filling it in.

1	2	3	4
Places I Have Worked Thus Far in My Life	Kinds of People I'd Most Like to Work With, in Order of Preference	Kinds of People Who Drove Me Nuts	Kinds of People I'd Prefer Not to Have to Work With, in Order of Preference
	Think back on your favorite people in the workplace. Who supported you? Who always pitched in and helped? Write down the characteristics of your favorite people at work. When you finish Column 4, return to this column, add in any newly discovered items, and reorder your favorite traits, if needed. 1b. 2b. 3b. 4b. 5b.	No names, but describe what made them difficult; e.g., bossy, micromanagers, talking too much about their personal problems, always left early before the job was done. List these in any order; it doesn't matter.	Review column 3 and rank your top three to five most difficult people. Consider the opposite trait or characteristic and add that to your list in column 2. 1a. 2a. 3a. 4a. 5a.

Start, of course, by filling in column 1 in the table, and then column 2. This will bring you to column 3, where you can fill in the items that you don't like about certain coworkers, clients, and others. In column 4 you will want to prioritize your least favorite kinds of people. How do you do that? Well, you can "eyeball" it and notice which ones jump out at you from column 3, or you can use the Prioritizing Grid. The following page shows an example, which illustrates how you use the ten-item grid.

(I originally had more than ten items as a result of this exercise, but by guess and by gosh I narrowed them down to my top ten, and then worked just with them here.)

How to Complete the Prioritizing Grid

Section A. Here I put my list of ten items, in any order I choose. So, as you can see, the people I'd prefer not to have to work with are those who *are bossy, never thank anyone, are messy in dress or office space, claim too much, are uncompassionate, never tell the truth, are always late, are totally undependable, feel superior to others,* or *never have any ideas.* The order in which I list these items here in Section A doesn't matter at all.

Section B. Here are displayed all the possible pairs among those ten. Each pair is in a little box, or rather the *numbers* that represent each pair are in a little box. You ask each box a question. The framing of the question is crucial. The question you address to each box is: "Between these two items, which is more important to me?" Or, since this is a grid of dislikes, "Which of these two do I dislike more?" (Think of choosing between two hypothetical jobs.)

Let's see how this works. We'll start with the first little box at the top. The box has the numbers 1 and 2 in it. (#1 stands for *bossy,* while #2 stands for *never thanks anyone*). So, the question is: *Which do you dislike more: #1 or #2?* You circle your preference in that box. I circled #1—as you can see—because I dislike being around bossy people at work more than I dislike being around ungrateful people.

Next, you go on to the second box (down diagonally to the southeast) that has in it the second pairing—in this case, the numbers 2 and 3. The question, again: Which do you dislike more? I circled #3 in that box—as you can see—because

PRIORITIZING GRID
for 10 items or fewer

EXAMPLE

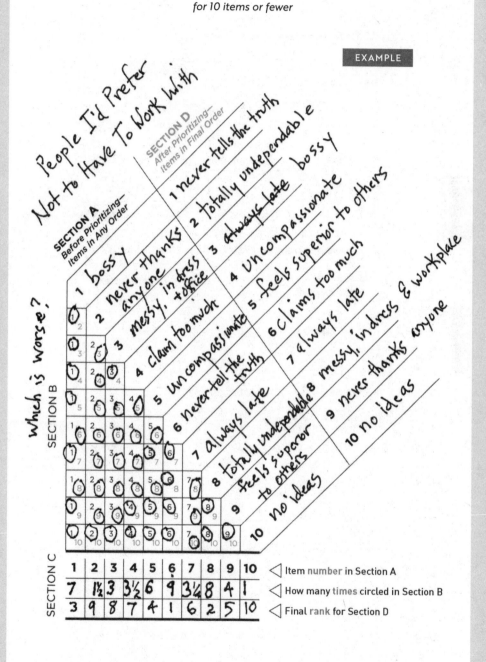

People I'd Prefer Not to Have To Work With

SECTION D
After Prioritizing—Items in Final Order

1 never tells the truth
2 totally undependable
3 always late
4 uncompassionate
5 feels superior to others
6 claims too much
7 always late
8 messy, in dress & workplace
9 never thanks anyone
10 no ideas

SECTION A
Before Prioritizing—Items in Any Order

1 bossy
2 never thanks anyone
3 messy, in dress & office
4 claim too much
5 uncompassionate
6 never tell the truth
7 always late
8 totally undependable feels superior to others
9 no ideas
10

Which is worse?

SECTION B

SECTION C	1	2	3	4	5	6	7	8	9	10	
	7	1½	3	3½	6	9	3⅛	8	4	1	◁ Item **number** in Section A ◁ How many **times** circled in Section B
	3	9	8	7	4	1	6	2	5	10	◁ Final **rank** for Section D

I dislike being around messy people at work more than I dislike being around people who never thank anyone.

And so it goes, until you've circled one number in each little box in Section B.

Section C. Section C has three rows, at the bottom of the grid, as you can see. The first row is just the ten numbers from Section A.

The second row is how many times each of those numbers just got circled in Section B. As you can see, item #1 got circled seven times, item #2 got circled one time (as did item #10—a tie—so, to break the tie, I look up in section B to find the little box that had both #2 and #10 in it, to see which I preferred at that time, and I see it was #2, so I give #2 an extra ½ point here, over #10). Item #3 I notice got circled three times, but so did item #4 and item #7—*a three-way tie!* How to break that tie? Well, here you'll just have to do some guessing. I guessed these were important to me in this order: #4, #7, and then #3. So I added ½ point to #4 and ¼ point to #7; I left #3 as it was.

In the third and bottommost row of Section C, I put the ranking according to the number of circles in the second row. Item #6 got the most circles—nine—so it is number 1 in ranking. Item #8 got the next most circles—eight—so it is number 2 in ranking. And so it goes, until that whole bottom line is filled in. Now the only task remaining on this grid is to copy the reorganized list onto Section D.

Section D. The aim here is to relist my ten items (from Section A) in the exact order of my preference or priority, using Section C as my guide. Item #6 got the most circles there, and it ranked number 1, so I copy the words for item #6 in the number 1 position in Section D. Item #8 ranked second, so I copy the words for item #8 into the second spot in Section D. Etc. Etc. What I am left with now, in Section D, is the ten items in the exact order of my preference and priority. *Nice!*

When you've completed the blank grid on the facing page for yourself, go back to the table on page 119. Copy the first five factors from Section D of the grid into the fourth column of the table. Now what you've got there is a list of negatives that you're trying to avoid. But what you want to end up with is a list of *positives* that you're trying to find.

So look at the five negative items you just put in column 4 of the table, and in column 2 write their opposite, or something near the opposite,

PRIORITIZING GRID
for 10 items or fewer

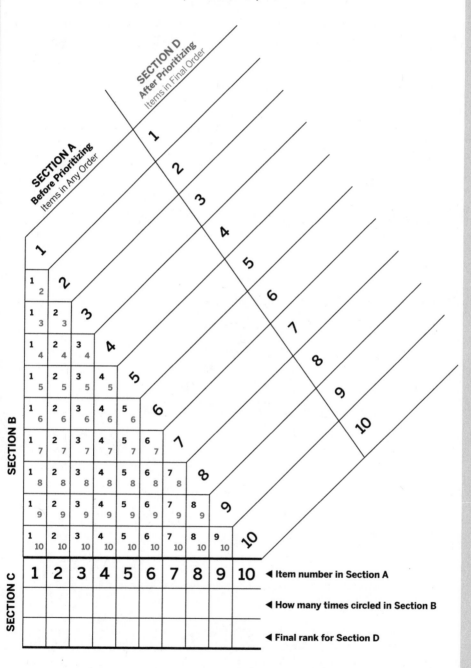

SECTION D
After Prioritizing
Items in Final Order

SECTION A
Before Prioritizing
Items in Any Order

SECTION B

SECTION C

◄ Item number in Section A

◄ How many times circled in Section B

◄ Final rank for Section D

directly beside each item. By "opposite" I don't necessarily mean the *exact* opposite. If one of your complaints in column 4 was "I was micromanaged, supervised every hour of my day," the opposite, in column 2, wouldn't necessarily be "No supervision." It might be "Limited supervision" or something like that. Your call. Note that you are adding these items to the list you already compiled in column 1. If there are duplicates, just leave them out. Highlight or place a star next to the positive items that are most important to you in column 1. Too many? Not sure? Then use the Prioritizing Grid again.

Now copy the top five from column 2 onto Petal One, My Preferred Kinds of People to Work With, on pages 186–187.

Congratulations! You did it—you're done with Petal One. Take a break or move on to Petal Two.

PETAL TWO

I Am a Person Who . . . Has these favorite working conditions

My Preferred Working Conditions

Goal in Filling Out This Petal: To state the physical working conditions and surroundings that would make you happiest, and therefore enable you to do your most effective work.

What You Are Looking For: Setting yourself up for a great work environment and avoiding past bad experiences.

Form of the Entries on Your Petal: Descriptors of physical surroundings and general work environment.

Example of a Helpful Petal: A workspace with lots of windows, nice view of greenery, relatively quiet, decent lunch period, flexibility about clocking in and clocking out, lots of shops nearby.

Your physical setting where you work can cheer you up or drag you down. It's important to know this before you weigh whether to take a particular job offer. The most useful way to do this has proved to be starting with working conditions that have made you unhappy in the past, and then flip them over into positives, just as we did in the previous exercise.

Plants that grow beautifully at sea level often perish if they're taken ten thousand feet up the mountain. Likewise, we do our best work under certain conditions but not under others. Thus, the question "What are your favorite working conditions?" actually is "Under what circumstances do you do your most effective work?"

Before you get started, again, this petal is about physical space and location—not people. To add more about people, go back to Petal One.

PETAL TWO, WORKSHEET #1
A TABLE: PHYSICAL ENVIRONMENTS WHERE I WOULD THRIVE

The best way to approach this chart is to focus on both the good and bad aspects of previous jobs. Work each of the columns as you think about your past work experiences. In column 1, list all the places where you have worked. When you think of something positive ("nice view" or "casual environment"), write that in column 2. When you think of things you would prefer to not experience again ("outdoors in the hot sun" or "cubicle"), write them in column 3. Rank order the worst experiences from column 3 (again, by "eyeballing" it or by using the Prioritizing Grid on the facing page) and write the rank-ordered list in column 4. Then consider the opposite ("indoor air-conditioned environment" or "personal office with walls") and write those items in column 2 if they are not already there. Copy the key items (you choose how many) from column 2 onto Petal Two, the Favorite Working Conditions petal of your Flower Diagram, pages 186–187. (For some people it's easier to remember all the things you *disliked* about *any* previous job. If that's the case for you, just start with column 3 and go from there.)

Preferences for Working Conditions

1	2	3	4
Places I Have Worked	The Keys to My Effectiveness at Work—What I Like or Need	Distasteful Working Conditions	Distasteful Working Conditions, Ranked
	I believe my effectiveness would be at an absolute maximum if I could work under these conditions. (List ideal aspects of previous jobs.)	I have learned from the past that my effectiveness at work is decreased when I have to work under these conditions. (List less desirable or bad conditions you experienced.) 1a. 2a. 3a. 4a. 5a.	Among the factors or qualities listed in column 3, these are the ones I dislike absolutely the most (rank in order of decreasing dislike). Consider the opposite of these conditions and place that in column 2. 1b. 2b. 3b. 4b. 5b.

PRIORITIZING GRID

for 10 items or fewer

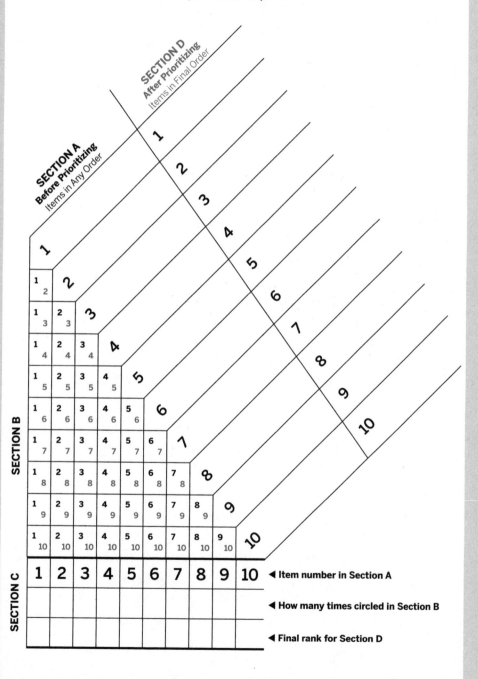

SECTION D
After Prioritizing
Items in Final Order

SECTION A
Before Prioritizing
Items in Any Order

SECTION B

SECTION C

◀ Item number in Section A

◀ How many times circled in Section B

◀ Final rank for Section D

PETAL TWO, WORKSHEET #2

CREATE A VISION OF YOUR IDEAL WORK ENVIRONMENT

Worksheet #1 helped you organize your thoughts in a logical manner, but your worksheet might be limited by what you already know. Creating a Vision Board of possibilities and ideas could help open your mind to new ideas and possibilities. Please keep in mind that this Vision Board is not magic. Its purpose is to help you think visually about your future workplace and expand your thinking with new images. You will still have to set goals and take action to make any "vision" real. You can create your Vision Board in two ways: on paper or online.

Paper version: Get a large sheet of paper or a poster board and go through magazines, cutting out pictures that fit your ideal environment. Don't censor yourself by saying *there's no point in including that picture. That will never happen.* Glue the picture onto your paper anyway. When you're done adding the images you've chosen (and if you can't find enough magazines, go online and print out pictures), analyze your results. Do you find a lot of certain kinds of images? Are they formal environments or more casual? Are they located in a city or near the seashore? Are there certain elements present, such as a medical/hospital setting, or a college setting, or a modern technology firm?

Online version: Instead of using paper, just open a blank Word document and copy and paste pictures from various websites. (One caution: sometimes pictures can have viruses attached to them, so be sure to keep your virus protector active while you're doing this exercise, and consider only using safe picture sites like Pixabay.com or Unsplash.com.) You will analyze your online Vision Board in the same way as the paper one.

Sometimes it helps to have your friends or relatives look at your board. They might see trends or spot new ideas you've missed. When you've completed Worksheet #2, write down the key elements you identified from your board. If there are new insights, consider adding them to column 2 of Worksheet #1 and including them on Petal Two if they are significant and important factors.

And you're done with Petal Two for the moment. Keep in mind you can always add extra items as you think about them. It's not unusual to complete a petal one day, only to think of more things to add the next day. This is a living document, so don't hesitate to add more ideas as they occur to you.

Time for a break? Or ready to move on?

PETAL THREE

I Am a Person Who . . . can do these particular things in these particular ways

---

My Favorite Transferable Skills and Traits

Goal in Filling Out This Petal: To discover your favorite functional skills and personal traits, which can be transferred to any field of interest. They are things you probably were born knowing how to do, or at least you began with a natural gift and have honed and sharpened it since.

What You Are Looking For: Not just what you can do, but more particularly which of those skills and traits you most love to use.

Form of the Entries on Your Petal: Verbs, usually in pure form (for example, analyze, write, draw, coach), though they may sometimes be expressed as actions (for example, analyzing, writing, drawing, coaching).

Example of a Helpful Petal: (These stories show that I can) innovate, analyze, classify, coach, negotiate; or (These stories show that I am good at) innovating, analyzing, classifying, coaching, negotiating.

A Crash Course in Skills, Talents, Abilities, and Traits

"Skills" is one of the most misunderstood words in all the world of work. It begins with high school job hunters: "I haven't really got any skills," they say. *Wrong!*

It continues with college students: "I've spent four years in college. I haven't had time to pick up any skills." *Wrong!*

And it lasts through the middle years, especially when a person is thinking of changing his or her career: "I'll have to go back to college and get retrained, because otherwise I won't have any skills in my new field." Or: "Well, if I claim any skills, I'll have to start at a very entry kind of level." *Wrong!*

All of this confusion about the word "skills" stems from a total misunderstanding of what the word means. A misunderstanding that is shared, we might add, by altogether too many employers, and human resources departments, and other so-called vocational experts. So let's clarify what we mean here.

Skills are simply something you are good at. They can also be called talents or abilities. They can also be divided into categories like "soft" or "hard," or "transferable." Basically, hard skills refer back to the "what," and soft skills refer more to the style in which you do something—the "how." Sometimes soft skills illustrate personality traits. And just to confuse the issue more, sometimes soft skills are also called "self-management skills." And what about "transferable skills"? That basically means that the hard and soft skills—and traits—that you perform in one setting can be useful in another setting. Sometimes it isn't just the specific skill, but rather the thinking required to do the skill that is transferable.

Finally, there's another term that is becoming more common in the job-search world: "competencies." In many ways, the word "competencies" is just a fancier name for skills, but it is often used to categorize a larger set of skills. For instance, a competency in communications might include writing skills, speaking skills, leadership skills, and so on.

Okay, let's get out of the weeds. In this section, with this petal, we are going to focus on the skills and traits you possess, with an emphasis on which ones are most transferable to other jobs and roles.

It's important to do a thorough assessment of your skills and traits, because too many people assume they don't have the needed skills for a new job and end up returning to school and spending money on a formal degree they might not have needed. I've said it before, and I'll say it again: *maybe* you need some further schooling, but very often it is possible to make a dramatic career change without any retraining. It all depends. And you won't really *know* whether or not you need further schooling until you have finished all the exercises in this self-inventory. Knowing and analyzing your skills seems basic, but it's amazing how many job seekers don't take the time to do this.

All skills have the potential to be transferable. So let's start with some assumptions about skills.

1. **Your skills are the most basic unit—the atoms—of whatever job or career you may choose.**

2. **You should always claim the highest skills you legitimately can, as demonstrated by your past performance.**

When you list your skills (which you will do shortly), consider which skills are the most difficult or complex. Those skills are likely to be more valued by a future employer.

3. **The higher your transferable skills, the more freedom you will have on the job.**

The more complex and valuable your skills are, the more opportunities you will have to carve out a job that truly fits you. For instance, most workplaces and positions require computer or other technical skills. If you know how to use a word processing program, that's a great skill, but it's a skill that many others possess as well. However, if you also know how to use a graphic design program, that is an additional skill that may add to your value to an employer (particularly if you can demonstrate why this skill could help). And if you can also code or write apps, well, then your technical skills are likely to land you a job.

4. **The higher your transferable skills, the less competition you will face for whatever job you are seeking.**

The essence of this approach to job hunting or career changing is that once you have identified your favorite transferable skills and your favorite special knowledges, you may then approach any organization that interests you, whether they have a known vacancy or not. Naturally, whatever places you visit—and particularly those that have not advertised any vacancy—you will find far fewer job hunters whom you have to compete with.

In fact, if the employers you visit happen to like you well enough, they may be willing to create for you a job that does not presently exist. *In which case, you will be competing with no one, since you will be the sole applicant for that newly created job.* While this doesn't happen all the time, it is astounding to me how many times it *does* happen. The *reason* it does is that the employers often have been *thinking* about creating a new job within their organization, for quite some time—but with this and that, they just have never gotten around to *doing* it. Until you walk in.

Then they decide they don't want to let you get away, since *good employees are as hard to find as good employers*. And they suddenly remember that job they have been thinking about creating for many weeks or months now. So they dust off their *intention*, create the job on the spot, and offer it to you! And if that new job is not only what *they* need, but exactly what *you* were looking for, then you have a dream job. Match-match. Win-win.

PETAL THREE, WORKSHEET #1
A SKILLS CHART: ANALYZING SEVEN STORIES WHEN YOU WERE ENJOYING YOURSELF

Now that you know what transferable skills *are*, the challenge that awaits you is figuring out your own. If you are one of the lucky few people who already know what their transferable skills are, write them down and put them in your order of preference on your Flower Diagram (pages 186–187).

If, however, you don't know what your skills are (and 95 percent of all workers *don't*), you will need some help. Fortunately, there is an exercise to help.

It involves the following steps.

1. **Write One Story About Some Episode in Your Life (the First of Seven)**
Yes, I know, I know. You are avoiding this exercise because you don't like to write. *Writers are a very rare breed.* That's what thousands of job hunters have told me, over the years. And yet, how often during the day

do you text or email? You are a writer every day and just don't realize it. Let's face it: we human beings are a writing species, and we only need a topic we have a real passion for, or interest in—such as our life—for the writing genie to spring forth from within each of us, pen or keyboard in hand.

So, call the *Seven Stories from your life* that you're about to write your personal *offline blog*, if you prefer. But start writing. Please.

Okay, the next step is actually writing. Here is one person's first story:

Several years ago, our family adopted a mixed-breed puppy from a shelter. Based on her appearance, she seemed to be part Poodle, part Labrador, and maybe part Border Collie. We named her Ruffles. Not only was Ruffles adorable, she had the sweetest, gentlest nature and loved everyone. She was a hit at the local dog park and everywhere I took her. The only challenge was her high energy level: she jumped around and pulled on her leash; she got bored easily and chewed up the furniture, and anything else, if I didn't keep her busy. A friend suggested I get her obedience training, so I enrolled her in puppy kindergarten at a local pet store. We failed miserably. She preferred socializing with the other dogs and people and had no interest in listening to me.

Something about this experience triggered my own stubborn nature, so I decided to train her myself. In fact, I had a secret goal: I would train her to be a therapy dog and take her to a local children's hospital. I started by getting some books from the library on dog training. I watched TV programs on the topic and started trying the various techniques to see which worked best. She was doing great at home, but I still had challenges with her in public. I looked up therapy dog training and discovered that the American Kennel Club has a Canine Good Citizen program for training dogs. The training I had done at home helped Ruffles quickly succeed in the group environment, and she was able to complete the ten-step test (which included sitting politely for petting and ignoring distractions in her environment) and achieve her Canine Good Citizen certificate.

After that, I checked with the local children's hospital and learned that Ruffles and I needed to go through another program to certify her as a therapy dog, so we enrolled in online training through a nonprofit organization. Once she was through the training process and attained her "novice" status, we started visiting the children's hospital.

I didn't realize what a commitment I had made when I set my first goal with Ruffles, but the experience was incredible. I met so many wonderful children and families who were going through a terrible time in their lives, and watching their faces light up when they saw Ruffles was the highlight of my week. As I look back, I think I benefited more than anyone from the experience.

As this example illustrates, each story should have the following points:

- **Your goal/what you wanted to accomplish:** "I wanted my dog to stop chewing up the furniture, and I also wanted to find an outlet for her energy and friendly personality."

- **Some kind of hurdle, obstacle, or constraint you faced:** "She and I failed miserably in puppy kindergarten. She was stubborn and too interested in other dogs and people. I couldn't control her, and I was sure I wouldn't be able to train her."

- **A description of what you did, step by step, to ultimately achieve your goal:** "I read everything I could about training dogs. I watched TV shows, too, and I tried all the techniques. I kept taking her to the park and working on her socialization skills. I searched out local training programs for preparing her to be a therapy dog. I enrolled in several programs both in person and online. I then started taking her to the hospital to try out and improve her skills."

- **A description of the outcome or result:** "Ruffles received the appropriate certificate and was able to volunteer at the local children's hospital."

- **Any measurable/quantifiable statement of that outcome:** "I'd have to say that the outcome is more emotional than financial. I learned a lot about myself, particularly my tenacity and my patience. I also learned a lot about compassion and kindness, and the value of small experiences that can make someone's day. I think working with Ruffles made me a better person."

Now write *your* story, using the sample as a guide.

Don't pick a story where you achieved something *big*, like "how I got my college degree over a period of ten years." At least to begin with, write a story about some brief episode or task you accomplished, in which you also had fun!

Do not try to be *too* brief. This isn't Twitter.

2. Analyze Your First Story, Using the Skills Grid, to See What Transferable Skills You Used

Above the number 1 in the grid on page 140, write a brief title for your first story. Then work your way down column 1, asking yourself for each skill in the right-hand column: "Did I use this skill in this story?"

If the answer is "Yes," color in the little square for that skill, in that column, with a red pen or whatever.

Work your way through the entire Parachute Skills Grid that way, with your first story.

As an example, if we were to analyze the "Ruffles" story to identify some key skills used by Ruffles's owner, we might select training, follow-through, assessing and evaluating, communicating well, problem solving, and goal setting.

3. Write Six Other Stories, and Analyze Them for Transferable Skills

Voilà! You are done with Story #1. However, "one swallow doth not a summer make," so the fact that you used certain skills in this first story doesn't tell you much. You have to keep writing stories—seven is the ideal, five is the minimum to be of any use—because what you are looking for is patterns—transferable skills that keep reappearing in story after story. They keep reappearing because they are your favorites (assuming you chose stories where you were *really* enjoying yourself).

If you are finding it difficult to come up with seven stories, here are some ideas that might inspire you. Write a story about:

- A situation that made you feel part of something larger than yourself
- An experience that stood out because you were proud of what you accomplished
- Helping someone, or making someone else's life better
- Something you did despite others saying you couldn't do it
- Something you did that you would like to do again
- A strong skill or interest of yours and how you used it

- Something that was exciting or inspiring to you
- An experience you look back on fondly
- An experience that taught you something, even if it wasn't fun at the time
- An experience that required you to take a risk

Don't forget to look for skills that you use outside of work. For instance, if you enjoy playing video games, it is possible that you have developed skills such as strategic planning, navigating changing environments, active listening, communicating, or collaborating. Not only are those skills useful in various jobs and fields, but if you want a career in video game development, video game skills can get you a scholarship to college—more than thirty colleges, including NYU, offer scholarships to study gaming.

Are you still stuck? If you absolutely can't think of any experiences you've had where you enjoyed yourself, and accomplished something, then try this: describe the seven most enjoyable jobs that you've had; or seven roles you've had so far in your life, such as spouse, parent, tutor, homemaker, handyman, gardener, community volunteer, citizen, student, etc. Tell us something you did or accomplished, in each role. In his excellent book *The Seven Habits of Highly Effective People*, Stephen Covey encourages readers to identify seven roles they play or want to play in their lives. Check this book out if you'd like to learn more about thinking of yourself in terms of roles that you play.

So, write your Story #2, from any period in your life, and analyze it using the skills grid. And keep this process up, until you have written, and analyzed, all your stories. A weekend should do it! In a weekend, you can inventory your *past* sufficiently so that you have a good picture of the *kind* of work you would love to be doing *in the future*. (You can, of course, stretch the inventory over a number of weeks, maybe doing an hour or two one night a week, if you prefer. It's up to you as to how fast you do it.)

The Parachute Skills Grid

Your Seven Stories
In the space to the left, write above each number, in turn, the name you give to each story. Begin with Story #1. Then go down the list and mark the box if you used that skill in each story.

1	2	3	4	5	6	7	SKILLS WITH PEOPLE As my story shows, I can . . .
							Initiate, lead, be a pioneer
							Supervise, manage
							Follow through, get things done
							Motivate
							Persuade, sell, recruit
							Consult
							Advise
							Coordinate
							Negotiate, resolve conflicts
							Help people link up or connect
							Heal, cure
							Assess, evaluate, treat
							Convey warmth and empathy
							Interview, draw out
							Raise people's self-esteem
							Instruct
							Teach, tutor, or train (individuals, groups, animals)

1	2	3	4	5	6	7	SKILLS WITH PEOPLE continued
							Speak
							Listen
							Counsel, guide, mentor
							Communicate well, in person
							Communicate well, in writing
							Divert, amuse, entertain, perform, act
							Play an instrument
							Interpret, speak, or read a foreign language
							Serve, care for, follow instructions faithfully

1	2	3	4	5	6	7	SKILLS WITH DATA/IDEAS As my story shows, I can . . .
							Use my intuition
							Create, innovate, invent
							Design, use artistic abilities, be original
							Visualize, including in three dimensions
							Imagine
							Use my brain
							Synthesize, combine parts into a whole
							Systematize, prioritize
							Organize, classify
							Perceive patterns
							Analyze, break down into parts
							Work with numbers, compute
							Remember people, or data, to unusual degree
							Develop, improve

continued ▶

1	2	3	4	5	6	7	SKILLS WITH DATA/IDEAS continued
							Solve problems
							Plan
							Program
							Research
							Examine, inspect, compare, see similarities and differences
							Use acute senses (hearing, smell, taste, sight)
							Study, observe
							Compile, keep records, file, retrieve
							Copy

1	2	3	4	5	6	7	SKILLS WITH THINGS As my story shows, I can . . .
							Control, expedite things
							Make, produce, manufacture
							Repair
							Finish, restore, preserve
							Construct
							Shape, model, sculpt
							Cut, carve, chisel
							Set up, assemble
							Handle, tend, feed
							Operate, drive
							Manipulate
							Use my body, hands, fingers, with unusual dexterity or strength

4. **Discover Patterns and Priorities**

Okay, when you've finished this whole inventory, for all seven of your accomplishments/achievements/jobs/roles or whatever, you want to look down your completed Skills Grid to discover any **patterns** or **priorities**.

Patterns, because it isn't a matter of whether you used a skill once only, but rather whether you used it again and again. "Once" proves nothing; "again and again" is very convincing.

Priorities (that is, which skills are most important to you), because as we saw earlier, the job you eventually choose may not enable you to use all of your skills. You need to know *what you are willing to trade off, and what you are not.* This requires that you know which skills, or family of skills, are most important to you.

So, after finishing your seven stories (or if you're in a hurry, at least five), look through that Skills Grid and *guess* which *might* be your top ten favorite skills. These should be your best *guesses,* and they should be about *your favorite* skills: not the ones you think the job market will like the best, but the ones *you* enjoy using the most.

At this point, now that you've guessed your top ten, you want to be able to prioritize those ten *in exact order of priority.* Run your *guesses* through the Prioritizing Grid on the facing page, and when you're done with that grid's Section D, copy the top ten onto the building blocks diagram on page 146, as well as onto your Favorite Transferable Skills petal, on pages 186–187.

PRIORITIZING GRID

for 10 items or fewer

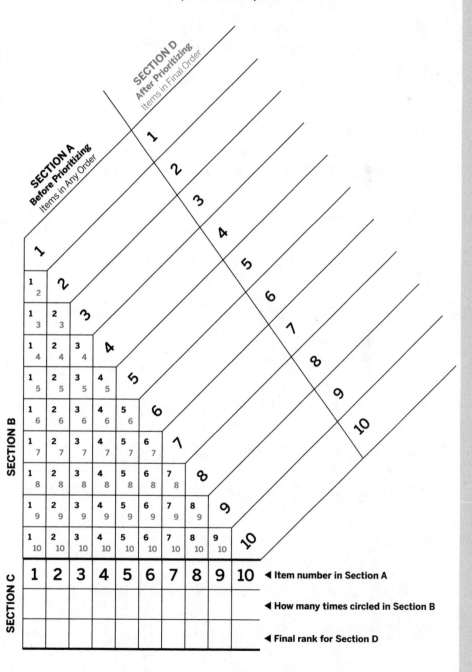

SECTION D
After Prioritizing
Items in Final Order

SECTION A
Before Prioritizing
Items in Any Order

SECTION B

SECTION C

◄ Item number in Section A

◄ How many times circled in Section B

◄ Final rank for Section D

The Virtue of Depicting Your Transferable Skills in Terms of Building Blocks

Suppose it turns out that the following are your top ten favorite skills: *analyzing, teaching, researching, writing, synthesizing, entertaining, classifying, conveying warmth, leading,* and *motivating.*

If you then enter these terms onto a diagram of Building Blocks in the order of your personal priority, the top one defines the kind of job or career you are looking for. If you put "analyzing" in the top block, you might seek a job as an analyst. But if instead you move "teaching" to the top block, then you might seek a job as a teacher. And so on, with "researching," "writing," "diagnosing," and the rest. You can choose among several goals.

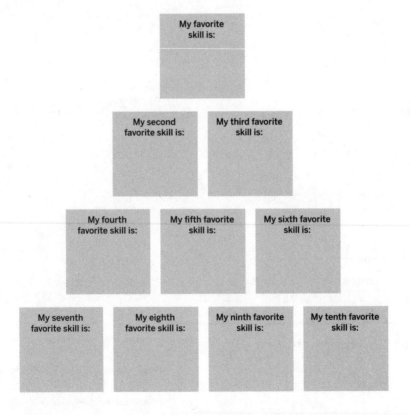

PETAL THREE, WORKSHEET #2

MY MOST IMPORTANT TRAITS

While your stories in Worksheet #1 focused on your **skills**, let's take those same stories and see if we can find transferable **traits** that employers would value. For instance, if we go back to the "Ruffles" story, what traits can you identify in that writer? I would select patience, tenacity, compassion, and achievement orientation. Any employer would likely want someone with these traits in almost any field of employment. So go through your stories again and use the checklist on the following page to identify the traits you exhibited. See which ones appear more than once on the grid, and make a list of your "top ten" to place on Petal Three.

Now, let's go a little deeper.

In general, your traits describe how you deal with:

- Time and promptness
- People and emotions
- Authority and being told what to do at your job
- Supervision and being told how to do your job
- Impulse versus self-discipline, within yourself
- Initiative versus response, within yourself
- Crises or problems

If you want to know what your traits or self-management skills are, popular tests such as the MBTI (the Myers-Briggs Type Indicator) measure that sort of thing.

If you have access to the internet, there are clues, at least, about your traits or "type." Here are three sites to check out:

Working Out Your Myers-Briggs Type

www.teamtechnology.co.uk/tt/t-articl/mb-simpl.htm

An informative article about the MBTI

A Checklist of My Strongest Traits

I am very . . .

- ☐ Accurate
- ☐ Achievement-oriented
- ☐ Adaptable
- ☐ Adept
- ☐ Adept at having fun
- ☐ Adventuresome
- ☐ Alert
- ☐ Appreciative
- ☐ Assertive
- ☐ Astute
- ☐ Authoritative
- ☐ Calm
- ☐ Cautious
- ☐ Charismatic
- ☐ Compassionate
- ☐ Competent
- ☐ Consistent
- ☐ Contagious in my enthusiasm
- ☐ Cooperative
- ☐ Courageous
- ☐ Creative
- ☐ Decisive
- ☐ Deliberate
- ☐ Dependable
- ☐ Diligent
- ☐ Diplomatic
- ☐ Discreet
- ☐ Driven

- ☐ Dynamic
- ☐ Effective
- ☐ Energetic
- ☐ Enthusiastic
- ☐ Exceptional
- ☐ Exhaustive
- ☐ Experienced
- ☐ Expert
- ☐ Economical
- ☐ Firm
- ☐ Flexible
- ☐ Human-oriented
- ☐ Inclusive
- ☐ Impulsive
- ☐ Independent
- ☐ Innovative
- ☐ Kind
- ☐ Knowledgeable
- ☐ Loyal
- ☐ Methodical
- ☐ Objective
- ☐ Open-minded
- ☐ Outgoing
- ☐ Outstanding
- ☐ Patient
- ☐ Penetrating
- ☐ Perceptive
- ☐ Persevering
- ☐ Persistent

- ☐ Pioneering
- ☐ Practical
- ☐ Professional
- ☐ Protective
- ☐ Punctual
- ☐ Quick in my work
- ☐ Rational
- ☐ Realistic
- ☐ Reliable
- ☐ Resourceful
- ☐ Responsible
- ☐ Responsive
- ☐ Safeguarding
- ☐ Self-motivated
- ☐ Self-reliant
- ☐ Sensitive
- ☐ Sophisticated
- ☐ Strong
- ☐ Supportive
- ☐ Tactful
- ☐ Tenacious
- ☐ Thorough
- ☐ Unique
- ☐ Unusual
- ☐ Versatile
- ☐ Vigorous

The 16 Personality Types

www.personalitypage.com/high-level.html

A helpful site about Myers types

Myers-Briggs Foundation home page

www.myersbriggs.org

The official website of the foundation; lots of testing resources

Another excellent test to learn more about your values is the Values-in-Action (VIA) assessment, which you can take for free online at www.authentichappiness.sas.upenn.edu/testcenter. This site, developed by the Positive Psychology Center at the University of Pennsylvania, contains several interesting and helpful work-related assessments. Try experimenting; they are free, although you have to register.

You can use your self-management skills to flesh out each of your favorite transferable skills so that you are able to describe each of your talents or skills with more than just a one-word verb or gerund.

Let's take *organizing* as our example. You tell us proudly: "I'm good at organizing." That's a fine *start* at defining your traits, but unfortunately it doesn't yet tell us much. Organizing *what*? People, as at a party? Nuts and bolts, as on a workbench? Or lots of information, as on a computer? These are three entirely different skills. The one word *organizing* doesn't tell us which one is yours.

So, please look at your favorite transferable skills or traits, and ask yourself if you want to flesh out any of them with **an object**—some kind of data/information, or some kind of people, or some kind of thing or even an idea—plus **a self-management skill or trait or style** (adverb or adjective).

Why is the trait important here? Well, "I'm good at organizing information painstakingly and logically" and "I'm good at organizing information in a flash, by intuition" are two entirely different skills. The difference between them is spelled out not in the verb, nor in the object, but in the adjectival or adverbial phrase there at the end. So, expand the definition of any of your ten favorite skills that you choose, in the fashion I have just described.

When you are face to face with a person who has the power to hire you, you want to be able to explain what makes you different from nineteen other people who can basically do the same thing that you can do. It is often the self-management skill, the trait, the adjective or adverb that will save your life, during that explanation.

Now, on to the next petal of Who You Are.

PETAL FOUR

I Am a Person Who . . . already has (and loves) these particular knowledges (or interests)

My Favorite Knowledges, Interests, Subjects

Goal in Filling Out This Petal: To summarize all that you have stored in your brain. Required: From your past, subjects you already know a lot about and enjoy talking about. Optional: For your future, what you would like to learn.

What You Are Looking For: Some guidance as to what field you would most enjoy working in.

Example of a Helpful Petal: Graphic design, data analysis, mathematics, how to repair a car, video games, cooking, music, principles of mechanical engineering, how to run an organization, Chinese language.

As mentioned in Petal Three, there are three things traditionally called skills: **knowledges**, as here; **functions**, also known as transferable skills; and **traits** or **self-management skills**. And as we saw there, a general rule throughout this inventory is that *knowledges are nouns*; *transferable skills are verbs*; and *traits are adjectives or adverbs*. If it helps knowing that, great; if not, *forget it!* Our overarching principle throughout this book is that if a generalization, metaphor, or example helps you, use it. But if it just confuses you, then ignore it!!!

On Petal Four, you will eventually write your final results—your Favorite Knowledges/Fields of Interest, prioritized in the order of their importance to you—on pages 186–187.

PETAL FOUR, WORKSHEET #1
TEN PROMPTS FOR IDENTIFYING YOUR FAVORITE KNOWLEDGES, SUBJECTS, FIELDS, OR INTERESTS (WHATEVER YOU WISH TO CALL THEM)

On a blank sheet of paper, jot down your answers to any or all of these ten prompts:

1. What are your favorite subjects or hobbies to explore (Computers? Gardening? Spanish? Law? Physics? Music?) and/or places where you like to spend your time (Museums? Medical settings? Clothing stores? Libraries? and so on)? Start a list.

2. What do you love to talk about? Ask yourself: If you were stuck on a desert island with a person who only had the capacity to speak on a few subjects, what would you pray those subjects were?

    If you were at a get-together, talking with someone who was covering two of your favorite subjects at once, which way would you hope the conversation would go? Toward which subject?

If you could talk about something with some world expert, all day long, day after day, what would that subject or field of interest be? Add any ideas that these questions spark in you to your list.

3. What magazine articles or blogs do you love to read? You get really interested when you see a blog that deals with . . . what subject? Add any ideas to your list.

4. What newspaper articles do you love to read or podcasts do you listen to? You get really interested when you see a TV news special report that deals with . . . what subject? Add any ideas to your list.

5. If you're browsing in a bookstore, what sections of the bookstore do you tend to gravitate toward? What subjects there do you find really fascinating? Add any ideas to your list.

6. What sites on the internet do you tend to gravitate toward? What subjects do these sites deal with? Do any of these really fascinate you? Add any ideas to your list.

7. What television shows do you tend to watch? What do you enjoy about them? Add any ideas to your list.

8. When you look at a catalog of courses that you could take in your town or city (or on the internet), which subjects really interest you? Add any ideas to your list.

9. If you could write a book, and it wasn't about your own life or somebody else's, what would be the subject of the book? Add it to your list.

10. There are moments, in most of our lives, when we are so engrossed in a task that we lose all track of time. (Someone has to remind us that it's time for supper, or whatever.) If this ever happens to you, what task, what subject, so absorbs your attention that you lose all track of time? Add it to your list.

PETAL FOUR, WORKSHEET #2

CHART OF ALL THE THINGS YOU'VE LEARNED: THE FISHERMAN'S NET

You may want to copy the following chart onto a larger piece of paper, leaving much more space beneath the title for each of the four parts, before you start filling it in. This chart is like **a commercial fisherman's net**, which you want to cast into the sea to capture the largest haul of fish possible, and only later do you pick out the best from your haul. But we start *big*.

How to fill out this chart? Well, that's your choice. You may want to fill this out at one sitting, or you may prefer to keep it in your pocket and jot down anything that occurs to you over a period of two or three weeks: every bright idea, every hunch, every remembered dream, every intuition that pops up. *This is an important petal—very important—as it may help you unearth a field or fields where you would really like to work. So it's worth spending some time on.*

Now here are some hints to help you fill in the first three parts of the chart on the next page.

The Fisherman's Net

Notes About the Knowledges, Subjects, or Interests I've Picked Up Thus Far in My Life	
1. What I know from my previous jobs	2. What I know about or picked up, outside of work
3. What fields, careers, or industries sound interesting to me	4. Any other hunches, bright ideas, great ideas, and the like that occur to me

Part 1. What You Know from Your Previous Jobs

If you've been out there in the world of work for some time, you've probably learned a lot of things that you now just take for granted. "Of course I know that!" But such knowledges may be important, in and of themselves, or they may point you to something important down the line. So don't be afraid to really get detailed.

Examples: It can be work like bookkeeping, handling applications, credit collection of overdue accounts, hiring, international business, management, marketing, sales, merchandising, packaging, policy development, problem solving, troubleshooting, public speaking, recruiting, conference planning, systems analysis, the culture of other countries, other languages, government contract procedures, and so on.

Think of each job you've ever held, and then for each job jot down any system or procedure that you learned there. For example: "Worked in a warehouse: learned how to use a forklift and crane, inventory control, logistics automation software, warehouse management systems, team-work principles, and how to supervise employees."

Or "Worked at a fast food place: learned how to prepare and serve food, how to wait on customers, how to make change, how to deal with complaints, how to train new employees."

Part 2. What You Know Outside of Work

Jot down any bodies of knowledge that you picked up on your own just because the subject fascinated you, such as: antiques, gardening, cooking, budgeting, decorating, photography, crafts, spirituality, sports, camping, travel, repairing things, flea markets, scrapbooking, sewing, art appreci-ation at museums, how to run or work in a volunteer organization, and so on.

- Also think of anything you learned in high school (or college) that you prize knowing today: keyboarding, Chinese, accounting, geography? Is this knowledge important to you? Figure that out later; for now, your goal is to just cast as wide a net as possible.

- Think of anything you learned at training seminars, workshops, conferences, and so on, possibly in connection with a job you had at the time. Or something you decided to attend on your own. Jot it all down. Is this knowledge important to you? Figure that out later; for now, your goal is to just cast as wide a net as possible.

- Think of anything you've studied at home, via online courses, mobile apps, podcasts, YouTube videos, PBS television or pro-grams. Is this knowledge important to you? Figure that out later; for now, your goal is to just cast as wide a net as possible. Jot it all down.

- Think of anything you learned out there in the world, such as *how to assemble a flash mob, how to organize a protest, how to fundraise for a particular cause, how to run a marathon, how to repair a toilet.* Is this knowledge important to you? Figure that out later; for now, your goal is to just cast as wide a net as possible. Jot it all down, in the second section of the chart.

Part 3. What Fields, Careers, or Industries Sound Interesting to You
Broadly speaking, the workplace consists of the following six fields: *agriculture, manufacturing, information, technology, finance,* and *services.* Any ideas about which of these six is most attractive to you, right off the bat? If so, jot your answer down in the third section of the chart.

To drill down further into these six, your best bet is the government's O*NET OnLine (www.onetonline.org).

O*NET OnLine has various lists of **career clusters** or **industries** or **job families**. The following list is a mashup of these. Please read over it and copy down any of these that you want to explore further in the third section of the chart. Multiple choices are preferred here, in order to have alternatives and therefore hope.

- ☐ Accommodation and Food Services
- ☐ Administrative and Support Services
- ☐ Agriculture, Food, and Natural Resources
- ☐ Architecture, Engineering, and Construction
- ☐ Arts, Audio/Video Technology, and Communications
- ☐ Business, Operations, Management, and Administration
- ☐ Community and Social Services
- ☐ Computer and Mathematical
- ☐ Design, Entertainment, Sports, and Media
- ☐ Distribution and Logistics
- ☐ Education, Training, and Library
- ☐ Entertainment and Recreation
- ☐ Farming, Forestry, Fishing, and Hunting
- ☐ Finance and Insurance

☐ Food Preparation and Serving

☐ Government and Public Administration

☐ Green Industries or Jobs

☐ Health Care, Health Science, and Social Assistance

☐ Hospitality and Tourism

☐ Human Services

☐ Information and Information Technology

☐ Law, Public Safety, Corrections, and Security

☐ Life, Physical, and Social Sciences

☐ Management of Companies and Enterprises

☐ Manufacturing

☐ Marketing, Sales, and Service

☐ Military Related

☐ Mining, Quarrying, and Oil and Gas Extraction

☐ Personal Care and Service

☐ Production

☐ Professional, Scientific, and Technical Services

☐ Protective Services

☐ Real Estate, Rental, and Leasing

☐ Religion, Faith, and Related

☐ Retail Trade, Sales, and Related

☐ Science, Technology, Engineering, and Mathematics

☐ Self-Employment

☐ Transportation, Warehousing, and Material Moving

☐ Utilities

With the O*NET OnLine, when you have chosen any items on this list, drop-down menus allow you to go deeper into each *career cluster, industry,* or *job family* that you have checked off. These drill down to **career pathways**, and then drill down further to **individual occupations**, and then drill down still further to **tasks, tools, technologies, knowledges, skills, abilities, work activities, education, interests, work styles, work values, related occupations,** and **salary.**

Remember: Jobs, industries, and careers are *mortal*; they are born, they grow, they mature, they flourish, then decline and ultimately die. Sometimes it takes centuries, sometimes merely decades, sometimes even less time than that. But eventually most jobs, industries, and careers are mortal.

We are mortal. So are jobs. Understand that truth, and you will avoid a life of bitterness and blame. In today's world, you must *always* have a plan B up your sleeve.

PETAL FOUR, WORKSHEET #3

PRIORITIZING YOUR KNOWLEDGES: FAVORITE SUBJECTS MATRIX

Okay, now you've completed Worksheet #2. You've cast as wide a commercial fisherman's net—so to speak—as possible, using Worksheet #1 and Worksheet #2 for this Petal. What now?

Well, it's time to pick the best of your haul, as we indicated earlier. Time to look it all over and decide which knowledges, subjects, or interests are your favorites. Time for prioritizing. But we're going to use a different kind of prioritizing aid here: not our familiar Grid, but four boxes/compartments/"bins" along the axes of Expertise and Enthusiasm. In other words, a matrix.

Before you begin, copy the matrix on the facing page onto a much larger piece of paper.

Then copy everything—*everything*—you have written down on Worksheet #1 (Ten Prompts) and Worksheet #2 (the Chart) and decide which of the four bins it belongs in, as you weigh your expertise (or lack of it) and your enthusiasm (or lack of it) with that particular subject or knowledge.

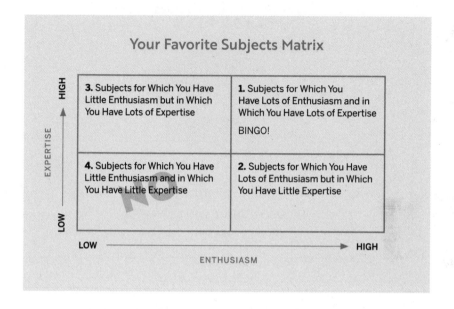

(You don't have to copy anything into bin #4 if you don't want to—except if you want bin #4 to stand there, filled with subjects and knowledges that you don't care about, as a cautionary tale. I'll state the obvious: any knowledge that you have neither any expertise in nor any enthusiasm for is a knowledge you will want to avoid at all costs in a future job, if it's up to you. And it is.)

Once you have finished copying the knowledge from Worksheets #1 and #2 into these bins, go back and study only what you put into bin #1: *High Expertise, High Enthusiasm.* Copy what you consider to be your top four or five favorites from that bin—*use a Prioritizing Grid if you need to*—and maybe, just maybe, one item from bin #2, and put them on Petal Four, found on pages 186–187.

Bueno! Your Favorite Subjects, Knowledges, Fields, Interests—whatever you want to call them—is done. Now you're ready to move on, to consider the fifth side of Who You Are.

PETAL FIVE

I Am a Person Who . . . prefers a certain level of responsibility and salary

---

My Preferred Level of Responsibility and Salary

Goal in Filling Out This Petal: To gain a realistic picture of how much money you will need to earn, or want to earn, at whatever job you find.

What You Are Looking For: A range, because most employers are thinking in terms of a range, too. When you negotiate salary—as you will almost certainly have to, if the employer is of any significant size—you want to get the best outcome for your needs.

Form of the Entries on Your Petal: Total dollars needed, weekly, monthly, or annually. Stated in thousands (symbol: K).

Example of a Helpful Petal: $75K to $85K (good because it's a range, is realistic based on your research into the career field, and is justifiable based on your levels of experience and education).

A Crash Course in Money

Money is important. Or else we're reduced to bartering for our food, clothing, and shelter. So, when we're out of work, unless we have huge amounts of money in our savings account or investments, we are inevitably thinking: *What am I going to do so that I have enough money to put food on the table, clothes on my back, and a roof over our heads for myself—and for my family or partner (if I have one)?*

Happiness is important, too. So we may find ourselves thinking: *How much do I really need to be earning, for me to be truly happy with my life?*

Are these two worries—money and happiness—related? Can money buy happiness?

Partly, it turns out. Partly. A study, published in 2010, of the responses of 450,000 people in the US to a daily survey, found that the less money they made, the more unhappy they tended to be, day after day.[18] No surprise there. And, obviously, the more money they made, measured in terms of percentage improvement, the happier they tended to be, *as measured by the frequency and intensity of moments of smiling, laughter, affection, and joy all day long, versus moments of sadness, worry, and stress.*

So money does buy happiness. *But only up to a point.* That point was found to be around $75,000 annual income, with a satiation point at $95,000. If people made more money annually than $75,000, it of course further improved their *satisfaction* with how their life was going, but it did not increase their *happiness*. Above $75,000, they started to report reduced ability to spend time with people they liked, to enjoy leisure, and to savor small pleasures. Happiness depends on things like that, and on other factors too: good health; a loving relationship; loving friends; and a feeling of competence—gaining mastery, respect, praise, or even love because we are really good at what we do.

So this petal cannot be filled out all by itself. It is inextricably tied to the other petals—most particularly, to what you love to do and where you love to do it.

Still, salary is something you must think about ahead of time, when you're contemplating your ideal job or career. Level goes hand in hand with salary, of course. So here are a few of questions you should be asking yourself:

1. **At what level would you like to work, in your ideal job?**

Level is a matter of how much responsibility you want in an organization:

- Boss or CEO (this may mean you'll have to form your own business)
- Manager or someone under the boss who carries out orders
- The head of a team
- A member of a team of equals
- One who works in tandem with one other partner
- One who works alone, as an employee, a consultant to an organization, or a one-person business

Think carefully about your answer, talk it over with your friends or family, then enter a two- or three-word summary of your answer (for now) on Petal Six, the Preferred Salary and Level of Responsibility, of your Flower Diagram, pages 186–187.

2. **What salary would you like to be aiming for?**

Here you have to think in terms of a range, not a single figure. It's a mistake to hyperfocus on one number, as you will see in chapter 10 on salary negotiation. One way to do this is to think of your minimum or maximum desired.

Minimum is what you would need to make to just barely get by. And incidentally, you do need to know this *before* you go in for a job interview with anyone (or before you form your own business, and need to know how much profit you must make, just to survive). You can't survive on a negative income stream.

Maximum could be any astronomical figure you can think of, but it is more useful here to put down the salary you realistically think you could make, with your present competency and experience, were you working for a real, *but generous*, boss. (If this maximum figure is still depressingly low, then put down the salary you would like to be making five years from now.)

3. What benefits package would you like to aim for?

Keep in mind that a better benefits package than you currently have can offset a slightly lower salary offer than you would like. Once again, you must know what's most important about your compensation. Even though there are copays and other costs associated with benefits, a strong benefits package can increase your overall compensation by as much as 30 percent beyond your salary. Some possible benefits include:

- Healthcare (medical, dental, vision)
- Bonuses
- Disability insurance (long-term and short-term)
- Free meals
- Retirement (401[k] or 403[b]) or pension
- Sick/parental leave
- Vacation time/holidays
- Child care (free or low-cost)
- Stock options
- Tuition reimbursement for self or children
- Work-from-home flexibility

Are any of these benefits imperative for you? Which ones are unnecessary? Knowing what you need in terms of benefits can help you greatly in your salary negotiations.

PETAL FIVE, WORKSHEET #1

A BUDGET: KEEPING TRACK OF HOW MUCH YOU DO SPEND AND HOW MUCH YOU'D LIKE TO SPEND

We all think we know how much money we need to earn. But one of the best ways to really know is by making a budget. On the next page you will find a simple guide to the categories you will need to think about. Figure out what you think you will need *monthly* in each category. And if you see any categories missing, do not hesitate to add them.

One of the best ways to start determining your necessary income is to keep track of how you actually spend your money. You can just jot down notes at the end of each day. Lots of apps make this task much easier. For example, there is Spending Tracker, Pocket Expense, Goodbudget, and for all those who want to sync with their bank accounts, Mint.com.

The good news: all are simple, and all are free.

Once you figure out what you *actually* spend, you'll be much better able to lay out a realistic budget of what you *want* to spend.

In any event, by hook or by crook, once you have your monthly budget it's time to do some math. Fill out your monthly expenses chart on the next two pages.

Multiply the total amount you need each month by 12, to get the yearly figure.

Divide the yearly figure by 2,000, and you will be reasonably near the *minimum* hourly wage that you need. Thus, if you need $3,333 per month, multiplied by 12 that's $40,000 a year, and then divided by 2,000, that's $20 an hour.

You will also want to put down the *maximum* salary you would like to make (dream, dream, dream). Once you are done, enter both salary figures—minimum and maximum—and any notes you want to add, such as to justify the maximum (you may also want to add any nonmonetary rewards you seek from the Optional Exercise on page 167) and add all of this on Petal Six, the Preferred Salary and Level of Responsibility petal, found on pages 186–187.

Housing

Rent or mortgage payments . . . . $_____

Electricity/gas. . . . . $_____

Water . . . . $_____

Phone/internet. . . . . $_____

Garbage removal . . . . $_____

Cleaning, maintenance, repairs . . . . $_____

Food

What you spend at the supermarket

and/or farmers' market . . . . $_____

Eating out . . . . $_____

Clothing

Purchase of new or used clothing . . . . $_____

Cleaning, dry cleaning, laundry . . . . $_____

Automobile/transportation

Car payments . . . . $_____

Gas . . . . $_____

Repairs. . . . . $_____

Public transportation (bus, train, plane). . . . . $_____

Insurance

Car . . . . $_____

Medical or health care . . . . $_____

House and personal possessions. . . . . $_____

Life . . . . $_____

Medical expenses

Doctors' visits. . . . . $_____

Prescriptions. . . . . $_____

Fitness costs . . . . $_____

Support for other family members

Child care costs (if you have children) . . . . $_____

Child support (if you're paying that). . . . . $_____

Support for your parents (if you're helping out). . . . . . $_____

Charity giving/tithe (to help others) . . . . $_____

School/learning

    Children's costs (if you have children in school) . . . . . $_____

    Your learning costs (adult education,

        job-hunting classes) . . . . $_____

Pet care (if you have pets). . . . . $_____

Bills and debts (usual monthly payments)

    Credit cards . . . . $_____

    Other obligations you pay off monthly. . . . . $_____

Taxes

    Federal (annual return, divided by twelve months) . . . $_____

    State (likewise). . . . . $_____

    Local/property (annual, divided by twelve months). . . $_____

    Tax help (if you ever use an accountant, or

        pay a friend to help you with taxes) . . . . $_____

Savings (what you currently deposit each month) . . . . . . $_____

Retirement Contributions . . . . $_____

Amusement/discretionary spending

    Movies, Netflix, other. . . . . $_____

    Other entertainment. . . . . $_____

    Reading: newspapers, magazines, books . . . . $_____

    Gifts (birthdays, holidays, anniversaries) . . . . $_____

    Vacations. . . . . $_____

Total Amount You Need Each Month. . . . . $_____

PETAL FIVE, WORKSHEET #2

AN OPTIONAL EXERCISE:
OTHER REWARDS BESIDES MONEY

If you do check off things on this list, arrange your answers in order of importance to you, and then add them to the petal.

You may wish to put down other rewards, besides money, that you would hope for from your next job or career. These might be:

- ☐ Adventure
- ☐ A chance to be creative
- ☐ A chance to exercise leadership
- ☐ A chance to help others
- ☐ A chance to make decisions
- ☐ A chance to use your expertise
- ☐ A diverse work environment
- ☐ Challenge
- ☐ Fame
- ☐ Influence
- ☐ Intellectual stimulation
- ☐ Popularity
- ☐ Power
- ☐ Respect
- ☐ Other

Now, on to the seventh side of Who You Are.

PETAL SIX

I Am a Person Who . . . prefers certain places to live

My Preferred Place(s) to Live

Goal in Filling Out This Petal: To define in what part of the country or the world you would most like to work and live, and would be happiest, if you ever have a choice. Also to resolve any conflict (should it arise) between you and your partner as to where you want to live after you retire or make your next career move.

What You Are Looking For: Forming a clearer picture about what you hope for in life, now or later. Now, if you're able to move and want to make a wise decision as to where. Later, if you're currently tied down to a particular place because "I need to be near my kids or my ailing parents," or whatever, in which case this becomes a planning for the future: retirement, or earlier. It's important to think about the future now, because an opportunity may come along when you least expect it, and you might pass right by it, unless you've given it some thought and instantly recognize it.

Form of the Entries on Your Petal: You can stay general (city, suburbs, rural, up in the mountains, on the coast, or overseas) or you can get very specific if you're really ready to move, naming names and places—as this exercise will teach you to do.

Example of a Helpful Petal: First preference, San Francisco; second preference, Honolulu; third preference, New York City.

PETAL SIX, WORKSHEET #1
A CHART: WHAT I LIKED OR DISLIKED ABOUT PLACES I HAVE LIVED

Copy the chart found on pages 170–171, onto a larger (11 by 17 inches) piece of paper or cardboard. And if you are doing this exercise with a partner, make a copy for them too, so that each of you is working on a clean copy of your own and can follow these instructions independently. Ask your partner to complete the same list with the first four columns, and have them create a page with the list of possible locations that fit their characteristics.

Now, to fill out this chart:

Column 1. List all the places where you have ever lived.

Column 2. List all the factors you disliked about each place.

Column 3. List what you liked about living in those places. Keep going until you have listed all the factors you disliked or hated about each and every place you named in column 1.

Review column 2, your list of negative factors, and in column 3 try to list each one's opposite (or near opposite). For example, "the sun never shone there" would, in column 3, be turned into "mostly sunny, all year round." It will not always be the exact opposite. For example, the negative factor "rains all the time" does not necessarily translate into the positive "sunny all the time." It might be something like "sunny at least 200 days a year." It's your call. Keep going until every negative factor in column 2 has an opposite, positive factor, in column 3.

(At this point, you don't really need column 1. Its purpose was to jog your memory.)

Column 4. In column 4, list the positive factors in column 3, from most important to you to least important. For example, if you were looking at and trying to name a new town, city, or place where you could be happy and flourish, what is the first thing you would look for? Would it

My Geographical Preferences

Decision Making for Just You

COLUMN 1	COLUMN 2	COLUMN 3	COLUMN 4
Names of Places I Have Lived	From the Past: Negatives	Translating the Negatives into Positives	Ranking of My Positives
	Factors I Disliked and Still Dislike About Any Place	Factors I Liked and Still Like About Any Place	1.
			2.
			3.
			4.
			5.
			6.
			7.
			8.
			9.
			10.

Our Geographical Preferences

Decision Making for You and a Partner

COLUMN 5	COLUMN 6	COLUMN 7	COLUMN 8
Places That Fit These Criteria	Ranking of Their Preferences	Combining Our Two Lists (columns 4 & 6)	Places That Fit These Criteria
	a.	a.	
		1.	
	b.	b.	
		2.	
	c.	c.	
		3.	
	d.	d.	
		4.	
	e.	e.	
	f.	5.	
		f.	
	g.	6.	
		g.	
	h.	7.	
		h.	
	i.	8.	
		i.	
	j.	9.	
		j.	
		10.	

PRIORITIZING GRID
for 10 items or fewer

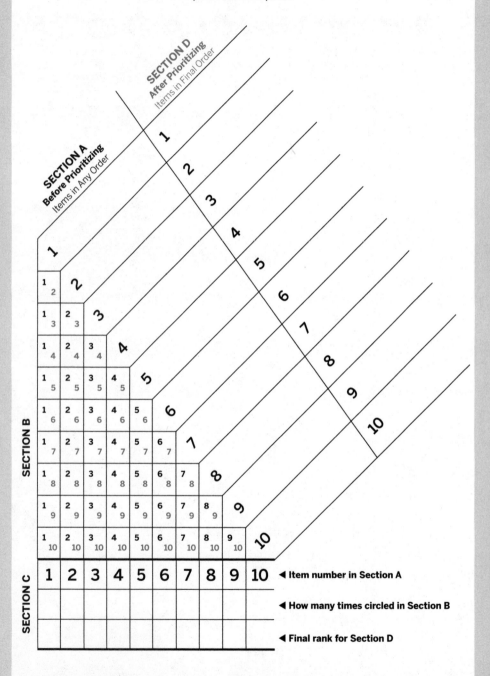

SECTION D
After Prioritizing
Items in Final Order

SECTION A
Before Prioritizing
Items in Any Order

SECTION B

SECTION C

◀ Item number in Section A

◀ How many times circled in Section B

◀ Final rank for Section D

be good weather? Lack of crime? Good schools? Access to cultural opportunities, such as music, art, museums, or whatever? Inexpensive housing? Rank all the factors in column 4. If you need an organizing tool, use the ten-item Prioritizing Grid on the facing page.

Show and tell. Once you're done, on a fresh blank sheet of paper list those top ten factors, in order of importance to you. For the next ten days, show it to everyone you meet and ask them: "Can you think of any place that has all ten of these factors, or at least the top five?" Jot down any and all of their suggestions on the back of the sheet. When the ten days are up, look at the back of that sheet and circle the three places that seem the most interesting to you. If there is only a partial overlap between your dream factors and the places your friends and acquaintances can come up with, *make sure the overlap is in the factors that count the most.* Google can help, too. Try searching "cities with lowest crime rates" or "best places for sunshine in US" and see what shows up. Just keep in mind that some of those lists are not neutral. They may be influenced by a sponsor or whatever group produced it, such as a tourism company or the local chamber of commerce.

Column 5. You now have some locations you will want to find out more about, so that you can eventually figure out which would be your absolute favorite place to live, and your second, and your third, as backups. Enter those top three places in column 5, then copy these, plus your top five geographical factors, onto Petal Six, Preferred Place(s) to Live, on the Flower Diagram on pages 186–187.

Column 6. If you're working with a partner, it's time to compare your lists. In column 6, place your partner's top choices.

Column 7. Alternate writing your partner's and your ranked choices

Did you find any places where your lists agree or at least complement each other? Did you select the same cities? Same general geographic areas?

Column 8. Try coming up with a prioritized list you both can agree on and list those places (or criteria) and place them here.

By looking at columns 7 and 8, you will now know the key elements that are important to each of you and both of you. You will also have a list of places that might work for each of you—and both of you. Review these columns together and start developing your top five places that you both would feel comfortable about. That's the list that can go on Petal Six, Preferred Places to Live.

Finally, both of you should put the names of those top three places, plus your top five geographical factors, onto Petal Six, the Preferred Place(s) to Live petal, on both of your Flower Diagrams, pages 186–187.

Conclusion for Petal Six

Does all this seem like just too much work? Well, there are a few options you *may* want to try. The first is a website called Teleport (teleport.org). Try it! See if it helps you at all. One reader said, about a similar site, "I found it useful. It showed me towns I'd never thought about." Consider vacationing in your top choice locations. Spend at least a week and pretend you live there. Talk to a real estate agent or look at where apartments are available in which neighborhoods. Take time to visit grocery stores, shops, and restaurants.

The third alternative: Have everyone in the house throw darts at a map (of the US or wherever) that you've pinned to a dartboard. See what place the most darts came near. (One family did this after they couldn't agree on any location. For them it came out: Denver. So, Denver it was!)

PETAL SEVEN

I Am a Person Who . . . has a certain goal, purpose, or mission in life

---

My Purpose or Sense of Mission for My Life

Goal in Filling Out This Petal: To know the moral compass or spiritual values by which you want to guide your life, or the overall goals that inspire you.

What You Are Looking For: Some definition of your overall goals, purpose, and/or mission of your life. This may help you pick out the kinds of organizations or companies you'd like to work for, if you find ones that are serving the same mission as yours.

Form of the Entries on Your Petal: A description of what sphere of life you want to make better, with some attending details.

Example of a Helpful Petal: My purpose in life is to help others through my teaching. I want there to be more knowledge, more compassion, more forgiveness, in those I have worked or lived with, because I have taught them.

You need to dream about the broad outcome of your life, and not just this year's job search. What kind of footprint do you want to leave on this Earth, after your journey here is done? Figure that out, and you're well on your way to defining your life as having purpose and a mission. As John Holland famously said, "We need to look further down the road than just headlight range at night." The road is the road of life.

PETAL SEVEN, WORKSHEET #1

DIAGRAM: THE NINE SPHERES OF PURPOSE OR MISSION

Generally speaking, purpose can be broken down into nine spheres, corresponding to our nature. As you look these over in the diagram on the facing page, which one appeals to *you* the most? Time for some hard thinking (ouch!). So study this diagram *slowly*. Take time to ponder and think. Consider circling the elements that are most important to you.

Now let's look at these in more detail. Consider these as spheres, environments, or arenas in which you like to play.

1. **The Sphere of the Senses.** When you have finished your life here on Earth, do you want there to be more beauty in the world because you were here? If so, what kind of beauty entrances you? Is it art, music, flowers, photography, painting, staging, crafts, clothing, jewelry, or something else? If this is your main purpose in life, then write one paragraph about it.

2. **The Sphere of the Body.** When you have finished your life here on Earth, do you want there to be more wholeness, fitness, or health in the world, more healing of the body's wounds, more feeding of the hungry and clothing of the poor, because you were here? What issue in particular? If this is your main purpose in life, then write one paragraph about it.

3. **The Sphere of Our Possessions.** Is your major concern the often false love of possessions in this world? When you have finished your life here on Earth, do you want there to be better stewardship of what we possess—as individuals, as a community, as a nation—in the world, because you were here? Do you want to see simplicity, quality (rather than quantity), and a broader emphasis on the word

The Purpose for My Life:
I Want There to Be More . . . (choose)

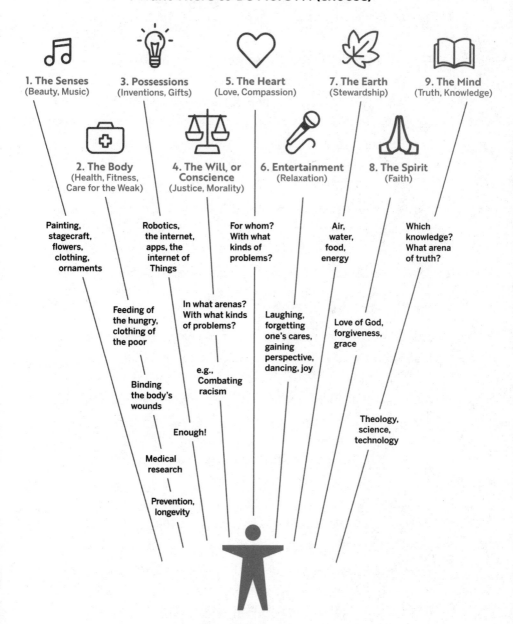

1. The Senses
(Beauty, Music)

3. Possessions
(Inventions, Gifts)

5. The Heart
(Love, Compassion)

7. The Earth
(Stewardship)

9. The Mind
(Truth, Knowledge)

2. The Body
(Health, Fitness,
Care for the Weak)

4. The Will, or
Conscience
(Justice, Morality)

6. Entertainment
(Relaxation)

8. The Spirit
(Faith)

Painting,
stagecraft,
flowers,
clothing,
ornaments

Robotics,
the internet,
apps, the
internet of
Things

For whom?
With what
kinds of
problems?

Air,
water,
food,
energy

Which
knowledge?
What arena
of truth?

Feeding of
the hungry,
clothing of
the poor

In what arenas?
With what kinds
of problems?

Laughing,
forgetting
one's cares,
gaining
perspective,
dancing, joy

Love of God,
forgiveness,
grace

Binding
the body's
wounds

e.g.,
Combating
racism

Theology,
science,
technology

Enough!

Medical
research

Prevention,
longevity

. . . in the World Because I Was Here

You may pick more than one. Write a one-page essay. Summarize it on the
Goal, Purpose, or Mission in Life petal, pages 186–187.

"enough," rather than on the words "more, more"? If so, in what areas of human life in particular? If this is your main purpose in life, then write one paragraph about it.

4. **The Sphere of the Will or Conscience.** When you have finished your life here on Earth, do you want there to be more morality, more justice, more righteousness, more honesty in the world, because you were here? In what areas of human life or history, in particular? And in what geographical area? If this is your main purpose in life, then write one paragraph about it.

5. **The Sphere of the Heart.** When you have finished your life here on Earth, do you want there to be more love and compassion in the world, because you were here? Love or compassion for whom? Or for what? If this is your main purpose in life, then write one paragraph about it.

6. **The Sphere of Entertainment.** When you have finished your life here on Earth, do you want there to be more lightening of people's loads, more giving them perspective, more helping them to forget their cares for a spell; do you want there to be more laughter in the world, and joy, because you were here? If so, what particular kind of entertainment do you want to contribute to the world? If this is your main purpose in life, then write one paragraph about it.

7. **The Sphere of the Earth.** Is the planet on which we stand your major concern? When you have finished your life here on Earth, do you want there to be better protection of this fragile planet, more exploration of the world or the universe—exploration, not exploitation—more dealing with its problems and its energy, because you were here? If so, which problems or challenges, in particular, draw your heart and soul? If this is your main purpose in life, then write one paragraph about it.

8. **The Sphere of the Spirit.** When you have finished your life here on Earth, do you want there to be more spirituality in the world, more faith, more compassion, more forgiveness, more love for a higher power and the human family in all its diversity, because you were here? If so, with what ages, people, or with what parts of human life? If this is you, then your sense of purpose is pointing you toward the sphere of the spirit. Write one paragraph about it.

9. **The Sphere of the Mind.** When you have finished your life here on Earth, do you want there to be more knowledge, truth, or clarity in the world, because you were here? Knowledge, truth, or clarity concerning what in particular? If this is your main purpose in life, then write one paragraph about it.

In sum, remember that all of these are worthwhile purposes and missions, all of these are necessary and needed in this world. The question is, Which one in particular draws you to it *the most*? Which one do you most want to lend your brain, your energies, your skills and gifts, your life, to serve while you are here on this Earth?

When you are done, enter a summary paragraph or essay of what you have decided your purpose or mission is (you may pick more than one) on Petal Seven, your Goal, Purpose, or Mission in Life, on pages 186–187.

PETAL SEVEN, WORKSHEET #2

ESSAY: YOUR PHILOSOPHY ABOUT LIFE

There are two challenges you may run into with this petal.

First Challenge: You just come up empty on this exercise, despite hard thinking. No harm done. If you want an answer, just keep the question on the back burner of your mind; eventually, some insight is going to break through—tomorrow, next week, next month, or a year from now. Be patient with yourself.

Second Challenge: This subject doesn't interest you at all. Okay. Then instead of writing a statement of purpose or mission for your life, you can instead write a statement outlining what you think about *life*: why are we here, why are *you* here, and so on. This is often called your philosophy of life.

In writing a philosophy of life, aim for it to run no more than two pages, single spaced, and it can be less. It should address whichever of the following elements you think are most important; pick and choose. You do *not* have to write about all of them. In most cases, you will only need two or three sentences about each element you choose to comment on.

- **Beauty:** what kind of beauty stirs you; the function of beauty in the world
- **Behavior:** how you think we should behave in this world
- **Beliefs:** your strongest beliefs
- **Celebration:** how you like to play or celebrate
- **Choice:** its nature and importance to you
- **Community:** your concept of belonging to each other; what you think is our responsibility to each other
- **Compassion:** how you demonstrate it to yourself and others
- **Confusion:** how you live with it and deal with it
- **Death:** what you think about it and what you think happens after it
- **Events:** what you think makes things happen; how you explain why they happen
- **Free will:** whether our lives are "predetermined" or we have free will
- **Happiness:** what makes for the truest human happiness
- **Heroes and heroines:** who yours are, and why
- **Humanity:** what you think is important about being human, what you think is our function
- **Love:** what you think about its nature and importance, along with all its related words: compassion, forgiveness, grace

- **Moral issues:** which ones you believe are the most important for us to pay attention to, wrestle with, help solve
- **Paradox:** your attitude toward its presence in life
- **Purpose:** why we are here, what life is all about
- **Reality:** what you think is its nature and components
- **Self:** whether physical self is the limit of your being; what trust-in-self means
- **Spirituality:** its place in human life, how we should treat it
- **Stewardship:** what we should do with the gifts we have been given
- **Truth:** what you think about it; which truths are most important
- **Uniqueness:** what you think makes each of us unique
- **Universe:** your concept of what holds the universe together—a supreme being or other force
- **Values:** what you think about humanity, what you think about the world, ranked by what matters most (to you)

When you are done writing, put a summary paragraph on Petal Seven, your Goal, Purpose, or Mission in Life, on pages 186–187. And you're done!

I Am a Person Who . . . Has Completed My Flower

Readers have asked to see an example of "that one piece of paper" all filled out. Rich W. Feller—a student of mine (RB) back in 1982, now a world-famous professor and past president of the National Career Development Association—filled out his flower as you see on the following pages. He said that one piece of paper has been his lifelong companion ever since, and his guiding star. (The petals then were slightly different.)

Rich Feller first put his personal picture together over thirty years ago. Here are his comments about its usefulness since, and how that one piece of paper helped him, how he's used it, and how it's changed.

Rich Feller's Flower

EXAMPLE

Favorite Working Conditions

1. Receive clinical supervision 2. Mentor relationship 3. Excellent secretary 4. Part of larger, highly respected organization with clear direction 5. Near gourmet and health food specialty shops 6. Heterogeneous colleagues (race, sex, age) 7. Flexible dress code 8. Merit system 9. Can bike/bus/walk to work 10. Private office with window

Favorite People Environment

1. Strong social, perceptual skills 2. Emotionally and physically healthy 3. Enthusiastically include others 4. Heterogeneous in interests and skills 5. Social changers, innovators 6. Politically, economically astute 7. Confident enough to confront/cry and be foolish 8. Sensitive to nontraditional issues 9. I and R (see page 115) 10. Nonmaterialistic

Favorite Skills

1. Observational/learning skills • continually expose self to new experiences • perceptive in identifying and assessing potential of others 2. Leadership skills • continually search for more responsibility • see a problem/act to solve it 3. Instructing/interpreting/guiding • committed to learning as a lifelong process • create atmosphere of acceptance 4. Serving/helping/human relations skills • shape atmosphere of particular place

Favorite Values

1. Improve the human condition 2. Promote interdependence and futuristic principles 3. Maximize productive use of human/material resources 4. Teach people to be self-directed/self-responsible 5. Free people from self-defeating controls (thoughts, rules, barriers) 6. Promote capitalistic principles 7. Reduce exploitation 8. Promote political participation 9. Acknowledge those who give to the community 10. Give away ideas

Favorite Interests

1. Large conference planning
2. Regional geography & culture
3. Traveling on $20/day
4. Career planning seminars
5. Counseling techniques/theories
6. American policies
7. Fundamentals of sports
8. Fighting sexism
9. NASCAR auto racing
10. Interior design

• relate well in dealing with public **5.** Detail/follow-through skills • handle great variety of tasks • resource broker **6.** Influencing/persuading skills • recruiting talent/leadership • inspiring trust **7.** Performing skills • getting up in front of a group (if I'm in control) • addressing small and large groups **8.** Intuitional/innovative skills • continually develop/ generate new ideas **9.** Develop/plan/ organize/execute • designing projects • utilizing skills of others **10.** Language/read/write • communicate effectively • can think quickly on my feet

Salary and Level of Responsibility

1. Can determine 9/12 month contract
2. Can determine own projects
3. Considerable clout in organization's direction without administrative responsibilities
4. Able to select colleagues **5.** 3 to 5 assistants **6.** $35K to $50K **7.** Serve on various important boards **8.** Can defer clerical and budget decisions and tasks **9.** Speak before large groups **10.** Can run for elected office

Geography

1. Close to major city
2. Mild winters/low humidity
3. Change in seasons **4.** Clean and green **5.** 100,000 people **6.** Nice shopping malls **7.** Wide range of athletic options **8.** Diverse economic base **9.** Ample local culture **10.** Sense of community (pride)

What the Parachute Flower Has Meant to Me

More than anything I've gained from an academic life, my Flower has given me hope, direction, and a lens to satisfaction. Using it to assess my life direction during crisis, career moves, and stretch assignments, it helps me define and hold to personal commitments. In many ways it's my "guiding light." Data within my Flower became and remain the core of any success and satisfaction I have achieved.

After I first filled out my own Flower Diagram in a two-week workshop with Dick Bolles back in 1982, I decided to teach the Flower to others. My academic position has allowed me to do this, abundantly. Having now taught the Flower to thousands of counselors and career development and human resource specialists, I continually use it with clients and in my own transitional retirement planning.

I'm overwhelmed with how little has changed within my Flower, over the years. My Flower is the best of what I am. Its petals are my compass, and using my "favorite skills" is the mirror to a joyful day. I trust the wisdom within that one piece of paper. It has guided my work and my life, ever since 1982, and it has helped my wife and me define our hopes for our son.

The process of filling out and acting on that one piece of paper taught me a lot. Specifically, it taught me *the importance of the following ten things, often running contrary to what my studies and doctoral work had taught me previously.*

I learned from my Flower the importance of:

1. Chasing after passions, honoring strengths, and respecting skill identification
2. Challenging societal definitions of balance and success
3. Committing to something bigger than oneself
4. Living authentically and with joy
5. Being good at what matters to oneself and its relationship to opportunity
6. Finding pleasure in all that one does
7. Staying focused on well-being and life satisfaction
8. Personal clarity and responsibility for designing "possible selves"
9. Letting the world know, humbly but clearly, what we want

10. "Coaching" people amidst a world of abundance where individuals yearn for meaning and purpose more than they hunger for possessions, abject compliance with society's expectations, or simply fitting in

This technologically enhanced, global workplace we now face in the twenty-first century certainly challenges all we thought we knew about our life roles. Maintaining clarity, learning agility, and identifying development plans have become elevated to new and critical importance, if we are to maintain choice. As a result I've added the following four emphases to "Rich's Flower"; that is to say, I try to keep a running list (constantly updated) of ten things that I want to:

1. Have
2. Do
3. Learn
4. Give

Through the practice of keeping these in mind, I can measure change in my growth and development.

I feel so fortunate to have the opportunity to share with others how much I gained from the wisdom and hope embedded within "Rich's Flower."

I humbly offer my resume, home location and design, and family commitments on my website at www.richfeller.com. I'd be honored to share my journey, and encourage others to nurture and shine light on their garden as well. I believe you'll find about 90 percent of the Flower's items influence our daily experience.

Rich Feller
Professor of Counseling and Career Development
University Distinguished Teaching Scholar
Colorado State University
Fort Collins, CO

Okay: like Rich, you've now got your completed Flower.
Nice diagram. What do you do with it?
Well, that's the subject of our next chapter.

The Flower

"That One Piece of Paper"

1

My Preferred Kinds of PEOPLE TO WORK WITH:

1

2

3

4

5

My Holland Code:

2

My Favorite WORKING CONDITIONS:

1

2

3

4

5

7

My GOAL, PURPOSE, or MISSION IN LIFE
(or my philosophy about life):

3

What I Can Do and Love to Do (My Favorite TRANSFERABLE SKILLS):

1

2

3

4

5

6

7

8

9

10

4

My Favorite KNOWLEDGES or Fields of Interest:

1

2

3

4

5

5

Level of Responsibility I'd Like:

My preferred SALARY RANGE:

Other Rewards Hoped For:

1

2

3

6

My Preferred Kinds of PLACES TO LIVE:

My Preferred GEORGRAPHICAL FACTORS:

1

2

3

1

2

3

This is the real secret of life—to be completely engaged with what you are doing in the here and now. And instead of calling it work, realize it is play.

—ALAN WATTS

CHAPTER 7

YOU GET TO CHOOSE WHERE YOU WORK

Some of you will look at your completed Flower Exercise and have an instant flash of recognition. *Wow, I see what I want to do with my life! I'm excited.* Others of you will say *Well, I finished it. Now what?* And you will need a more carefully reasoned series of steps to find that out.

So here are the ten next steps, which will be explained further in the rest of this book:

1. Find out what careers or work your Flower points to.
2. Try on some of those jobs before you decide which ones to pursue.
3. Find out what kinds of organizations have such jobs.
4. Find names of particular places that interest you.
5. Research those places thoroughly before formally approaching them.
6. Prepare your targeted job-search materials (such as resume, social media profiles, and so on; chapter 8).
7. Approach potential employers through a variety of methods including online applications, networking, social media, and so on (chapters 7 and 8).
8. Prepare strong responses and stories for your interviews (chapter 9).
9. Consider offers and negotiate salary (chapter 10).
10. Start your new/improved/different career!

First, You Need to Find Out What Careers or Jobs Your Flower Points To

Look at your completed Flower Diagram, and from Petal Five choose the top *three* of your favorite **Knowledges** (or fields of interest, favorite fields, or fields of fascination—whatever you want to call them). All nouns. On one piece of blank paper, say, 8½ by 11 inches, or on a screen, copy these in the top half of that page, in their order of importance to you (most important at the top). Beneath them all, midway down the page, draw a line, straight across.

Next, look at the Skills petal on your completed Flower Diagram and choose your top *five* favorite **Transferable Skills**. All verbs. Copy them down, in order, below the line.

Start researching online. Search on phrases like "careers with _____" and insert the skills or knowledges you want to use in the workplace. Consider what level of education or skills is needed to work in those fields.

Go into Indeed.com and enter your skills or knowledges as a keyword under the "what" tab, then see what jobs show up. For instance, let's say one of your skills is speaking French. Go to Indeed and type "French" in the "what" box and your desired geographic location in the "where" box. Anything interesting show up? I tried this search using New York City and found a wide variety of job openings, from administrative aides to teachers to customer support to interpreter to marketing. The jobs were located in banks, hospitals, schools, businesses, and even the United Nations.

Once you have done your basic searches, try taking your list of knowledges and skills and showing it to at least five friends, family members, or professionals you know. Ask them what jobs or work these skills suggest to them. Tell them you just want them to take some wild guesses, combining as many of the eight factors on that paper or screen as possible. If possible, you or they must combine two or three of your knowledges (fields) into one specialty: that's what can make you unique, with very little competition from others.

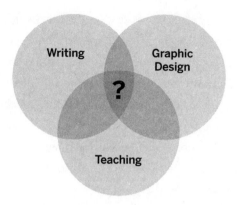

Here's how: Let us say your three favorite knowledges are writing, graphic design, and teaching. If you possibly can, use all three areas of expertise, not just one. So put those three favorite knowledges on a series of overlapping circles, as shown. Next, to figure out how to combine these three, imagine that each circle is a person; in this case, writer, graphic designer, and teacher.

- You can start by identifying anyone you know who already works in these fields. (You can also read about each of these fields on the internet.) When you meet with people who work in one of these fields, ask them what careers they think could combine those three skills.

- Jot down *everything* these people suggest to you, on your computer, tablet, smartphone, or paper. Whether you like their suggestions or not. This is just brainstorming, for the moment.

- After you have done this for a week or so, review all your notes. Anything helpful or valuable here? If you see some useful suggestions, circle them and determine to explore them. If nothing looks interesting, go talk to five more of your friends, acquaintances, or people you know in the business world or nonprofit sector. Repeat as necessary.

- As you ponder any suggestions that look worth exploring, what interests you the most? Consider that all jobs can be described as working primarily with *people* or working primarily with *information/data* or working primarily with *things*. Most jobs involve all three, but which is your *primary* preference? Often your *favorite* skill will give you the best clue. If it *doesn't*, then go back and look at the *whole* Transferable Skills petal on your Flower Diagram. What do you think? Are your favorite skills weighted more toward working with *people*, *information/data*, or *things*?

- Just remember what you are trying to do here: find some career suggestions for your Flower. Typically, if you show it to enough family, friends, or colleagues, you will end up with about forty suggestions.

In the case of the individual who was interested in careers related to teaching, graphic design, and writing, by taking these steps he was able to find some interesting career ideas including graphics design instructor, game designer, web designer, and email marketing designer. All of these ideas sounded interesting to him, so he will be following the suggestions in the rest of this chapter to continue his research and move closer to his dream job. He even found a graphic design instructor position in his geographic area and plans to apply for it while still researching these other opportunities.

Don't ever think to yourself: *Well, I see what it is that I would love to be able to do, but I know there is no job in the world like that.* Dear friend, you don't know any such thing. Now I grant you that after you have completed these steps, you may not be able to find all that you want down to the last detail. But you'd be surprised at how much of your dream you may be able to find. Sometimes you will find it in stages. One retired man I know, who had been a senior executive with a publishing company, found himself bored to death in retirement after he turned sixty-five. He decided he didn't care what field he worked in at that point, so he contacted his favorite business acquaintance, who told him apologetically, "Times are tough. We just don't have anything open that matches or requires your abilities; right now all we need is someone in our mail room." The sixty-five-year-old executive said, "I'll take that job!" He did, and over the ensuing years steadily advanced once again, to just the job he wanted: as a senior executive in that organization, where he utilized all his prized skills for a number of years. Finally, he retired for the second time, at the age of eighty-five.

Always keep in mind your dream. Get as close to it as you can. Then be patient. You never know what doors will open up.

The O'NET

Go to this site and you will see all kinds of careers related to your interests that you might not have considered (www.onetonline.org/find or www.onetonline.org/search). Suggested careers (or occupations) are grouped or classified by any or all of the following: industries in great demand; green economies; largest number of openings anticipated; STEM disciplines (that would be science, technology, engineering, and math); amount of preparation or training required; Military Occupation Classification (equivalencies); abilities required; occupational knowledge required; interests, skill sets, work values, and work activities required; values you want at work; tasks and duties involved; tools, technology, machines, equipment, and software used; and so on.

Once you find an occupation you want to know more about, use the specially developed Content Model (www.onetcenter.org/content.html), which can run ten to twelve pages of printouts for each occupation. Maintained by the US Department of Labor, it is very thorough, and you may find a lot of helpful information.

Second, You Need to Try On Jobs Before You Decide Which Ones to Pursue

When you go shopping at a clothing store, you try on different outfits that you see in the window or on the racks. Why do you try them on? Well, the clothes that look *terrific* in the window don't always look so hot when you see them on *you*. They don't hang quite right, they don't flatter your shape, or they are sized oddly.

It's the same with careers. Ones that *sound* terrific in your imagination don't always look so great when you actually see them up close and personal.

What you want, of course, is a career that looks terrific—in the window *and* on you. So you need to go talk to people who are already doing the kind of job or career that you're thinking about. LinkedIn should be invaluable to you for locating the names of such people. But before you reach out to people, make sure you have researched what you can on the internet. There's no point in wasting someone's time asking them basic questions that can easily be answered by a website. Just search online, "how do you start a graphics business" or "how do you get into a finance career"—you'll find lots of basic information. That way, when you do connect with someone who is an expert in the field, you won't have to ask the basic questions. You can ask whether what you have read is accurate. And you can focus on *them* and their career path.

Once you find them, if they live nearby, ask for nineteen minutes of their time face to face—say, at a coffee shop—and keep to your word, unless during the chat they *insist* they want to go on talking. You can also ask for a phone call or quick Zoom meeting, if you can't meet in person. *Some* workers—not all—are desperate to find someone who will actually listen to them; you may come as an answer to their prayers. Keep the focus on *them—their* story.

Here are some questions that will help when you're talking with workers who are actually doing the career or job you think you might like to do:

- "How did *you* get into this work?"
- "What do *you* like the most about it?"
- "What do *you* like the least about it?"
- And "Where else could I find people who do this kind of work?" (You should always ask them for more than one name here, so that if you run into a dead end at any point, you can easily reach out to the other name[s] they suggested.)

If at any point in these informational interviews with workers it becomes more and more clear to you that this career, occupation, or job you are exploring definitely doesn't fit you, then the last question (above) gets turned into a different kind of inquiry:

- "Do you have any ideas as to who else I could talk to—*about my skills and special knowledges or interests*—who might know what other careers use the same skills and knowledges?" If they come up with names, go visit the people they suggest. If they can't think of anyone, ask them, "If you don't know of anyone, who do you think might know of someone?"

Sooner or later, as you do this informational interviewing with workers, you'll find a career that fits you just fine. It uses your favorite skills. It employs your favorite special knowledges or fields of interest. When this happens, you must ask the people you have been talking to **how much training it takes to get into that field or career**.

More times than not, you will hear *bad news*. They will tell you something like: "In order to be hired for this job, you have to have a master's degree and ten years' experience at it."

Is that so? Keep in mind that no matter how many people tell you that such-and-such are the rules about getting into a particular occupation— and there are no exceptions—believe me, there *are* exceptions to almost *every* rule, except for those few professions that have rigid entrance examinations—say, medicine or law. Otherwise, *somebody* has figured out a way around the rules. You want to find out who these people are and go talk to them, to find out *how they did it*.

So, in your informational interviewing, you press deeper; you search for *exceptions*:

- "Yes, but do you know of anyone in this field who got into it without that master's degree and ten years' experience?"
- "And where might I find him or her?"
- "And if you don't know of any such person, who do you think might know?"

In the end, maybe—just maybe—you can't find any exceptions. It's not that they aren't out there; it's just that you don't know how to find them. So what do you do when everyone tells you that such-and-such a career takes *years* to prepare for, and you can't find *anyone* who took a shortcut? What then?

Good news. Every professional specialty has one or more *shadow* professions, which require much less training. For example, instead of becoming a doctor, you can go into paramedical work; instead of becoming a lawyer, you can go into paralegal work; instead of becoming a licensed career counselor, you can become a career coach. There is always a way to get *close*, at least, to what you dream of. Think about your career ideas more broadly. You can search on "careers related to ____" and discover ideas you've never considered.

Third, You Need to Find Out What Kinds of Organizations Have Such Jobs

Before you think of individual places where you might like to work, it is helpful to stop and think of all the *kinds* of places where you might get hired, so you can be sure you're casting the widest net possible.

Let's take an example. Suppose in your new career you want to be a teacher. You must then ask yourself: *What kinds of places hire teachers?* You might answer, *Just schools*—and, finding that schools in your geographical area have no openings, you might assume, *Well, there are no jobs for people in this career.*

But wait a minute! There are countless other *kinds* of organizations and agencies out there, besides schools, that employ *teachers*. For example, corporate training and educational departments, workshop sponsors, foundations, private research firms, educational consultants, teachers' associations, professional and trade societies, military bases, state and local councils on higher education, fire and police training academies, and so on and so forth.

"*Kinds* of places" also means places with different *hiring options*, besides full-time, such as:

- Places that would employ you part-time (maybe you'll end up deciding, or having, to hold down two or even three part-time jobs, which together add up to one full-time job)
- Places that take temporary workers, on assignment for one project at a time
- Places that take consultants, one project at a time
- Places that operate primarily with volunteers
- Places that are nonprofit
- Places that are for-profit
- And, don't forget, places that you yourself could start up, should you decide to be your own boss (see chapter 11)

During this interviewing for information, you should not only talk to people who can give you a broad overview of the career that you are considering. You should also talk with actual workers, who can tell you in more detail what the tasks are in the kinds of organizations that interest you.

Fourth, You Need to Find Names of Particular Places That Interest You

As you interview workers about their jobs or careers, somebody will probably innocently mention, somewhere along the way, actual names of organizations that have such kinds of workers—plus what's good or bad about the place. This is important information for you. Jot it all down. Keep notes religiously!

But you will want to supplement what they have told you, by seeking out other people to whom you can simply say: "I'm interested in this kind of organization, because I want to do this kind of work; do you know of particular places like that, that I might investigate? And if so, where they are located?" Use face-to-face interviews, use LinkedIn, use search engines, to try to find the answer(s) to that question. Incidentally, you must not care, at this point, if they have *known* vacancies or not. The only question that should concern you for the moment is whether or not the place looks interesting, or even intriguing to you. (The only caveat is that you will probably want to investigate smaller places—one hundred or fewer employees—rather than larger; and newer places, rather than older.) **For a successful job hunt you should choose places based on your interest in them, and not wait for them to open up a vacancy.** Vacancies can suddenly open up in a moment, and without warning.

What will you end up with, when this step is done? Well, you'll likely have either *too few names* or *too many* to go investigate. There are ways of dealing with either of these eventualities.

Too Many Names

You will want to cut the territory down, to a manageable number of *targets*.

Let's take an example. Suppose you discover that the career that interests you the most is *financial services*. You want to be a financial adviser. Well, that's a beginning. You've cut the 23 million US job markets down to:

I want to work in a place that hires financial advisers. But the territory is still too large. There are thousands of places in the country that use financial advisers. You can't go visit them all. So, you've got to cut down the territory further. Suppose that on your Preferred Place to Live petal you said that you really want to live and work in the San Jose area of California. That's helpful: that cuts down the territory further. Now your goal is:

I want to work in a place that hires financial advisers, within the San Jose area. But the territory is still too large. There could be 100, 200, 300 organizations that fit that description. So you look at your Flower Diagram for further help, and you notice that under *working conditions* you said you wanted to work for an organization with fifty or fewer employees. Good, now your goal is:

I want to work in a place that hires financial advisers, within the San Jose area, that has fifty or fewer employees. This territory may still be too large. So you look again at your Flower Diagram for further guidance, and you see that you said you wanted to work for an organization that works with people who are close to retiring. So now your statement of what you're looking for becomes:

I want to work in a place that hires financial advisers, within the San Jose area, has fifty or fewer employees, and helps people with their pending retirement. Using your Flower Diagram, you can thus keep cutting down the territory, until the "*targets*" of your job hunt are no more than ten places. That's a manageable number of places for you to *start with.* You can always expand the list later, if none of these ten turns out to be promising or interesting.

Too Few Names

In this case, you want to expand the territory. Your salvation here is probably not going to be informational interviewing face to face, but digital directories. Indeed.com can give you a general idea of the openings and opportunities in your area. Also, see if the local chamber of commerce publishes a business directory; often it will list not only small companies but also local divisions of larger companies, with names of department heads; sometimes they will even include the North American Industry Classification System (NAICS) codes, which is useful if you want to search by the code of your chosen field. Thirdly, see if your town or city publishes a business newsletter, directory, or even a Book of Lists on its own. It will, of course, cost you, but it may be worth it. Some metropolitan areas (San Francisco comes to mind) have particularly helpful ones. Forty of them are listed at www.bizjournals.com. Your local public library can be a terrific source of free assistance. Ask a librarian to help you find print and online resources, including databases like Reference USA or the Small Business Resource Center.

If you are diligent here, you won't lack for names, believe me—unless it's a very small town you live in, in which case you'll just have to cast your net a little wider, to include other towns, villages, or cities that are within commuting distance from you.

Fifth, Research That Place Thoroughly Before Formally Approaching Them

At some point you will be happy. You've found a career that you would do just about anything to have. You've interviewed people *actually doing that work*, and you like it even more. You've found names of places that hire people for that career.

Okay, now what? Do you rush right over there? No. You research those places first. This is an absolute *must*. Remember, companies and organizations love to be loved. You demonstrate you love them when you have taken the trouble to find out all about them, before you walk in. That's called *research*.

What should you research about places before you approach them for a hiring interview? Well, first of all, you want to know something about the organization from the inside. What kind of work they do there. Their style of working. Their *corporate culture*. And what kinds of goals they are trying to achieve, what obstacles or challenges they are running into, and how your skills and knowledges can help them. In the interview you must be prepared to demonstrate that you have something they need. That begins with finding out *what* they need.

Secondly, you want to find out if you would enjoy working there. You want to take the measure of those organizations. Everybody takes the measure of a workplace, but most job hunters or career changers do it only *after* they are hired there. In the US, for example, a survey of the federal/state employment service once found that 57 percent of those who found a job through that service were not working at that job just thirty days later—*because* within their first ten or twenty days *on the job* they found out they didn't really like it there at all.

You, by doing this research ahead of time, are choosing a better path by far. Yes, even in tough times, you do want to be picky. Otherwise, you'll take the job in desperation, thinking, *Oh, I could put up with anything*, and then find out after you take the job that you were kidding yourself. Then you have to quit, and start your job hunt all over again. By doing this research now, you are saving yourself a lot of grief. So you need to know ahead of time whether this place just doesn't fit.

How do you find that out? There are several ways—some face to face, some not:

- **Friends and Neighbors.** Ask *everyone* you know if they know anyone who works at the places that interest you. If they do, ask them if they could arrange for you and that person to get together, for lunch, coffee, or tea. When you meet, tell them why the place interests you, and indicate you'd like to know more about it. (It helps a lot if your mutual friend is sitting there with the two of you, so the purpose of this little chat won't be misconstrued.) This is the vastly preferred way to find out about a place. However, obviously you need a couple of additional alternatives up your sleeve, in case you run into a dead end here.

- **People at the Organizations in Question, or Similar.** LinkedIn has an extensive menu where you can find the names of companies. It will tell you who works there or used to work there. An email will sometimes produce an interesting contact, but in this increasingly busy, busy life, even the best-hearted people may sometimes say they just cannot give you any time, due to overload. If so, respect that.

  You can go in person to organizations and ask questions about the place. This is not recommended with large organizations that have security guards and so on. But with small organizations (say, fifty employees or fewer) you sometimes can find out quite a bit by just showing up. Here, however, I must caution you about several *dangers*.

  First, make sure you're not asking them questions that are readily available in print or online, which you could easily have read for yourself instead of bothering *them*. This irritates people.

  Second, make sure that you approach the gateway people—front desk, receptionists, customer service, and the like—*before* you ever approach people higher up in that organization.

  Third, make sure that you approach subordinates rather than the top person in the place, if the subordinates would know the answer to your questions. Bothering the boss there with some simple questions that someone else could have answered is committing job-hunting suicide.

  Fourth, make sure you're not using this approach simply as a sneaky way to get in to see the boss and make a pitch for them to hire you. You said this was just information gathering. Don't lie.

Don't ever lie. They will remember you, but not in the way you want to be remembered.

- **What's on the Internet.** Many job hunters or career changers think that every organization, company, or nonprofit has its own website these days. Not true. Sometimes they do, sometimes they don't. It often has to do with the size of the place, its access to a good web designer, its desperation for customers, that kind of thing. Easy way to find out: type the name of the place into your favorite search engine and see what turns up. Try more than one search engine. Sometimes one returns results the others don't. There are, in fact, sites particularly devoted to getting feedback on organizations from actual employees who are working there or recently used to. The best known is Glassdoor (www.glassdoor.com/Reviews/index.htm). Approximately half of all job seekers consult Glassdoor.[19] It has employee reviews from almost eight hundred thousand companies or organizations worldwide. It will even tell you which companies are (supposedly) the best to work for. Similar review sites include

  FairyGodBoss (https://fairygodboss.com/company-reviews),
  Indeed (https://www.indeed.com/companies?from=gnav
  -acme—acme-webapp),
  Vault (https://www.vault.com/company-ratings-research),
  and Career Bliss (www.careerbliss.com/reviews).

- **What's in Print.** Published books are not good resources for current company information; their time lag is too great. But often the organization has timely stuff—in print, or on its website—about its business, purpose, and so on. Also, the CEO or head of the organization may have given talks, and the front desk there may have copies of those talks. In addition, there may be brochures, annual reports, and such that the organization has put out about itself. How can you get copies? The person who answers the phone there will know or at least know who to refer you to. Also, if it's a decent-size organization, public libraries in that town or city may have files on that organization—newspaper clippings, articles, etc. You never know; and it never hurts to ask your friendly neighborhood research librarian.

• **Temporary Agencies.** Many job hunters and career changers have found that a useful way to explore organizations is to find positions through temporary agencies. To find these, search Google for the name of your town or city with "temp agencies" or "employment agencies." Employers turn to such agencies in order to find (1) job hunters who can work part-time for a limited number of days, and (2) job hunters who can work full-time for a limited number of days. The advantage to you of temporary work is that if there is an agency that loans out people with your particular skills and expertise, you get a chance to be sent to a number of different employers over a period of several days or weeks and see each one from the inside. Maybe the temp agency won't send you to exactly the place you hoped for, but sometimes you can develop contacts in the place you love, even while you're temporarily working somewhere else, if both organizations are in the same field. At the very least you'll pick up experience that you can later cite on your resume.

• **Volunteering.** If you're okay financially for a while but you can't find work, you can volunteer to work for nothing, short term, at a place with a cause or mission that interests you. You can find a directory of such organizations that offer internships (unpaid, or sometimes offering a stipend; www.internships.com) or volunteer opportunities (listed at www.volunteeringinamerica.gov—see their data infographic about volunteering leading to employment—and www.volunteermatch.org). Also, you can search on the name of your city or town with "volunteer opportunities" and see what that turns up. Or you can just walk into an organization or company of your choice and ask if they would let you volunteer your time there.

Your goal is, first of all, to find out more about the place.

Second, if you've been out of work a lengthy period of time, your goal is to feel useful. You're making your life count for something.

Third, your distant hope is that maybe somewhere down the line they'll actually want to hire you to stay on, for pay. The odds of that happening are pretty remote, so don't count on it and don't push it, but *sometimes* they may ask you to stay. For pay. The success rate of this as a method for finding jobs isn't terrific. But it does happen. And even if it doesn't, you have likely built up new transferable skills and a new entry for your resume.

A Public Service Announcement: You Must Send Thank-You Notes, Please, Please, Please!

After anyone has done you a favor, anytime during your job hunt, you must be sure to send them a thank-you note by the very next day, at the latest. Send the note to *anyone* who helps you or talks with you. That means friends, people at the organization in question, temporary agency people, receptionists, librarians, workers, or whomever.

Ask them, when face to face with them, for their business card (if they have one), or ask them to write their name and work address on a piece of paper for you. You don't want to misspell their name. It can be difficult to figure out how to spell people's names simply from the sound of them. What sounds like "Laura" may actually be "Lara"; what sounds like "Smith" may actually be "Smythe," and so on. Get that name and address, but get it right, please.

And let me reiterate: thank-you notes must be prompt. Email the thank-you note that same night, or the very next day at the latest. Follow it with a lovely copy, handwritten or printed, nicely formatted, and sent through the mail. Most employers these days prefer a printed letter to a handwritten one, but if your handwriting is beautiful, then go for it.

Don't ramble on and on. Your mailed thank-you note can be just two or three sentences. Something like: "I wanted to thank you for talking with me yesterday. It was very helpful to me. I much appreciated your taking the time out of your busy schedule to do this. Best wishes to you," and then sign it. Of course, if you have any additional thoughts to add, then add them. And when you're done, remember to sign it.

What If I Get Offered a Job Along the Way, While I'm Just Gathering Information?

It happens. Particularly when the economy is strong and employers are looking. An occasional employer *may* stray across your path during all this informational interviewing. And that employer *may* be so impressed with you that they want to hire you on the spot. So, it's *possible* that you'd get offered a job while you're still doing your information gathering. And if that happens, what should you say?

Consider it carefully. If you're desperate, you will probably have to say *yes*. I remember one wintertime when I was in my thirties, with a family of five; I had just gone through the knee of my last pair of pants, we were burning pieces of old furniture in our fireplace to stay warm, the legs on our bed had just broken, and we were eating spaghetti until it was coming out our ears. In such a situation, you can't afford to be picky. You've got to put food on the table and stave off the debt collectors. Now.

But if you have time to be more careful, then you respond to the job offer in a way that will buy you some time. You tell them what you're doing: you are examining careers, fields, industries, jobs, and particular organizations *before* you decide where you would do your best and most effective work. And you're sure this employer would do the same if they were in your shoes. (If they're not impressed with your thoroughness and professionalism at this point, then I assure you this is not a place where you want to work.)

Add that your informational interviewing isn't finished yet, so it would be premature for you to accept their job offer until you're *sure* that this is the place where you could be most effective and do your best work.

Then you add: "Of course, I'm excited that you would want me to be working here. And when I've finished my personal survey, I'll be glad to get back to you about this, as my preliminary impression is that this is the kind of place I'd like to work in, and the kind of people I'd like to work for, and the kind of people I'd like to work with."

In other words, *if you're not desperate yet*, you don't walk immediately through any opened doors, but neither should you allow them to shut.

As I said, this scenario is highly unlikely. You're networking with *workers*. But it's nice to be prepared ahead of time, in your mind, just in case it ever does happen.

Final Suggestions About Contacts

A word about contacts in general: Research has revealed that in general the more of a social life you have, the more people you know, the more time you spend with people outside of work, the more likely you are to find a job. Some surveys estimate that as many as 85 percent of positions are found through networking.[20] And the more people you know who are in other fields than your own, the more likely you are to be able to effectively change careers. Often, in fact, your contacts will turn up job opportunities for you even before you go out formally searching. Problem: one in four workers don't network at all. And 41 percent would like to network more but don't feel they have time. Those statistics are for the UK,[21] but similar stats are found around the world.

Another research discovery is that the further afield these contacts are from your usual social circles, the more likely they are to help your job hunt. Ask yourself how much time you spend with your contacts; you can generally divide them into those with whom you have strong ties (self-explanatory) and those with whom you have weak ties: people you see only occasionally or rarely—maybe only once a year or even less. These weak ties will strengthen your job search immeasurably.

These research findings have been summed up by Stanford professor Mark Granovetter as "the strength of weak ties." As he writes in his classic *Getting a Job*, "There is . . . a structural tendency for those to whom one is only *weakly* tied, to have better access to job information one does not already have. Acquaintances, as compared to close friends, are more prone to move in different circles than one's self. Those to whom one is closest are likely to have the greater overlap with those one already knows, so that the information to which they are privy is likely to be much the same as that which one already has."[22]

Now, once you've found a place that interests you and you want to get an interview there, there is a particular kind of contact that will save your neck. I call such a contact a "bridge person"—meaning they know **you**, and they know **them** (your target), and thus they bridge the gap between you and a job there.

You can't identify a bridge person until you have a target company or organization in mind. But when that time comes, here's how you go about identifying *bridge people*:

1. LinkedIn is your best friend here. Each employer you want to pursue should have a Company Profile page. (Unless the company is just *too small*.) Identify which place you want to approach, look up its Company Profile page, and go there.

2. Start with the company. LinkedIn will identify people in your network who work for the company you are targeting. You can then sort that list by the titles of the *employees* there, as well as people who share other commonalities with you, such as LinkedIn groups, former employers, schools attended, or even previous places you've lived.

3. Then go to your school's profile page. If you ever attended vo-tech school, community college, college, university, or grad school, ask LinkedIn to tell you who among your fellow alumni work for the company or organization you are targeting.

4. Then go to the company activity. On that same Company Profile page, ask LinkedIn about new hires (who), departures (who), job-title changes, job postings, number of employees who use LinkedIn, where current employees work, where current employees worked before they worked for *this* company, where former employees went after they worked for this company, and so on. Insightful statistics!

5. As for connecting with the bridge people whose names you discover, currently LinkedIn requires you to have one of their *paid* memberships, rather than the *free* one, to send a note to someone who's not a direct connection. But if they're still working at the company, you can search for their contact information through a larger search engine (Google their name!).

6. If you come up blank, both on LinkedIn and all the other places you search for names—family, friends, Facebook—so it seems no bridge person can be found who knows *you* and also knows *them*—you can advertise on LinkedIn for such connections. "Ads by LinkedIn Members" are available for a modest cost. You can also browse LinkedIn groups and join those (ten at the most) most likely to be seen by the kinds of companies you are trying to reach. However, don't just join them! Post intelligent questions, and respond to intelligent "post-ers." In other words, attain as high visibility there as you can; maybe *employers* will then come after *you*.

Once you get an introduction to a place, follow the instructions about interviews in chapter 9 of this book. And, good luck!

He or she who gets hired is not necessarily
the one who can do that job best;
but, the one who knows the most
about how to get hired.

—RICHARD LATHROP

CHAPTER 8

YOUR RESUME IS ALREADY ONLINE

Maybe you remember the old days—when you needed a job, you wrote a resume and sent it out. You probably wrote whatever looked good about your past work, confident that employers would know only what you chose to tell them.

Short of their hiring a private detective or talking to your previous employers, a prospective employer couldn't find out much about you.

Yeah, those days are gone. (And maybe you're young enough that those days never existed for you.) Remember back in chapter 1 where we discussed how employers are looking for reasons to exclude you from the candidate pool? Thanks to the internet, with a few simple clicks, employers can find out almost anything they want.

All any prospective employer has to do now is *Google* your name—and there's your new resume, using the word "resume" loosely.

If you've posted anything on Facebook, Twitter, LinkedIn, Instagram, Pinterest, or YouTube, or you have your own website or webcasts or photo album or blog, or you've been on anyone else's Facebook page, you have left a trail. *Bye, bye, control.*

The numbers vary depending on which study you read, but it's safe to say that virtually all recruiters will look at your social media presence, and more than 60 percent of employers have rejected some applicants on the basis of what they found. Things that can get you rejected: bad grammar or gross misspelling on your Facebook or LinkedIn profile; anything indicating you lied on your resume; any bad-mouthing of previous employers; any signs of racism, prejudice, or weird opinions about stuff;

anything indicating alcohol or drug abuse; and any—to put it delicately—*inappropriate content*.

The good news is that this works both ways. Employers are constantly searching LinkedIn for potential candidates. Sometimes an employer will offer someone a job because they liked what Google turned up about them. Online evidence like the creativity or professionalism you demonstrate; expressing yourself extremely well; their overall impression of your personality; the wide range of interests you exhibit; and evidence that you get along well and communicate well with other people.

And if you're thinking the easiest way to avoid problems is to not use social media, think again. According to a survey conducted by the Harris Poll for CareerBuilder in 2018, about 47 percent of employers indicate that if they can't find a social media presence for someone, they won't bring them in for an interview.[23]

So is there anything you can do about this Google "resume" of yours? Well yes, actually, there are two key things you can do. You can edit, and you can build.

Let's see what each of these involves.

Edit What's Already Out There

First of all, think of how you would like to come across when you are being considered for a job. Make a list of adjectives you'd like the employer to think of when they consider hiring you. For example, how about professional? Experienced? Inventive? Hardworking? Disciplined? Honest? Trustworthy? Kind?

What else? Make a list.

Then search your name online and read over every relevant entry that comes up. Go over any posts you have put up on social media platforms like Facebook, LinkedIn, Twitter, Instagram, Pinterest, or YouTube, and remove anything you posted there, or allowed others to post, that contradicts the impression you would like to make, or anything that might cause a would-be employer to think, *Uh, let's not call them in after all.* You have your list of what you need to look for. This is also a good time to check your privacy settings on any platforms you are using. Make sure that your Facebook profile (which you likely use for fun or personal connections with friends and interest groups) is set to allow only friends to access. Just remember, no matter how "private" your settings are, you're still on a public forum, so there's always a chance someone can access or share your information. Your LinkedIn profile, on the other hand, should be public, because you want employers to find you.

If you don't know how to remove an item from a particular site, type or speak the following into a search engine such as Google: "How to remove an item from [Facebook]" or wherever. The site itself may not tell you, but by using your favorite search engine you should have no trouble finding detailed, step-by-step instructions for scrubbing any site.

I guarantee you're hardly the first one with this need, so someone clever has already figured out how to do it and posted the answer. But you want current instructions, so look at the date on the list of items the search engine pops up. Pick the most recent and do what they say.

If you want to be thorough, you should do this editing on any and all sites that you find you're on.

Now to the second thing you can do about your Google "resume."

Build Your New Online Profile

Whatever sites you are using, if they allow you to fill out a profile, fill it out completely: cross every *t*, dot every *i*, and have someone check your spelling. Leave no part of the profile blank unless you have a very good reason.

Most importantly, be sure to keep each profile up to date. Really up to date. Week by week, or at the least, month by month. You'll look less professional if you have an obviously outdated profile.

Let's look at key social media sites to consider if you're job searching.

LinkedIn

The most important site for job seekers and employers is LinkedIn. Be sure to get on it, if you're not there already (www.linkedin.com/reg/join). LinkedIn has excellent search engine optimization (SEO), which means it will likely be the first item that appears when someone searches your name online.

Any job hunter should focus first on LinkedIn. Here's how and why:

- LinkedIn gives you a highly visible online presence, even if you don't use any other social media. You can easily highlight your expertise and experience for all potential employers to see.

- Many corporate and agency headhunters avoid advertising an open position, but nonetheless search on LinkedIn for what employers call "passive job seekers." In other words, you might not be looking for them, but they are looking for you. Of course, you have no control over whether they find you, except for being sure you have a completely filled-out profile. They search by keywords, so it's important to know the keywords for your industry or job title and use them.

- You can develop and grow your network through LinkedIn. You can search LinkedIn for people who graduated from your high school, college, and graduate or professional school. You can find people who are doing the type of work you would like to do. You can find people who work for an employer you'd like to work for. You can grow your network by contacting those individuals and asking to connect with them. But this is important: *don't* just hit the Invite button; it's essential to include a short, personalized message when you reach out. It can be something simple like "I read your profile,

and I'm interested in the type of work you do. I would like to connect with you here on LinkedIn."

- LinkedIn is an excellent research tool for the job seeker. You can
research companies and discover if you already know someone
who works there. (Now you have a potentially friendly connection.)
You can get email alerts for job openings. You can search company
sites and read their job postings. You can apply online for openings
through LinkedIn and attach your resume and cover letter. You can
even follow companies to be kept informed of any new information
that might affect your ability to get a job with them.

Have I convinced you of the value of LinkedIn? Spend some time
online with it and explore individual profiles. Read how others have
completed their profiles, noting what you like or don't like. If setting
up a profile seems intimidating, take advantage of LinkedIn's variety
of helpful trainings as well as YouTube videos (www.youtube.com/user
/Linkedin).

Here are twelve suggestions for improving your profile—and thus
your chances of having any employer seek you out. If you've already created a profile, go through this list to make sure you have followed these
suggestions:

1. Sign in with an email account you use regularly so you will be aware
   of any messages or updates to your site.

   Once you create an account, immediately go to "Settings and
   Privacy" and find the listings "How Others See Your Profile" and
   "How Others See Your LinkedIn Activity." Under those headings you
   will have several options for when people are notified about edits to
   your profile. Turn off most notifications so they won't see every time
   you make a minor change to your account. You will still be able to
   share a major update (like new employment status). Also, customize

your profile URL so it contains only your name and not a lot of strange numbers or characters. There's a quick link on your profile page to do this.

2. Select and post a professional photo (headshot). Surveys have revealed that not having your photo posted is a turnoff for most employers. The likelihood that your LinkedIn profile will get viewed increases sevenfold if you include a photo. Fill the frame with just your head and shoulders. The picture should be sharply focused and well lit, even if taken with your cell phone. Dress up for this one. And smile. Behind your headshot at the top of your profile is a generic blue background space. Consider inserting another image that might further describe you. Some people place a picture of their current employment site; others show a book or product they created. Any picture that highlights your area of expertise would be good. Review other profiles and see if you like anything in particular. Just remember that this is professional: this is not the place for a picture of your pets (unless you're a veterinarian) or your family (unless you're in a family business).

3. Your "headline" is the short description you can enter after your name. You are limited to 120 characters, so fill the headline section with keywords related to your job or industry. Keywords will attract potential employers because they search for candidates using keywords. Look at other profiles to see how others have described themselves.

4. In the "About" section, state whatever you think gives you a competitive advantage in your field—that is, what makes you a better hire than the nineteen (or ninety!) other people who might compete for the kind of job you want. This is a place to highlight what makes you the best choice (or, for the modest, a better choice) for that kind of job. Think of this section as an opportunity to tell

your story. You will want to include entries from your resume, but you are not limited to strict resume format; you can craft a story that highlights what you are seeking or what an employer should know about you. You can add attachments (PDFs) or links in this section.

5. Describe your past jobs or experience, and list all the jobs you have held most recently. Unless relevant, you probably don't need to go back more than ten years. Again, LinkedIn gives you enough space to tell a story, so tell a story. Summarize some major achievement of yours in that job, and then tell a story of how you did it and what the measurable results were (time or money saved, the profit created, and so on). List your skills and use keywords to describe your activities to increase the value and strength of your profile.

6. Under "Skills and Endorsements," include at least five skills, and list every keyword you can think of that would lead a search engine to find you for the job you want. You can always Google "keywords in _____" and indicate your industry, such as "keywords in marketing" or "keywords in real estate." Also, try finding someone on LinkedIn who already has a job like the one you want, and see what keywords *they* listed. Copy the ones that seem relevant in your case.

7. Fill out the "Education" section completely, including listing any additional training you might have received on the job. Include your high school; that increases the odds that someone might find you through a school search. And don't forget to do your own searches for people from your high school, college, and others. They might be the best support and network you will have.

8. List any licenses or certificates you have obtained. Keep relevance in mind: what certificates or training might an employer be interested in?

9. Add links to any website or other professional social media you use. What would help you stand out:

    • Your blog? If you have one, and posts there are *solely* devoted to your area of expertise.

    • Your Twitter account? If you have one, and if you've only been posting tweets that support your expertise in your field.

    • Your Facebook profile? Probably not, unless you have an account dedicated to your career, looking very focused and professional. If it's a typical personal account, more related to your friends and hobbies, don't bother linking to it.

10. This is purely optional, but if it would help sell your expertise, consider filming a video of yourself discussing some area of your expertise (with numbers, if possible), posting it on YouTube, and linking to it from your LinkedIn profile. If you don't know how to shoot and upload the video, there are loads of free instructions (even on YouTube) telling you step by step how to do this. (Just remember, this needs to be professional—a poor video could detract from your profile.)

11. Get recommendations from colleagues, former supervisors, and others who have worked with you and know your skills.

12. Join one or more LinkedIn groups related to your expertise. Post sparingly but regularly, when they are discussing something you are an expert on. You want to get a name and reputation in your field. You can use "groups" as a search category and type in keywords related to your career field or interests.

Want to see how your LinkedIn profile measures up? Here's a rubric you can use. Compare your profile with the recommendations in this diagram. Any time you're not measuring up to the Competitive column, you have some work to do.

LinkedIn Rubric for Job Seekers

	COMPETITIVE	SATISFACTORY	NEEDS IMPROVEMENT
Picture	Professional headshot Clear and non-distracting background Attire appropriate for field	Professional appearance, but poor background Unprofessional attire	No picture or unprofessional Picture with someone cut out
Headline	Focuses on titles, skills, and keywords for industry Articulates professional goal Indicates what you're seeking	Some titles and skills listed No mention of industry or professional goal	Job title only Just indicates "job seeker" If student, just says "Student at . . ." Doesn't highlight skills or expertise
"About" Section (Summary)	Clear description of skills, strengths, and accomplishments Use of relevant keywords to target industry Follows and enhances resume	Description of skills and achievements, but too short (lacks detail) or too long (to be read)	No summary Poorly written or contains misspellings Discrepancy between resume and content
Experience	Relevant skills, responsibilities, or achievements highlighted No typos or grammar issues Dates accurate and current Uses keywords and language relevant to target industry	Lists main skills and responsibilities, is either incomplete or too detailed	Leaves out key information; no description of skills, responsibilities, or achievements Dates are missing or confusing Typos or grammatical errors

continued ▶

	COMPETITIVE	SATISFACTORY	NEEDS IMPROVEMENT
Education	Clear listing of undergraduate and graduate schools attended Includes other relevant training programs, including high school (for networking purposes) Major and other relevant information included	Lists high school and college but provides no details	Failure to list colleges or other education Typos or grammatical errors Dates are missing or confusing
Skills and Recommendations	Skills listed are relevant to desired industry Skills are described elsewhere in profile Skills are endorsed by others Recommendations are visible	Skills listed, but not all relevant to target industries Recommendations are provided, but not relevant for target industries	No skills listed in the skill section No recommendations

If you are comfortable with social media and can keep it current, consider expanding your online presence. Here are several ways:

Use Hashtags

Most social media forums allow you to use hashtags (#) to find related links and information. As you work with all your media outlets, try using some of these hashtags to find potential career information and job openings:

#Careers
#CareerAdvice
#CareerDevelopment
#Employment
#HireMe
#Hiring

#JobOpening
#Jobs
#JobSearch
#JobSearching
#JobSearchTips
#Jobseeking

#JoinOurTeam   #CareerSuccess
#NowHiring   #PersonalBranding
#Recruiting   #PersonalDevelopment
#Resume   #ResumeTips

Forums and Groups

Professional sites like LinkedIn have forums, or groups, organized by subject matter. Other social networking sites, like Facebook, have pages and groups devoted to particular subjects. Look through the directory of those groups or forums, choose one or two that are related to your industry or interests, and after signing up, speak up regularly whenever you have something to say that will quietly demonstrate you are an expert in your chosen subject area. Otherwise, keep quiet. Don't speak up about just anything. You want to be seen as a specialist—knowledgeable and focused. You want to get noticed by employers when they're searching for expert talent in your field or specialty. Examples of Facebook groups you could join include:

Job Opportunities & Careers in US
Jobs in NYC
Social Media, Marketing & PR Jobs
Digital Nomad Jobs: Remote Job Opportunities
Women's Job-Search Network
Media, Marketing & PR Jobs

Meet-up.com offers a variety of career-related groups, but they vary by location. Do a search for your region in Meet-up to see if any groups meeting your needs have meet-ups close to you. Some groups are specifically focused on the job search, but others are industry-focused, and you could meet people in your industry. Be open-minded: for instance, if you use WordPress in your job, you might seek out a group of WordPress users. Even if they don't work in your field, you will learn about other employers and career fields where people who use WordPress work. And you might even improve your WordPress skills. If you can't find a group related to your needs, consider starting your own group. You will have a chance to meet like-minded people in your community, and you never know what type of connections you'll be able to develop.

There are many group conversation sites like Reddit and Quora. These sites can be helpful for getting answers to your career questions. You can also find subgroups designed for discussions about jobs and job search-ing. Use them if they are helpful. Just remember that you can't be sure of the expertise of the individuals responding to your questions, so try to find other ways to verify what you learn. That's where informational interviews can be especially helpful. You can ask someone in the career field you're seeking to verify information: "I was reading on a Reddit forum that this industry values . . ." Not only are you demonstrating that you are doing your research, but you also have a chance to learn whether what you have discovered is true or not.

Other apps like What'sApp, Slack, Apple's iMessage, and Facebook Messenger can be helpful if you get into the right conversations. Check them out and see what you discover. If you don't see anything helpful, just skip that resource and focus on one that works. It's hard to go wrong focusing on LinkedIn, for example.

Write a Blog
Consider starting a blog (if you don't already have one), particularly if you enjoy educating others and have good basic writing skills. It doesn't matter what your expertise is; if it's related to the job you are looking for, do a blog, and update it regularly. And if you don't know how to blog, there are helpful sites such as Blogger, WordPress, or Squarespace that give you detailed instructions. Incidentally, there are reportedly up to three hundred million blogs on the internet. Figure out how to make yours stand out. This is an optional step for most people, but if you're looking to stand out and want a "product" to show an employer, a blog could be a great sales tool.

If you already have a blog, but it ranges all over the countryside in terms of subject matter, then start a new blog that is more narrowly focused on your particular area of expertise. Post helpful articles there, focused on action steps, not just thoughts. Let's say you are an expert plumber; you can post entries on your blog that deal with such problems as "how to fix a leaky faucet." Generally speaking, employers are looking for blogs that deal with concrete action rather than lofty philosophical thought. Unless, of course, they represent a think tank.

Twitter

Some experts claim that blogs are so *yesterday*. Communication, they say, is moving toward brief, and briefer. Twenty-four percent of US adults use Twitter, and that number jumps to 40 percent in those aged eighteen to twenty-nine. Twitter's advantage is that it has hashtags, and Google is indexing all those tags and tweets. Savvy employers know how to do Twitter searches on Google (or on Twitter itself, for that matter). All you have to figure out is which hashtags employers are likely to look for when they want to find someone with your expertise and experience. Twitter can be an excellent way to connect with individuals who are interested in the same career areas as you. Here are some quick ways to get started:

- Create your account using a professional handle. Your name or a combination of name and career field could work, unless you plan to change career fields. Since you're using Twitter for professional reasons, stay away from tweets related to politics, sex, religion, or other issues that could cause controversy—unless, of course, your work is related to one of those fields. Twitter is fun and full of humor, so it's okay to occasionally post funny or cute pictures or clever tweets; just remember that it's all public and can be searched by a potential employer.

- Use the search box to find tweets related to your career interests; for example, finance, marketing, programming, writing, sales. Read the tweets, and if you find one you like, retweet it. Notice who posted it and check out their profile. If they post other items you might like, follow them. Their posts will start appearing in your feed.

- Continue this pattern of retweeting and following. Then start adding your own content based on links to articles you find on the internet. When possible, give credit to the author by including their Twitter handle (@Their Handle). They will be likely to follow you. Ultimately you start to connect with people and send direct messages (DMs) to exchange information.

- If you start posting interesting articles and content you find related to your career field, others will start following you. You can appear to be an expert in your field by consistently posting interesting news and articles about your field. Just keep in mind that Twitter is about conversations and responses. Be sure to like, retweet, and reply to postings you enjoy.

- Some employers (including the federal government) post their job opportunities on Twitter, sometimes before they even make it to the job boards or other sites. Make sure you're following key employers or job sites on Twitter to get the latest news.

YouTube

YouTube is a great way to both conduct career research and present yourself online. Simply enter whatever topic you're interested in in the search box, and you'll be amazed at the amount of free help available. A simple entry like "elevator pitch" brings up thousands of videos to help you learn and practice. TED Talks can be another great source of career information and provide great examples of strong presentation and storytelling skills.

Presentation is moving strongly these days toward the visual. People like to *see* you, not just *read* you. You don't need expensive equipment; smartphones can produce surprisingly good video. Depending on your career field, a creative and professional video might be a great sales tool to attract customers or potential employers. As for where to post your video, once you've shot and edited it, the champion of course is YouTube—1.5 billion monthly users, 5 billion views per day. Another site worth checking is Vimeo (https://vimeo.com/). As with all social media, use only what you need and what you're willing to keep up with. It takes time to keep various sites fresh and current, and you don't want to waste your time on social media that won't advance your career. Done cleverly and carefully, videos can be a great way to let a potential employer see your presentation or other skills.

Instagram

Because of its heavy emphasis on pictures, Instagram works best for communications-related fields such as public relations, marketing, sales, advertising, and tech, or for creative people such as artists, authors, chefs, or photographers. That's not to say it won't work for other careers such as finance or operations, but you probably won't find as much helpful information beyond companies that are promoting their brand. Even in those industries it's still worth a look. It can be a great way to do some inside research and learn about the company's culture by how they present themselves online.

Create a basic Instagram account (following the usual guidelines for social media security) and then look up and follow the Instagram profiles of any company you'd like to work for. If it's a product-based company (many on Instagram are), you'll learn more about their product and how they promote their brand. Do some posting yourself, but keep in mind that if you're going to promote yourself or your work, it's helpful to create a cohesive look, use good lighting, post a variety of content, engage with followers, and use your profile as a launch pad to other sites such as LinkedIn or a professional website. Note how often others in your field are posting and use that as a guideline.

If a company you're interested in posts items, "like" them as appropriate. You don't need to (and in fact you shouldn't) "like" everything. You want to demonstrate interest, not stalking. Chances are if you're following them and liking their posts, they will follow you. Check and see if their human resources department has its own Instagram account: it's a great way to find job openings before they are posted elsewhere.

For example: have you ever thought about working for the Disney corporation?

Disney Careers has its own Instagram account (https://www.instagram .com/disneycareers/).

If you scroll through the images, they often link to sites with more job information. A picture of one of their cruise ships leads you to their Instagram link, @DisneyCruiseJobs, and a hashtag (#ShipLife) you can click on to see more pictures and get more information related to working on a cruise ship.

Going Offline: Writing Your Resume

You might think that at this point no one needs a resume anymore. But you'd be wrong. People still use resumes, and employers still request them. If nothing else, they are a handy way to encapsulate key information about your past careers in a simple format that everyone understands. And not a lot changes about resume writing. The internet is loaded with templates and great examples you can use to create your resume. But the trick is, you actually have to follow the advice. Too many job seekers dislike writing resumes and try to spend as little time as possible writing them. This is a mistake. You really need to dig into this process. Sure, some people will tell you that resumes are a waste of time or "no one uses them anymore," but the truth is a one- or two-page document that summarizes the best of your past work experience is one of the best ways to show what your future potential is. So take the time to work on this; you'll be surprised at what a well-crafted resume might lead to.

Preparing to Write Your Resume: A Quick Guide to Jog Your Memory

When preparing to write your resume, take out a blank piece of paper, a notepad, or start a new document on the computer and write the places you have been employed, your job title(s), and the dates of your employment. Then write down your most important duties, activities, projects, accomplishments, and so on. Use numbers to support when possible.

Here are ten questions to jog your memory and get started:

1. What were you most proud of in your role at this organization?

2. What key projects did you work on? What was accomplished in these projects? What was the most important role or responsibility you had?

3. Who benefitted from your work and how?

4. What did you do to increase sales, revenue, bring in new clients or customers? How did you accomplish that? What skills or knowledge were needed?

5. How did you save money for your organization? What cost-cutting procedures did you implement? What skills or knowledge were needed?

6. What improvements did you make for the organization or your area? How was the organization or your team better because you were there?

7. What were the key skills you needed to succeed in your role?

8. What were the key personality traits needed to succeed in your role?

9. What are the keywords for your field or position, and how can you include them in your resume?

10. Where did you go above and beyond your job description to do something unique, creative, or inventive for the organization?

Now that you have some ideas about what you want to say in your resume, let's consider the four key formats:

Traditional. Also known as reverse chronological. In this format, you simply list all your past work in order, starting with the most recent.

Functional. This format focuses on the skills, functions, or activities you performed, with just a short listing of your employers toward the end.

Combination. This resume combines the best of the first two: it divides your experiences by the function you performed, but also lists your experiences in a reverse chronological format so it's easy to read and follow.

Creative. Creative resumes are just that: creative. They differ in style and form.

You can look up resume formats on a variety of internet sites. Even most word processing programs have sample templates that you can adjust to fit your needs. The table here illustrates the four main types of resumes and the situations in which it's best to use them. Search on each of the types to see a variety of examples and templates.

Types of Resumes Chart

	TRADITIONAL	FUNCTIONAL	COMBINATION	CREATIVE
Basic Structure	Divide resume into education, experience, and other sections. Place each section's entries in reverse chronological order, beginning with most recent.	Divide resume by skills or competencies. Use education and experiences to illustrate and support these competencies. Doesn't always include dates of experience or education.	Divide experience into categories based on work area ("marketing") or theme/skill ("leadership") most relevant to employer. Within each category use reverse chronological order.	Varies according to the position sought and skills needed. Can involve unique fonts, colors, structure, or illustrations.
Purpose/Value	Most traditional and common. Works for most stages of life. Easiest to construct. Works best when you have a consistent employment record that fits the field you're seeking.	By focusing on experiences and skills, and not dates, this resume can help when you want to highlight skills rather than how you attained them, when you're switching to a completely new career field, when there are gaps in employment, or when you're returning to the workplace after significant time away.	Generally, the most powerful format for most positions. Works best when you want to highlight related education and experience that may not be your most recent experience, or when you want to combine experience from different areas.	Directly demonstrates creative skills and ability to use Photoshop, Illustrator, or other creative computer software.

continued ▶

	TRADITIONAL	FUNCTIONAL	COMBINATION	CREATIVE
Downsides to This Approach	If your most recent education or experience doesn't fit the position you're seeking, this will not show you at your best.	Because it's generally used by people with gaps in experience, employers may be concerned that you're hiding something. (If you have gaps, be prepared to explain them in your cover letter or interview.)	Harder to write initially. Requires you to consider the subcategories you will create that an employer would want to see.	Creativity is subjective. What is creative to one employer may be seen as odd or inappropriate to another. Harder to gauge audience reaction, since resume may be viewed by noncreative types.
How to Choose Which to Use	Use when you have experience that directly relates to the position you seek.	Use, with caution, when you want the employer to focus on your skills and competencies rather than on dates or how you acquired the experience.	Use when you can divide your education or experience into categories that relate to your desired field.	Use, with caution, when a creative approach would fit directly with the position you seek. You might still want to create a more traditional resume to accompany your creative effort.

Key Tips for Designing Your Resume

It's impossible to show all the resume styles that you could consider—this entire book would have to be just about resumes! Because there are so many different styles of resumes and they fit certain fields, you will want to search online for resume templates or check out the websites listed here for great examples you can work with. But just to get you started, here is a sample of what a combination resume could look like.

Sample Combination Resume

NAME	City, State	Phone	Email	LinkedIn

Objective
This is an optional section. Keep it to one line. If you know the specific title you are seeking, place it here. You can also indicate your field of interest, as in "Sales position in the roofing industry."

Summary
Another optional area. Use bullet points and list three to five key skills you have related to the position you're seeking.

Related Experience
(Change "Related" to a word that describes what you're going for, such as "Sales Experience.")

Company Name. Location. *Title*   Dates

- Up to five bullet points illustrating key responsibilities and accomplishments.

- Use reverse chronological order. Start with most recent job related to this category first.

- Place in order of importance/relevance to job you are seeking

- If title is more impressive than company name, lead with title. Just be consistent.

- Use active verbs *(do not use "responsible for" or "duties included")*

Additional Experience
(If possible, change "Additional" to another relevant area of expertise, such as "Management.")

Company Name. Location. *Title*   Dates

- Same as above but limit to three bullet points if the category isn't as relevant.

- Focus on projects, achievements, and finance-related successes.

- Use data when relevant and helpful.

Education
(This section can be moved above Experience if it is more relevant to the employer or if you just graduated.)

Degree received, field of study. School Name, Location. Graduation Date

- Use bullets to highlight important accomplishments including GPA *(if over 3.0, honors, awards, relevant internships, and so on)*

You can use this template as a guideline, but it's best to do some online research to find examples that work for your situation. The following websites provide excellent examples of resumes. (Note: some may offer to write your resume for a fee. Generally that is not necessary or advisable. But if you choose to have someone write your resume, do your homework and make sure the person or the website is reliable.)

- **Glassdoor.com:** The Perfect Resume Looks Like This
  https://www.glassdoor.com/blog/anatomy-perfect-resume/
- **Novoresume.com:** How to Write a Resume
  https://novoresume.com/career-blog/how-to-write-a-resume-guide
- **The Interview Guys:** The Best Resume Format Guide for 2020
  https://theinterviewguys.com/best-resume-format-guide/
- **Indeed.com:** Resume Format Guide with Tips and Examples
  https://www.indeed.com/career-advice/resumes-cover-letters/
  resume-format-guide-with-examples
- **ResumeGenius.com:** How to Write a Resume: The Complete Guide
  https://resumegenius.com/how-to-write-a-resume-2

Regardless of which resume style you choose to use, certain rules apply to all. Keep the following in mind. Break them at your own risk.

1. Use your resume to tell your story. Describe all education and experience in ways that are relevant to the position you're seeking. Use action verbs and avoid phrases like "responsible for." For example, instead of "Responsible for managing team," use "Managed team."

2. List your experience either from most recent to most distant (reverse chronological) or by type (functional or combination). For instance, if you want a banking career and have worked in several banks, but most recently held a position in a retail store, you could create an experience section called "Banking Experience" and then

list just your banking jobs under that heading. The retail experience could go under "Other Experience," "Related Experience," or another category.

3. Sell your strengths. Don't make the employer dig for information.

4. Use keywords related to your field. Keywords are important if you're posting your resume without specific employers in mind. Good advice about keywords—what they are, and how to insert them into your resume—can be found in the Squawkfox article "8 Keywords That Set Your Resume on Fire."[24]

5. Avoid describing yourself in positive terms that can't be supported ("hardworking," "energetic," and the like). Focus on facts and what you did.

6. Include numbers and statistics when relevant. If you raised funds, indicate the amount; if you increased customer satisfaction, by how much?

7. Include contact information such as your name, city, state (if relevant; no need for street address), phone number, email, and LinkedIn address. (This applies to printed resumes; see the earlier caution about online resumes.)

8. Include education and training. If it's recent and most relevant to your work, place this before the experience section. If older or less relevant, place after the experience section. Include your GPA if it's 3.0 or above. Remember to include honors, awards, and scholarships.

9. Optional sections include a summary of your experiences at the top of the resume (generally not needed), a job objective (also not needed when there's a cover letter or when your objective is

clear), and a section for hobbies or interests. Hobbies or interests, if included, should always be at the end of the resume and limited to a few interesting and relevant selections.

10. If you're coming out of some subculture that has its own language (the military, the clergy), get some help in translating your experience into the language of employers. For example, "preached" should be replaced by "presented"; "commanded" should be replaced by "supervised," and so on.

11. Be prepared to alter and target your resume for every position you're applying to. Adjust your descriptions of your experience and education to best fit the skills needed for the position. A generic resume that isn't adjusted for a position will weaken your odds of being selected for an interview.

12. Always create a PDF document of your resume when you send it via email or upload to a website. The PDF document will preserve your resume's appearance and keep all the bullet points and fonts looking the way you intended.

13. Do not include photos, birthdate, marital status, information about children, and other private personal information.

14. Double-check spelling and grammar. Employers often eliminate resumes containing errors.

15. Show your resume to trusted friends and family and ask for feedback. They will often catch errors and typos, that might eliminate you from consideration. You can also show your resume to someone in your career field with whom you are conducting an informational interview. Ask for suggestions or ideas for improving it. And then follow through with the recommendations.

Once you find a template or style you like and have drafted your resume, use this resume rubric to determine if you've created one that employers will like.

Resume Rubric for Job Seekers

Go through your resume and note the items you want to change to make yours fit in the "competitive" column.

	COMPETITIVE	SATISFACTORY	NEEDS IMPROVEMENT
Format and Overall Content	Fills the page Not overcrowded or sparse No spelling or grammatical errors Consistent font size and type, bolding, and section titles Appropriate length for position and years of experience Name and contact info clear and complete Sections are ordered in optimal fashion Content within sections is in reverse chronological order	Fills one page Consistent font size and type, bolding, and section titles No spelling or grammatical errors Name and contact info clear and complete Experience generally in reverse chronological order	Inappropriate length for position: too short or too long Difficult to read Inconsistent font size and type, bolding, and section titles Multiple spelling or grammatical errors Fails to include contact info, or email address is unprofessional Inconsistent presentation of information Order of sections is not ideal Not in reverse chronological order

continued ▶

235

	COMPETITIVE	SATISFACTORY	NEEDS IMPROVEMENT
Experience Section	Title, Organization, Where and When Worked presented consistently Uses strong action verbs Descriptions highlight skills and accomplishments clearly, concisely, and effectively Skills relevant to position sought Focuses on relevance to employer	Uses some action verbs Descriptions highlight experience but not clearly or concisely No spelling or grammar errors Descriptions don't always consider relevance to employer Mixes use of active and passive tone	Uses "responsible for" Does not use action verbs Title, Organization, Where and When Worked not presented consistently Does not describe skills or accomplishments Descriptions do not highlight skills Presents information not relevant to employer Spelling or grammar errors
Education Section	Lists degrees received, dates, name of institution(s) and GPA (if 3.0 or better) Describes relevant coursework Describes relevant experience, including internships, honors, study abroad Presents information in a consistent and easy-to-read manner	Lists degrees received, name of institution and GPA (if 3.0 or better)	Does not list degree or graduation date Fails to include additional training or other relevant education Presents information inconsistently or is otherwise difficult to understand

The brutal truth is, no matter how skillfully you write and post your resume, some employers will like it, some won't. Trouble is, you don't know which category they fit into.

Post your resume on the website of companies that interest you, on their Human Resources page, if their site permits that. You can also post your resume on any of the major job-posting sites like Monster or CareerBuilder, although keep in mind that this will likely not be productive unless you have a unique and desirable skill. **I recommend you pay particular attention to small employers (first try those with up to** twenty-five employees, then up to fifty, and then up to one hundred). Also, you're likely to have better luck with newer organizations (seven years or less).

If you post your resume on the sites of particular employers, large or small, don't count on any acknowledgment or reply. Just post the thing, cross your fingers, and hope it arrives at the right time, at the right place, and gets into the hands of the right person: *the one who actually has the power to hire you*. Sad truth: Many employers don't even look at the resumes posted on their site.

Additional Job-Search Materials: Cover Letters and Portfolios

Your cover letter (or email) can greatly enhance your chances of getting the job. I get this kind of report all the time from successful job hunters: "Cover letter. Make it personal and specific to THAT job. I was directly told in two interviews that my unique cover letter got me in the door. I researched the companies . . ."

Your cover letter shouldn't be just a "here is my resume" note or a generic letter that fails to identify the employer by name or to connect the dots between your experience and what the position requires. If you don't know what a cover letter is, or how to write it, the internet can rescue you handily. Check out the Novoresume "How to Write a Cover Letter in 2020—Beginner's Guide."[25] You can also consult the cover letter chapter in my little book *What Color Is Your Parachute? Guide to Rethinking Resumes* (Ten Speed Press, 2014).

Another variation on the classic resume is a job or career portfolio. Artists have a portfolio with samples of their work. You probably knew that. But portfolios are equally apt in other fields. A portfolio may be electronic (posted on the internet) or on paper, in a notebook, or in a large display case (as with artists), demonstrating your accomplishments, experience, training, commendations, or awards from the past.

Instead of "portfolio" we might just call these "evidence of what I can do and have done" or "proof of performance." For guidance on how to prepare a job portfolio and what to include, simply search for "job or career portfolio"; you'll get a wealth of tips and information, such as www.livecareer.com/career/advice/jobs/job-search-portfolio.

Wild Life, by John Kovalic, ©1989 Shetland Productions. Reprinted with permission.

Some Friendly Tips for Making the Most of Your Resume

Your sole purpose for your resume, if you're targeting individual employers, is to get yourself invited in for an interview. The purpose of a resume is just to raise the employer's interest or curiosity and get invited in for an interview, where it will then be time for you to sell yourself. In person. Face to face. Not on paper. So go back and read over every single sentence in your resume and evaluate it by this one standard: *Will this item help to get me invited in? Or will this item seem too puzzling, or off-putting, or a red flag?* If you doubt a particular bullet point will help get you invited in for an interview, then omit it. If it's important to you, give yourself a note to be sure to cover it *in the interview*. And if there is something you feel you will ultimately need to explain, or expand upon, save that explanation also for the interview. Your resume is, above all, no place for "true confessions." This is not the place to indicate why you left a position. ("I kind of botched up, at the end, in that job; that's why they let me go, as

I'm sure they'll tell you when you check my references.") Save true confessions for the end of the interview, and only if you're confident at that point that they really want you, and you really want them, and they must know the information.

If you're putting your resume on your LinkedIn account or elsewhere online, be cautious about including any stuff on the resume that would help someone find out where you live or work. For your personal safety, leave out your address and phone number. Just an email address should more than suffice.

If you are sending your resume via email, first convert it to a PDF document, then send that as an attachment. A PDF format will keep the formatting consistent wherever it's opened.

If you're printing out a hard copy—to snail-mail to a target employer, drop off in person, or bring to an interview—pay attention to the paper you use. Picture this scenario: an employer is going through a whole stack of resumes, and on average he or she is giving each resume about eight seconds of their time (true: we checked!). Then that resume goes into either a pile we might call "Forget about it" or a pile we might call "Bears further investigation." And what determines which pile it goes into? *Surprise! It can be the feel of the paper.* Yes, that employer's first contact with your printed resume is with their fingers. By the pleasure or displeasure of their fingers as they first pick up your resume, they are prejudiced for or against you before they even start reading. Usually they are blissfully unaware of this. But this is why you want the paper to feel good. That usually means using paper rated at least 28 pounds (a paper's weight rating is on the packaging). And you want it to be easy to read, so be sure it's nicely laid out or formatted, using a decent-sized font, 12-point or even 14.

When discussing any nonvisible or nonobvious disability or issue you may have, generally speaking—there are exceptions—don't mention these issues on your resume or in your cover letter. And even when you're in the interview, don't discuss right off the bat what you *can't* do. Focus all their attention, initially, on what you *can* do—that you can perform all the tasks required in this job. Save what you can't do for the moment when they say they really want you.

Finally, don't include references on your resume. References go in a separate document with the words "References for" and your name. Then list three to five references by name, job title, employer, how they know you, and their phone number and email. *Never list somebody as a reference, at any time in your job hunt, without first getting their written permission to do so.* When you ask someone to serve as a reference, send them your latest resume and refresh their memory (if necessary) as to how they knew you.

Conclusion

Okay, one more time: *Do you need a resume?*

Well, no, you don't, and yes, you do.

You already have a kind of resume without lifting a finger, if you've been posting anything on the internet. Google is your newer resume. What an employer finds out about you by simply searching on your name helps determine whether you get hired or not.

You've got to clean up what they'll find, *before* they find it. Edit, fill in, expand, and add to it, before they see it.

But that alone is not enough. You need to summarize and organize the information about yourself in one place, online or off. And that means you need to write the traditional resume.[26]

Once written, you can go two ways with it. The first way is just to post it everywhere on the internet, which is akin to nailing it to a tree in the town square, where everyone can see it. You just post it *as is*.

The second way is to send it to particular employers whom you have targeted, hoping that resume will get you an interview. Here you will need to *edit it* before sending it to any employer. You will need to weigh every item in it by one criterion and one only: Will this help get me invited in, for an interview *at this place*? If the answer is *No*, you must edit or remove that item.

Because these are the most fundamental truths about approaching individual employers:

The primary purpose of a resume is *to get yourself invited in for an interview*.

The primary purpose of that interview is *to get yourself invited back for a second interview*.

The primary purpose of the second and subsequent interviews there is *to help them decide that they like you and want you,* once you've decided that you like them and could do some of your best work there.

No matter what you do,
your job is to tell your story.

—GARY VAYNERCHUK

CHAPTER 9

FIFTEEN TIPS ABOUT YOUR JOB INTERVIEW

Now, hunting for one of those millions of vacancies that are out there each month, will inevitably involve interviewing, sooner or later. And the word "interview" strikes terror into the hearts of many—if not most—job hunters. Well, it needn't. You actually have more practice at interviewing than you think, because not all interviews are for a job. There are many types of interviews. I can think of three kinds of interviews that arise during a job hunt. They are distinguished from each other by *what you are looking for*, and more importantly, *who you are talking to:*

1. **Interviews for fun or practice.** Here you are talking with **people who are passionate about something that you are, too**—be it football, scrapbooks, travel, physical fitness, running, or whatever. You ask them questions about their interests, and you share your thoughts. *Oh, you would just call these "conversations"? Okay, then: conversations.*

2. **Interviews for information,** where you are talking with **employees** who did or do the job you are exploring; or maybe you're talking with **information specialists**, or with **experts** in the industry that interests you. Again, you ask them questions and share your thoughts. *Oh, you would just call these "conversations"? Okay, then: conversations.*

3. **Interviews for a job,** where you are talking with **employers**, and most particularly with **the person who actually has the power to hire you for the job you want**. You want information about the position, and you provide information about yourself. *Oh, you wouldn't call these "conversations"? Well, I would.*

This chapter is about handling this third kind of interview or conversation: the one for a job. These interviews take many forms. It may be the traditional office interview where you are speaking with one interviewer. Or it may be conducted by phone or online via Skype or other video calling system. You might experience a panel interview, facing several people lined up along a table. Or you might have a group interview, in the case of several people from a particular office or team interviewing you at the same time. Some interviews include lunch and/or dinner; just remember, you are always being interviewed, even if someone says, "Let's just enjoy lunch." And you will likely experience more than one interview, unless the employer represents a small organization or even a one-person shop.

Your goal in the interview is to learn more about the position, to determine if you still want it, and, if so, to get hired for the position. You will want to develop responses to interview questions that will help connect the dots, so to speak, between your skills and talents and the position you are seeking. We already know that employers, above all else, are seeking individuals who have the skills they need and who are a good fit for their organization. Your role in the interview is to make sure the employer sees that in you.

By the way, there is no such thing as a generic "employer." Or employers, as in "Employers just won't hire me or someone with my background or someone with my disability." Just because you interviewed with two employers (or six, or twelve) and they wouldn't hire you. Those two. Those six. Or those twelve. They hardly speak for all twenty-eight-million-plus active businesses that are out there. Employers are individuals, as different from one another as night and day. Employers span a wide range of attitudes, wildly different ideas about how to hire, a wide range of ways to conduct hiring interviews, and as many different viewpoints as you can possibly think of. You cannot possibly predict the attitude of one employer based on the attitude of another. It's important not to generalize about all employers as if they are the same. And if you present yourself well and know what your skills and talents are, then some employer is looking for you. Guaranteed. Your job is to find *them*.

The bottom line is: don't get discouraged by your interview turn-downs. Job expert Tom Jackson brilliantly described the outcomes of job interviews at a whole bunch of places as follows:

NO NO NO NO NO NO NO NO NO NO NO NO NO NO
NO NO NO NO NO NO NO NO NO NO NO NO YES YES

As Tom points out, every "NO" you get out of the way gets you one step closer to YES.[27] (Or, preferably, two YESES.)

But, as with all things connected to the job search, the better prepared you are for these conversations we call interviews, the more likely it is you will succeed.

Here are fifteen tips about the hiring conversation(s) to keep in mind:

CONVERSATION TIP #1
DO YOUR HOMEWORK

Every interview should be prepared for, before you go in. Naturally, you want to go into the interview(s) with this employer curious to know more about *you*, but the employer is first of all curious about what you know about *them*. Do a lot of research on them before you go in. Why? Because organizations love to be loved. If you've gone to the trouble of finding out as much as you can about them before you interview with them, they will be flattered and impressed, believe me.

So don't skip this step. It may make the difference between your being hired or not being hired. Find out everything you can about them.

Google them. Go to their website, if they have one, and read all their press releases, plus everything there that is hidden under the heading "About Us." If this organization is local, and your town has a public library, ask your local librarian for help in finding any news clippings or other information about the place. And finally, ask all your friends if they know anyone who ever worked there or works there still, so you can take them to lunch or tea or Starbucks and find out any inside stories before you approach the place. (And, of course, maybe after you hear these stories you'll decide not to explore them any further. Better to know that now than later.)

Make sure you know the latest news about the company or industry. Be familiar with the job description or job posting about the position you're seeking. Be aware of the key duties or expectations about the position, and be prepared to discuss your ability to perform those duties. Know the names of your interviewers as well as their titles. If you know their names ahead of time, see if they have a LinkedIn profile. (Keep your research and conversation professional; this is not the time to find their Facebook page so you can find personal information. That's borderline stalking. Professional research is all that's necessary.)

CONVERSATION TIP #2
PREPARE STORIES

Storytelling is one of the most powerful techniques you can use in a job interview. Stories are memorable and illuminating, and when used properly can make the difference between an average interview and an interview that gets you the job. A bonus advantage of well-crafted stories is that you can apply to them to different questions. You don't have to know the questions you'll be asked if you have some well-prepared stories about your strengths and ability to overcome difficulties.

There are some basic guidelines to keep in mind when crafting your stories for an interview. Make sure they are interesting and directly relevant to the questions you might be asked. Focus on stories related to the workplace or professional behavior. If you haven't been in the workplace for a while, you can either refer to past situations or select stories that illustrate skills needed for the job you're seeking. Try to avoid stories that focus on your family or personal situations, unless you can craft them in a way that demonstrates skills or personality traits needed in the work setting. Don't tell stories that reveal information the employer doesn't need to know.

One way to structure your stories is to start with a simple setup: think about the "who, what, when, and where" of the situation. What is the context of your story?

For the main topic, focus your story on areas such as goals you've accomplished, obstacles you've overcome, decisions you've made, or problems you've solved. Think about stories that illustrate the skills, knowledge, and personality traits you identified in your Flower Exercise. If you're trying to transition into a new career field, tell stories that show how what you have done in your previous career directly relates to your desired field.

Here's an example: You've been a teacher for five years, and you hope to switch to a position with a tech company that has moved to your city. The starting position for this company is in customer service. You've already said to the employer, "You could argue that customer service is built into a teacher's DNA. We have a lot of people to please, including parents, students, and administrators. I received consistently positive feedback in my annual reviews."

That's a great start. But the interviewer will want to see behavioral examples of your skills in customer service. So the interviewer asks you, "Tell me about a challenging problem or situation you solved." Here's where a well-planned story will come into play. You want to select a story that focuses on the problems related to customer service. This would not be the time to tell a story about a student who lost their shoe and you found it. That's too simple and not as relevant. A better story would be: "Every student I work with is unique. One solution doesn't fit all, so I must listen and be creative. Recently I was trying to help a student prepare for an important test. We only had one night to get ready, and the student was tired and distracted. Instead of forcing him to sit at his desk and study, I asked him if he'd like to go for a walk. While walking, we talked about the test, and I gave him sample questions to try answering. We turned what could have been a grueling study session into a walk and a pleasant exchange of ideas. By the time we got back he was ready to open his books and study what he didn't know. He received the highest grade in his class. You just have to know your customer and respond in a way that's helpful." This story could be used to show the storyteller's creativity, ability to solve problems, empathy for others, and more.

Keep your stories positive. Even when describing a mistake you made or a problem you encountered, focus on what you learned or how it's something that won't happen again.

Finally, practice telling your stories. Try them out on family and friends, and take feedback to revise them until they are clear and concise. Your listeners can let you know if your story is going on too long (two minutes max) or if it is confusing or missing the point. You want to avoid rambling or unnecessary asides that don't relate to the main point.

CONVERSATION TIP #3
GET THE INFO

An interview for a job is a fact-finding mission. The goal, for both you and the employer, is to collect as much data as possible about each other to make a correct decision. This conversation is two people attempting to decide if you both want to keep the conversation going. And it's got to be a *two-way* decision. What the employer decides is critical, of course, but so is what you decide.

This interview is a data-collecting process for the employer. Whether one person or a team is interviewing you, they are using the interview to find out:

Do we like you?

Do we want you to work here?

Do you have the skills, knowledge, or experience that we really need?

Do you have the work ethic that we are looking for?

All well and good. But this interview is part of *your* data-collecting process, too—the one you have been engaged in, or should have been engaged in, throughout your whole job hunt. You are sitting there, now, with the employer or their team, and the question you are trying to find an answer to is *Do I like you all? Do I want to work here, or not?*

You don't have to begin an interview—as some so-called experts would have it—by "marketing yourself." Not yet. Not in the beginning. Not until you gather all the information you need to know about the place, and you are weighing the question *Do I want to work here?*—and have concluded *Yes* or *I think so*—do you then turn your energy toward *marketing* yourself. If you start to market yourself too early, you are likely to be focused on speaking instead of listening—and it's important that you spend the first part of the interview listening.

Let me emphasize this: there are two steps to your side of the conversation (or conversations): first, gentle questioning about the place, then quiet, self-confident marketing of yourself, if—but only if—you've decided this is the place for you. Because there are two steps, you'll save yourself a lot of grief if you realize that the first interview with this organization has only one main purpose: to be invited back for a second interview.

One way to think about this process is to consider what data you want the employer to know about you. Consider: *what are the three things I'd like this employer to remember about me?* If you plan that ahead of time, you can be sure to tell stories or provide information that will stick with the employer after you've left the interview.

CONVERSATION TIP #4

IT'S ALL ABOUT THE QUESTIONS

Questions to expect from them, then questions you can ask. The principal question, the first question, the most important question they are likely to ask you is "Tell me about yourself." How you answer that question will determine your fate during the rest of the interview. So, here are some key points to keep in mind as you answer:

- With this question they are giving you a kind of test. They want to see how you respond to an open-ended, unstructured situation, the kind of unanticipated challenge that life (and a job) are continually presenting to each of us. This is such a common question, employers expect you to have this answer at your fingertips, well-summarized, well-rehearsed. (This is the famous "elevator speech" job coaches are always recommending to job hunters. In the length of time it takes to ride an elevator up a tall building, you should be able to give your entire answer to *this question*, rehearsed and rehearsed beforehand, until you could say it in your sleep.)

- Employers feel you have flunked the test if you respond with a question instead of any answer. Every job hunter's favorite response— "Well, what do you want to know about me?"—is every employer's *least* favorite. They interpret this to mean you have no idea what to answer and are stalling for time.

- What employers are looking for here is an answer to a somewhat different question than the one they posed. The employer's unspoken real question is *What experience, skills, or knowledges do you have that are relevant to the job I am trying to fill?* That's what you should try to answer here. Remember, your goal is ultimately to connect the dots between you and the position. What you answer can help start that process. So this isn't the place for your personal history, where you grew up, your favorite food, your tastes, or hobbies. Employers want your work history, and more particularly your work history as it relates to this job.

- Incidentally, it will help if you ask yourself, before going to the interview(s), What are the three most important competencies *for this job?*" If you haven't a clue, then that's what you want to ask *them*, early on in the interview(s). Then, of course, during the interview(s) you will want to emphasize and demonstrate that you *have* those three competencies for the job that you are applying for. So you could say something like, "Well, I noticed in your job posting you are seeking a person who is _____, and I guess that's what most excited me about this position. I . . ." and then tell your story that relates to this trait.

Okay, what other questions might you expect the employer to ask you during your interview? Books on interviewing, of which there are many, often publish long lists of questions employers may ask you, along with some timeworn, semi-clever answers. Keep this in mind and be sure to *create your own answers*—not ones found in the books. Book lists include such questions as:

- What do you know about this company, business, or organization?
- Why are you applying for this job?
- How would you describe yourself?
- What are your major strengths?
- What is your greatest weakness?
- What type of work do you like to do best?
- What are your interests outside of work?
- What accomplishment thus far in your life gave you the greatest satisfaction?
- Why did you leave your last place of work?

- Where do you see yourself five years from now?
- What are your goals in life?
- How much did you make at your last job?

And the lists go on. But really, there are only *five basic questions* that you need pay attention to. The people who have the power to hire you are most curious about your answers to these five, which they may ask directly or try to find out without *even asking the questions per se:*

1. **"Why are you here?"** This means "Why are you knocking on my door, rather than someone else's door?"

2. **"What can you do for us?"** This means "If we were to hire you, will you help me with the challenges I face? What are your skills, and how much do you know about the subject or field that our organization is in?"

3. **"What kind of person are you?"** This means "Will you fit in or add a new perspective? Do you have the kind of personality that makes it easy for people to work with you, and do you share our vision?"

4. **"What exactly distinguishes you from nineteen or ninety other people who are applying for this job?"** This means "Do you have better work habits than the others, do you show up earlier, stay later, work more thoroughly, work faster, maintain higher standards, go the extra mile, or . . . what?"

5. **"Can I afford you?"** This means "If we decide we want you here, how much will it take to get you, and are we willing and able to pay that amount—governed, as we are, by our budget, and by our inability to pay you as much as the person who would be next above you on our organizational chart?"

These are the principal questions that employers want to know the answers to, even if the interview begins and ends with these five questions never once being asked explicitly by the employer. Nonetheless, these questions are still floating beneath the surface of the conversation, beneath all the things being discussed. So anything you can do during your interview(s) there to help the employer satisfy these five curiosities will make you stand out in the employer's mind.

Of course, it's not just the employer who has questions. This is a two-way conversation, remember? You have questions too. And—no surprise!—they are the same questions as the employer's (in only slightly different form). Here is what you are probably quietly thinking about during your half of the conversation:

1. **"What does this job involve?"** You want to understand exactly what tasks will be asked of you, so you can determine if these are the kinds of tasks you would really like to do, as well as can do.

2. **"What are the skills a top employee in this job would have to have?"** You want to find out if your skills match those that the employer thinks a top employee in this job has to have in order to do this job well.

3. **"Are these the kinds of people I would like to work with, or not?"** Do not ignore your intuition if it tells you that you would not be comfortable working with these people! You want to know if they have the kind of personalities that would enable you to accomplish your best work. If these people aren't it, keep looking!

4. **"If we like each other, and we both want to work together, can I persuade them there is something unique about me that makes me different from nineteen or ninety other people who are applying for this job?"** You need to think out, way ahead of time,

what does make you different from other people who can do the same job. For example, if you are good at analyzing problems, how do you do that? (a) Painstakingly? (b) Intuitively, in a flash? Or (c) by consulting with greater authorities in the field? You see the point. You are trying to put your finger on the style or manner in which you do your work that is distinctive—and hopefully appealing—to this employer, so that they choose you over other people they are interviewing. (These are your self-management or soft skills, as we saw in the Flower Exercise.)

5. **"Can I persuade them to hire me at the salary I need or want?"** This requires some knowledge on your part of how to conduct salary negotiation. (Key things to know: It should always take place at the end of the interviews, and whoever mentions a salary figure first generally loses in the negotiation.) That's covered in the next chapter.

You will probably want to ask questions #1 and #2 out loud. You should quietly *observe* the answer to question #3. You will be prepared to make the case for questions #4 and #5 when the *appropriate* opportunity in the interview arises.

Further questions you may want to ask:

- What significant changes has this company gone through in the past five years?
- What values are sacred to this company?
- What character traits do the most successful employees in this company have?
- What future changes do you see in the work here?
- Who do you see as your allies, colleagues, or competitors in this business?
- Who has succeeded in this role previously and how do you measure success?

How do you first raise these questions of yours, if you initiated the interview? Well, you might begin by reporting just exactly how you've been conducting your job hunt, and what it was that so impressed you about *this* organization during your research that you decided to come in and talk to them about a job. From there, and thereafter, you can fix your attention on the five questions that are inevitably on the employer's mind.

Incidentally, these five questions pop up (yet again) if you're there to talk *not* about a job that already exists, but rather a job that you hope they will *create* for you. In that case, these five questions change form only slightly. They get changed into five *statements* that you make to the person who has the power to *create* this job. Finally, knowing the five basic questions the employer is thinking of, here are some suggestions for how you might respond:

1. You tell them what you **like** about this organization.

2. You tell them what sorts of **needs** you find intriguing in this field, in general and in this organization in particular (by the way, unless you first hear the word coming out of their mouth, don't use the word "problems," as most employers prefer synonyms that sound gentler to their ears, such as "**challenges**" or "needs").

3. You tell them what seem to you to be necessary in order to meet such needs, and you give them brief stories from your past experience that demonstrate you have those very skills. Employers, in these days of behavioral interviews, are not impressed with vague statements like "I'm good at . . ." They want **concrete examples**, from your past experience, that prove you have the transferable skills, special knowledges skills, or self-management skills (that is, traits) that you claim to have.

4. You tell them what is **unique** about the way *you* perform those skills. Every prospective employer wants to know *what makes you different* from nineteen or ninety other people who can do the same kind of work as you. You *have* to know what that is. And then not merely talk about it, but actually demonstrate it by the way you conduct your side of the hiring interview.

5. And you tell them how the hiring of you will not cost them, in the long run. You need to be prepared to demonstrate that you will, in the long run, bring in more money than the salary they pay you. Emphasize this!

CONVERSATION TIP #5
NOT ALL INTERVIEWS ARE THE SAME

The style of interviewing and the questions you are asked at an interview can vary greatly, depending on several factors.

First, the Interviewer

Sometimes you'll be interviewing with professional interviewers: those who work in human resources and interview candidates daily. They know the laws and what questions are legal to ask and generally follow a standard interview format. Sometimes you'll interview with a line manager or division representative who occasionally interviews candidates but has many other responsibilities. This individual can be a wild card: some are well informed and prepared to interview; others adopt an off-the-cuff style and ask unusual questions. There's generally no way to prepare for this other than doing your homework, knowing as much about the company and position as possible, and having your prepared stories. You will likely interview with your future supervisor as well. This is the moment when you want to pay the most attention to fit. Do you like this person? Do you think they will be a good leader/manager? You can ask them what their management style is. You can also ask how they measure success in a worker. Remember, this is a conversation you are continuing to have until you have made up your mind that this position is for you.

Next, the Interview

Interviews come in all shapes and sizes. Depending on the position and the industry, you might have one interview and receive an offer—or at least learn your fate. Many organizations go through a multi-interview process, sometimes with one person at a time, sometimes a group interview. The questions can vary greatly, from the standard questions mentioned in Tip #4 to specific questions for certain fields. For example, in one popular style, the "behavioral interview," you're asked to specifically describe instances when you demonstrated certain traits or skills. As the name implies, they are focusing on your behavior, not just what you *say* you can do. So when you respond to a behavioral question like "Tell me about a time when you . . .", focus on a specific example where you demonstrated a particular skill or strength. Tell the employer the context of the situation, the task you were given, and how you accomplished it. As you think about the skills and traits you identified when creating your Flower, be sure to prepare stories that illustrate them. You will find that preparing these general stories about your skills will be helpful in your interviews. You can then adapt your stories to fit the specific questions asked.

Case interviews. If you're interviewing for a position in consulting, finance, or an executive role, you are likely to encounter a "case interview," in which you are presented with a situation and asked how you would handle it or how you would determine a plan of action. Case interviews can involve tricky questions that focus on your logical ability to solve problems. It's difficult to prepare for them, because it's hard to predict what you'll be asked. Check online for sample case questions. Bain & Company provides a helpful video and article called "What Is a Case Interview?" for preparing for case interviews.[28]

Behavioral exercises. You might be asked to perform certain tasks as part of the interview. Some interviews involve "inbox" exercises: they give you an inbox filled with memos and correspondence and ask you to quickly read through the materials and prioritize their importance and how you would handle them. If you are interviewing for a position that requires you to do presentations, you might be asked to give a sample presentation. (If you're lucky, you will know about this in advance and have time to prepare.) If you're interviewing for a technical position or knowledge of a specific program or software is expected (for example, Excel), don't be surprised if they place you at a computer and ask you to work with that program or software. In some cases, individuals who have indicated proficiency in a foreign language have suddenly been confronted with one of the interviewers speaking in that language. These examples illustrate why it is so important to be aware of the expectations of the position and the duties you would perform, and to be honest about your abilities.

Seven Tips for Managing Virtual or Online Interviews

Don't be surprised if your next interview isn't in person or on the phone. Skype, Zoom, and other internet-based video conferencing platforms are increasingly popular with employers. They eliminate the need for anyone to travel, they can be scheduled as easily as a call, and the video element allows both the interviewer and interviewee to have a closer connection with each other than they would in a regular phone call. But if you're new to this world, you might find these tips helpful in ensuring a successful online experience.

1. Do all your usual preparation for an interview, including research about the company and position. Place your resume on the desk with your computer so you can glance at it if needed. Remove other distracting papers that might rustle or fall during the interview.

2. Familiarize yourself with the technology you'll be using in advance, if possible. If the employer is using their own technology, practice with a program you're familiar with ahead of time so you'll be generally familiar with the process. Check your computer's camera angle so that it's on your face and upper body and not too close or far away. You might need to set your computer on a stack of books to bring the camera up to eye-level or slightly above your head. This will give you a better angle than if the camera is lower than your face.

3. Make sure your background is (ideally) a blank wall and the room is free from noise or distractions. Make sure the room has adequate lighting so the interviewer can see your face clearly. Don't sit in front of a window. Turn off your phone (unless you're using it for the interview!) and close the door to the room. If others are around, place a "Do Not Disturb" sign on the closed door. Keep pets and small children away as well.

4. Wear appropriate clothing (even for what can't be seen!); don't wear a nice top with shorts, for example. You might forget and stand up or drop something and need to move. Remember, the camera sees all. Make sure your clothing doesn't have stripes, strong patterns, or bright colors that might strobe or glare. Wear solid dark colors like blue, black, or dark gray.

5. Speak directly and look into the camera eye (which is likely at the top of your screen). Don't stare at the screen—you will appear to be looking down during much of the interview.

6. Take your time and pace your replies. Pause before responding. It's not unusual to experience sound delays, so be careful to wait for the full question or statement before you start talking.

7. Always have a backup plan if the technology fails. Get the phone number for the employer so you can call if needed. If you are showing a presentation, send a PDF copy in advance so your interviewer will have it regardless of technical issues.

CONVERSATION TIP #6

LISTEN, LISTEN, LISTEN

If I were asked to identify the number one behavior that can tank an interview, it's a candidate who talks too much. During the interview(s), be sure to observe the fifty-fifty rule. As a general rule, people who get hired are those who mix speaking and listening fifty-fifty in the interview. That is, half the time in the interview(s) they let the employer do the talking and half the time they do the talking. People who didn't achieve that balance are less likely to be hired. This is only common sense: if you talk too much about yourself, you come across as one who would ignore the needs of the organization; if you talk too little, you come across as too shy or introverted for the role.

Most experts agree that your responses to interview questions should be two minutes maximum, and often less. When you start to go beyond two minutes (unless you are explaining a technical issue relevant to the job and the question asked), you will lose the interviewer's attention, and the point you were making will likely be lost.

No matter how well prepared you are, how perfect your suit is, how impeccable your resume is, if you talk too much you will not get the job. This will take practice if it's not your standard style of speaking.

Be sensitive to cues that your response to a question has gone on too long. Watch the interviewer's face carefully for signs of boredom or a desire to respond to what you are saying. Remember that interviews are short—generally thirty minutes to an hour. Don't monopolize the conversation. You can't learn if you're not listening.

CONVERSATION TIP #7

DON'T BE A HIRING RISK

The employer is primarily concerned about risk. Employers *hate* risks. One risk stands above all the others: that they hire you and you don't work out. This would cost the employer a lot of money. Search on "cost of a bad hire" and see what it turns up. As you can see, the cost of hiring the wrong person can cost the employer one to five times the *bad hire's* annual salary, or more.

So during the interview, you may think you are sitting there, scared to death, while the employer (individual or team) is sitting there, blasé and confident. More likely both you and your interviewer may both be quite anxious.

The employer's anxieties include any or all of the following:

- You won't be able to do the job: that you lack the necessary skills or experience, and the hiring interview didn't uncover this.
- You'll stay around for only a few weeks or at most a few months, until you find a better job.
- It may take you too long to master the job, and thus it will be too long before you turn a profit for that organization.
- You won't get along with the other workers there, or you will develop a personality conflict with the boss.
- You will do only the minimum that you can get away with, rather than the maximum that the boss was hoping for. Since every boss these days is trying to keep their workforce as small as possible, they are hoping for the maximum productivity from each new hire.
- You will always have to be told what to do next, rather than taking initiative.
- You will turn out to have a disastrous character flaw not evident in the interview, and ultimately reveal yourself to be either dishonest, irresponsible, or to put it bluntly, an employer's worst nightmare.
- If this is a large organization, and your boss is not the top person there, that you will bring discredit upon them and their department/section/division for hiring you—making them lose face with the boss upstairs and possibly costing them a raise or a promotion.

In the end, employers want to hire people who can bring in more money than they are paid. Every organization has two main preoccupations for its day-by-day work: **challenges** they are facing, and what **solutions** to those challenges their employees and management are coming up with. Therefore, the main thing the employer is trying to figure out during the hiring interview with you is, **Will you be part of the solution there, or just another part of the challenge**?

In trying to allay their worries, you should figure out prior to the interview how a *bad* employee would screw up in the position you are discussing with the employer, individual, or team—things like coming in late, taking too much time off, following your own agenda instead of the employer's. So plan to show the employer, by your actions and words before, during, and after the interview, how much you are the very opposite. You show up on time or ahead of time. During the interview you are preoccupied with the employer's agenda, not your own. Your sole goal is to increase the organization's effectiveness, service, and bottom line.

CONVERSATION TIP #8
THE THINGS THAT CAN DO YOU IN

In a job interview, it's the small things that are the killers. Okay, you're in the interview. You're ready with your carefully rehearsed summary of your experience, skills, and knowledges. You are telling interesting stories and examples of your skills. *But the employer isn't listening.* Because, sitting across from you, they are noticing things about you that will kill the interview. And the job offer.

I think of this as losing to mosquitoes when you were prepared to fight dragons. And losing in the first two minutes (*ouch*).

So what's going on? Simply this.

The best interviewers operate intuitively on the principle that **microcosm reveals macrocosm.** They believe that what you do in some small arena reveals how you would and will act in a larger arena.

They watch you carefully, in the small arena of the interview, because they assume that each of your behaviors there reveals how you would act in a larger universe—like: *the job!*

They scrutinize your past, as in your resume, for the same reason: *microcosm* (your behavior in the past) *reveals macrocosm* (your likely behavior in the future).

So let us look at what mosquitoes (as it were) can fly in, during the first thirty seconds to two minutes of your interview so that the person who has the power to hire you doesn't start muttering to themself, "I sure hope we have some other candidates besides this one":

1. **Your appearance and personal habits.** Survey after survey has revealed that you are much more likely to get the job if:
    - You have obviously freshly bathed and groomed and you are professionally dressed.
    - You have freshly brushed and flossed your teeth.
    - You are not wafting tons of aftershave cologne or overwhelming perfume fifteen feet ahead of you when you enter the room. Employers have become super-sensitive these days to the fact that many employees (and employers!) are allergic to certain scents. Many interviews take place in small rooms and this can cause an employer to shorten the length of your interview.
    - You do not have a whole lot of tattoos clearly visible in the interview (unless it is an industry where tattoos are acceptable). Tattoos are everywhere these days: on movie stars, singers, dancers, athletes, and everyday people. If your body art is tiny and discreet, you need not be concerned. But if you have tattoos that might be off-putting, and you're afraid a particular employer that you want to work for is going to think badly of you upon seeing them, weigh carefully whether you value the tattoo more than a job (with this organization). At the very least, cover your tattoos with a long-sleeved shirt, blouse, or jacket.

2. **Nervous mannerisms.** It is a turnoff for many employers if:
    - You continually avoid eye contact with the employer (in fact, this is a big, big no-no).
    - You give a limp handshake.
    - You slouch in your chair, endlessly fidget with your hands, crack your knuckles, or constantly play with your hair during the interview. Note: Many of these mannerisms are unconscious

and increase under stress. One of the best ways to learn whether you're doing them is to record a mock interview on your phone or computer. Play it back, but turn off the sound, and watch.

3. **Lack of self-confidence.** It is a turnoff for many employers if:
   - You speak so softly you cannot be heard, or so loudly you can be heard two rooms away.
   - You give answers in an extremely hesitant fashion.
   - You give only the briefest answers (*no, yes, maybe, not yet, I think so*) to all the employer's questions.
   - You constantly interrupt the employer.
   - You downplay your achievements or abilities or are continuously self-critical.

4. **The consideration you show to other people.** It is a turnoff for many employers if:
   - You show a lack of courtesy to the receptionist, assistant, and (if at lunch) the server.
   - You are extremely critical of your previous employers.
   - You drink alcohol during the interview process. Ordering a drink if the employer takes you to lunch is a complete no-no, as it raises the question in the employer's mind *Do they normally stop with one, or do they normally keep on going?* Don't. Do. It! *Even if they do.*
   - You forget to thank the interviewer as you're leaving or forget to send a thank-you email afterward, that same day. Says one human resources expert: "A prompt, brief . . . letter thanking me for my time along with a (brief!) synopsis of his/her unique qualities communicates to me that this person is an assertive, motivated, customer-service-oriented salesperson who utilizes technology and knows the rules of the 'game.' These are qualities I am looking for. . . . At the moment I receive approximately one such letter . . . for every fifteen candidates interviewed."

5. **Your values.** It is a complete turnoff for many employers, if they see in you any sign of:
    - Arrogance or excessive aggressiveness.
    - Tardiness or failure to keep appointments and commitments on time, including these interviews.
    - Laziness or lack of motivation.
    - Constant complaining or blaming things on others.
    - Dishonesty or lying—especially on your resume or during the interviews.
    - Irresponsibility or tendency to goof off.
    - Not following instructions or obeying rules.
    - Lack of enthusiasm for this organization and what it is trying to do.
    - Instability, inappropriate response, and the like.
    - Poor preparation for this interview.

Incidentally, many employers have a non-smoking policy at their site. Today there are far fewer public places of business than in the past in which smoking is legal, so this is less of an issue than it once was. Just be aware of studies showing that in a competition between two equally qualified people, the nonsmoker will win out over the smoker a majority of the time. Sorry to report this, but take it seriously!

So there you have it: these are the *metaphorical* mosquitoes that can kill you when you're on the watch for dragons during hiring interviews.

This list can be frustrating, I know. I'm not reporting the world *as it should be*, and certainly not *as I would like it to be*. I'm only reporting what study after study has revealed about the world *as it is*. And how it affects your chances of getting hired.

But here's the good news, when all is said and done: you can kill all these mosquitoes. **Yes, you control and can change every one of these factors.** Go back and read the list and see!

CONVERSATION TIP #9

COMPETENCIES AND SKILLS

The word in hiring these days is competencies. Competencies are large overarching traits or abilities. For instance, while someone might have a skill in computer programming, they might also demonstrate competency in leadership. As mentioned in the Flower Exercise Skills Petal, competencies are broader categories of specific skills.

Competencies related to management, for example, might include fostering teamwork, motivating others, organizing projects, developing vision, or leading a team. You can learn more about competencies at this Workforce website, "31 Core Competencies Explained."[29]

By doing the Flower Exercise, you should already have a thorough list of your skills and competencies. Use this list to prepare your interview stories and responses to questions. But in addition to your already identified job-related skills and competencies, be aware of the general skills most employers are looking for, these days, regardless of the position you are seeking.

They are looking for employees who:

- Are punctual, arriving at work on time or better yet, early, and stay until quitting time or even leave late.
- Are dependable.
- Have a good attitude.
- Have drive, energy, and enthusiasm.
- Want more than a paycheck.
- Are self-disciplined, well-organized, highly motivated, and good at managing their time.
- Can handle people well.
- Can use language effectively.
- Can work on a computer.
- Are committed to teamwork.

- Are flexible and can respond to novel situations or adapt when circumstances at work change.
- Are trainable and love to learn.
- Are project-oriented and goal-oriented.
- Have creativity and are good at problem solving.
- Have integrity.
- Are loyal to the organization.
- Can identify opportunities, markets, and coming trends.

So plan on claiming all of these competencies that you *legitimately* can. Prior to the interview, sit down, make a list (or add to the list you already have), and jot down some experience you have had, for each of these, that proves you have that skill.

CONVERSATION TIP #10

PROVIDE EVIDENCE

Try to think of some way to bring evidence of your skills to the hiring interview. As mentioned previously, telling a good story is one of the best ways to provide evidence. Every candidate might say they are hardworking, but if you tell a story about the time someone on your team quit and you had to assume their job duties in addition to yours until a replacement was hired, you have provided a concrete example. And if you are an artist, a craftsperson, or anyone who produces a product, try to bring a sample of what you have made or produced—in scrapbook or portfolio form, on a flash drive, on YouTube, in photos, or, if you are a programmer, examples of your code. Just keep relevance in mind. Only bring evidence of skills needed in this new position.

CONVERSATION TIP #11
STAY POSITIVE

Do not bad-mouth your previous employer(s) during the interview, even if they were terrible people. Bad-mouthing a previous employer only makes this employer who is interviewing you worry about what you would say about *them*, after they hire you.

(I learned this in my own experience. I once spoke graciously about a previous employer during a job interview. Unbeknownst to me, the interviewer already knew that my previous employer had badly mistreated me. He therefore thought very highly of me because I didn't bad-mouth the guy. In fact, he never forgot this incident; talked about it for years afterward.)

Plan on saying something nice about any previous employer, or if you are pretty sure that the fact you and they didn't get along will surely come out, then try to nullify this ahead of time, by saying something simple like, "I usually get along with everybody, but for some reason, my past employer and I just didn't get along. Don't know why. It's never happened to me before. Hope it never happens again."

CONVERSATION TIP #12
KNOW WHAT'S BEHIND THE QUESTIONS

Throughout the interview, keep this in mind: employers don't really care about your past; they ask about it only to try to predict your future (behavior) with them, if they decide to hire you. They have fears, of course; don't we all?

Legally, US employers may ask you only questions that are related to the requirements and expectations of the job. They cannot ask about such things as your creed, religion, race, age, sexual orientation, or marital status. But any other questions about your past are *fair game*. And they *will* ask them, if they know what they're doing.

Therefore, during the hiring interview, before you answer any question the employer asks you about your past, you should pause to ask yourself *What fear about the future caused them to ask this question about my past?* and then address *that fear*, subtly or directly.

Here are some examples:

EMPLOYER'S QUESTION	THE FEAR BEHIND THE QUESTION	THE POINT YOU TRY TO GET ACROSS	PHRASES YOU MIGHT USE TO GET THIS ACROSS
"Tell me about yourself."	The employer is afraid he/she isn't going to conduct a very good interview, by failing to ask the right questions. Or is afraid there is something wrong with you, and is hoping you will blurt it out.	You are a good employee, as you have proved in the past at your other jobs. (Give the briefest history of who you are, interests, hobbies, and kind of work you have enjoyed the most to date.) Keep it to two minutes, max.	In describing your work history, use any honest phrases you can about your work history that are self-complimentary: "Hard worker." "Came in early, left late." "Always did more than was expected of me." And so on. Back up your statements with examples.
"What kind of work are you looking for?"	The employer is afraid that you are looking for a different job than that which the employer is trying to fill; for example, they want an assistant, but you want to be an office supervisor.	You are looking for precisely the kind of work the employer is offering (but don't say that if it isn't true). Repeat back to the employer, in your own words, what they have said about the job, and emphasize the skills you have to do that.	If the employer hasn't described the job at all, say, "I'd be happy to answer that, but first I need to understand exactly what kind of work this job involves." Then answer, as at left.
"Have you ever done this kind of work before?"	The employer is afraid you don't possess the necessary skills and experience to do this job.	You have skills that are transferable, from whatever you used to do, and you did it well.	"I pick up stuff very quickly." "I have quickly mastered any job I have ever done." Share how your past relates, offering examples.

continued ▶

269

EMPLOYER'S QUESTION	THE FEAR BEHIND THE QUESTION	THE POINT YOU TRY TO GET ACROSS	PHRASES YOU MIGHT USE TO GET THIS ACROSS
"Why did you leave your last job?" Or "How did you get along with your former boss and coworkers?"	The employer is afraid you don't get along well with people, especially bosses, and is just waiting for you to bad-mouth your previous boss or coworkers as proof of that.	Say whatever positive things you possibly can about your former boss and coworkers (without telling lies). Emphasize that you usually get along very well with people—and then let your gracious attitude toward your previous boss(es) and coworkers prove it, right before this employer's very eyes (and ears).	If you left voluntarily: "My boss and I both felt I would be happier and more effective in a job where [here describe your strong points, such as 'I would have more room to use my initiative and creativity']." If you were fired: "Usually, I get along well with everyone, but in this particular case the boss and I just didn't get along with each other. Difficult to say why." You don't need to say anything more than that. If you were laid off and your job wasn't filled after you left: "My job was terminated."
"How is your health?" Or "How much were you absent from work during your last job?"	The employer is afraid you will be absent from work a lot if they hire you. **Unfortunately for them, and fortunately for you, this is a question they cannot legally ask you.**	Just because the question is illegal doesn't mean you can't address their hidden fear. Even if they never mention it, you can try to disarm that fear.	You can find a way to say, "My productivity always exceeded other workers' in my previous jobs." Share a story or example to back this up.
"Can you explain why you've been out of work so long?" Or "Can you tell me why there are these gaps in your work history?" (Usually said after studying your resume.)	The employer is afraid that you are the kind of person who quits a job the minute they don't like something about it; in other words, that you have no "stick-to-it-iveness."	You love to work, and you regard times when things aren't going well as challenges, which you enjoy learning how to conquer.	"During the gaps in my work record, I was studying/doing volunteer work/raising my children/doing some hard thinking about my mission in life/finding redirection." (Choose one.)

EMPLOYER'S QUESTION	THE FEAR BEHIND THE QUESTION	THE POINT YOU TRY TO GET ACROSS	PHRASES YOU MIGHT USE TO GET THIS ACROSS
"Wouldn't this job represent a step down for you?" Or "I think this job would be way beneath your talents and experience." Or "Don't you think you would be underemployed if you took this job?"	The employer is afraid you could command a bigger salary somewhere else and will therefore leave this employer as soon as something better turns up.	You will stick with this job as long as you and the employer agree this is where you should be working.	"I like the duties of this position, and I have the skills to do it well." "We have mutual fears; every employer is afraid a good employee will leave too soon, and every employee is afraid the employer might fire them, for no good reason." "I like to work, and I give my best to every job I've ever had."
And finally, "Tell me, what is your greatest weakness?"	The employer is afraid you have some character flaw, and hopes you will now rashly blurt it out.	You have limitations just like anyone else, but you work constantly to improve yourself and be a more and more effective worker.	Mention a weakness and then stress its positive aspect; for example, "I don't like to be over-supervised, because I have a great deal of initiative, and I like to anticipate problems before they even arise."

CONVERSATION TIP #13

THINK LIKE AN INTERVIEWER

While you might not see the interviewer writing down anything while speaking with you, you can bet that right after you leave the interview they are either taking copious notes of the conversation or completing an evaluation form. To better understand what an employer might be looking for in your interview, take a look at this sample Candidate Evaluation Rubric.

This evaluation form can help you prepare for your interview by knowing what the employer is focusing on.

Candidate Evaluation Form

Name of Candidate: _____ Position: _____ Date: _____

Interviewed by: _____

Ratings	5-6 Excellent	3-4 Average	1-2 Poor	Comments
Appearance: Well-dressed; neat appearance; appropriate clothing; professional demeanor. No fidgeting or distracting behavior.				
Resume and other materials: Professional and neat. Well-organized. Provided portfolio or other work examples.				
Interpersonal skills: Good handshake and eye contact. Friendly; courteous; enthusiastic/interested.				
Knowledge of position: Clear understanding of position. Researched the organization. Asked good questions. Conveyed knowledge.				
Skills to perform job well: Previous direct or related experience to key functions. Confidence in performance ability.				
Communication: Speaks clearly, concisely, and confidently. Strong answers to questions. Good grammar. Appropriate volume for setting. Listens well.				
Leadership potential: Demonstrates interest in others. Project management experience. Motivator.				
Overall evaluation:				

CONVERSATION TIP #14
WHAT HAPPENS NOW? ASK ABOUT THE NEXT STEP IN THE PROCESS

Before you leave the (final) interview there, assuming you have decided that you like them and maybe they like you, you have a decision to make. The last questions you ask in the process are going to be the most memorable, so tread carefully. In some situations a direct approach is appropriate, so you could ask:

"Can you offer me this job?" If, after hearing all about this job at this place, you decide you'd really like to have it, you can ask for it. The worst thing the employer can say is "No," or "We need some time to think about all the interviews we're conducting." Be prepared for the employer to say no.

If you're not sure about asking such a bold question, you could also ask, **"What is the next step in the hiring process?"** or **"When may I expect to hear from you?"** If the employer says, "We need some time to think about this," or "We will be calling you for another interview," you could then ask:

"Might I ask what would be the latest I can expect to hear from you?" The employer will probably give you their best guess, but just know that hiring is often a process with several layers of approval, and it can take longer than anyone, including your interviewer, thinks. A delay is not a denial.

You can then ask, **"May I contact you after that date, if for any reason you haven't gotten back to me by that time?"** Some employers resent this question. But most employers appreciate your offering them what is in essence a safety net. They know they can get busy, become overwhelmed with other things, forget their promise to you. It's reassuring, in such a case, for you to offer to rescue them. Just keep in mind it can be frustrating to have several candidates constantly checking in, so use this action judiciously, if at all. You can always call the human resources office and ask if the position has been filled.

If ultimately the employer says "No," you can ask, **"Can you think of anyone else who might be interested in my skills and experience?"** This question is invoked only if they replied "No" to your first question.

Jot down any answers they give you, then stand up, thank them sincerely for their time, give a firm handshake, and leave.

In the following days, rigorously keep to all that you said, and don't contact them except with that mandatory thank-you email, until after the latest deadline you two agreed upon. If you do have to contact them after that date, and if they tell you things are still up in the air, you could ask these questions again, but tread lightly.

CONVERSATION TIP #15
WRITE A THANK-YOU EMAIL

Every expert on interviewing will tell you two things:

Thank-you notes or emails must be sent after every interview, by every job hunter.

Most job hunters ignore this advice.

Indeed, it is safe to say that it is the most overlooked step in the entire job-hunting process.

If you want to stand out from the others applying for the same job, send thank-you notes or emails to everyone you met there that day. Ask if they have a business card, and if not, ask them to write down their name and email address. Do this with the administrative assistants (who often hold the keys to the kingdom) as well as with your interviewer.

If you need any additional encouragement to send thank-you letters (besides the fact that it may get you the job), here are six more reasons for sending a thank-you note, especially to the person who interviewed you:

First, you were presenting yourself as someone who has good people skills. Your actions with respect to the job interview must back this claim up. Sending a thank-you note does that. The employer can see you are good with people; you remembered to thank them.

Second, it helps the employer recall who you are. Very helpful if they've seen a dozen people that day.

Third, if a committee will be involved in the hiring process, but only one member was at the first interview, the man or woman who first interviewed you has something to show the others on the committee.

Fourth, if the interview went rather well, and the employer seemed to show an interest in further talks, the thank-you note can reiterate your interest in further talks.

Fifth, the thank-you note gives you an opportunity to correct any wrong impression you inadvertently left behind. You can add anything you forgot to tell them that you want them to know. And from among all the things you two discussed, you can underline the two or three points that you most want to stand out in their minds.

Lastly, if the interview did not go well, or you lost all interest in working there, and this thank-you note is sort of "goodbye, and thanks," keep in mind that they may hear of openings elsewhere that would be of interest to you. In the thank-you note, you can mention this, and ask them to please let you know if they hear of anything anywhere. If this was a kind person who interviewed you, they may send you additional leads.

Conclusion

There is no magic in job hunting. No techniques work all the time. I hear regularly from job hunters who report that they paid attention to all the tips I have mentioned in this chapter and the book and are quite skilled at securing interviews—but they never get hired. And they want to know what they're doing wrong.

Sometimes it is because there are levels of screening, some within your sight, some beyond your sight. And everything may appear to be going well on the levels you can see, but not necessarily on the levels you can't see.

Still puzzled about why you're not getting hired? Sometimes, unfortunately, the answer is: you're not doing anything wrong. I don't know how often this happens, but I know it does happen: sometimes an employer already has made a decision about hiring someone else. Sometimes they are looking for someone with different skills or education.

You might think your interview went well and then be baffled as to why you got turned down. Trouble is, you will never know.

Employers will rarely tell you why you were turned down. You will never hear them say something frank like, "You came across as just too arrogant during the interview." Or "You just didn't seem to have the energy and drive we were seeking." You will almost always be left in the dark as to what it is you're doing wrong.

If you feel daring, there is a strategy you can try. If you've been interviewed by a whole bunch of employers, whoever was the friendliest of them all may want to help you. I said *may*.

You can always try phoning, reminding them of who you are, and then asking the following question—deliberately kept generalized, vague, unrelated to just that place, and above all, future-directed. Something like: "I'd appreciate some advice. I've been on several interviews at several different places now. From what you've seen, is there something about me in an interview that you think might be causing me not to get hired at those places? If so, I'd really appreciate your giving me some pointers so I can do better in my future hiring interviews."

Most of the time they'll duck. Their legal adviser, if they have one, will certainly advise against it. First of all, they're afraid of lawsuits. Second, they don't know how you will use what they might have to say. (Said an old military veteran to me one day, "I used to think it was my duty to tell everyone the truth. Now I only give it to those who can use it.")

But occasionally you will run into a compassionate and kind employer who is willing to risk giving you the truth, because they think you will use it wisely. If so, thank them from the bottom of your heart, no matter how painful their feedback is. And listen with an open mind. Don't get defensive or try to argue with them. Listen and accept what you hear. Such advice, seriously heeded, can bring about just the changes in your interviewing strategy that you most need, in order to win during interviews in the future.

In the absence of any such help from employers who interviewed you, you might want to get a good business friend of yours to role-play a mock hiring interview with you, in case they immediately see something glaringly wrong with how you're coming across.

When all else fails, I recommend you go to a career coach who charges by the hour, and put yourself in their tender, knowledgeable hands. Role-play an interview with them, and take their advice seriously (you've just paid for it, after all).

In interviewing, as elsewhere in your job hunt, the secret is to find out anything that is within your control, even if it's only 2 percent—and change it!

And if you do get the job, make one resolution to yourself right there, on the spot: plan to keep track of your accomplishments at this new job, on a weekly basis—jotting them down, every weekend, in your own private log. Career experts recommend you do this without fail. You can then summarize these accomplishments annually on a one-page sheet, for your boss's eyes, when the question of a raise or promotion comes up.

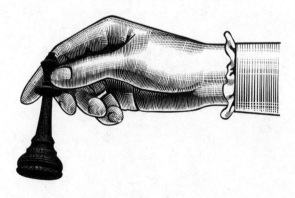

Pick up a camera. Shoot something. No matter how small, no matter how cheesy, no matter whether your friends and your sister star in it. Put your name on it as director. Now you're a director. Everything after that you're just negotiating your budget and your fee.

—JAMES CAMERON

CHAPTER 10

THE FIVE SECRETS OF SALARY NEGOTIATION

Salary. It must be discussed, before you finally agree to take the job. Once they've offered it to you.

Most employers will simply tell you the salary when they make you the offer (or send it in an offer letter).

But if they don't, just ask. And then be prepared to negotiate. You can generally assume that, unless the number is fixed by some corporate policy, there is some room to negotiate. Keep in mind that employers are always thinking about their budgets. If they can save some money when they hire you, they can use those funds elsewhere. So they likely have a range for the salary, and it's your job to learn as much as you can about that range to ensure that you get the best possible offer.

Keep in mind that salary isn't the entire issue. This is a perfect time to discuss any benefits that might go along with the position, including a health care plan, retirement fund, vacation days, or stock shares. All of these items are potential negotiating points in addition to the actual salary. Research ahead of time to learn what typical benefits are in your field of interest, because you might be willing to take a slightly lower salary if the benefits are particularly good. For example, salaries in higher education administration are often lower than comparable positions in the business world, but many colleges and universities provide tuition benefits for the children of administrators—a benefit that can be equal to several years' salary in the long run. So always ask, and always negotiate.

But know what you're negotiating for. Before you start the process, be prepared with your own limits. What is the minimum you can or will accept? What would a more ideal, yet realistic figure be? Be open to hearing whatever offer you are given, and don't get fixated on one figure. Try to negotiate all the variables at one time. Avoid coming back to the employer with another negotiating point. Lay your cards on the table during the discussion. For instance, if you need to take time off just two weeks after you plan to start the job (maybe you have to attend a wedding or there's another event you can't miss), negotiate that immediately. Don't wait until your first day on the job to bring that up.

Not everything is negotiable. Much of this has to do with how high up in the organization you will be: the lower the rank of the position, the less negotiation room exists. If many people are being hired into the same title, negotiation is less likely. If it's a highly desirable position, with lots of interested candidates, there will be less room for negotiation. This doesn't mean you can't ask; it's worth a try. Just be prepared to hear that it's not negotiable. You can then decide whether you are still interested.

If the prospect of negotiating throws fear into your heart, set your mind at ease; it's not all that difficult.

While whole books can be—and have been—written on this subject, there are basically just five secrets to keep in mind.

THE FIRST SECRET OF SALARY NEGOTIATION
Before You Go to the Interview, Do Some Careful Research on Typical Salaries for Your Field and in That Organization

Salary negotiation is required anytime the employer doesn't openly state the salary and doesn't indicate that it's not negotiable.

Okay, so here is the $64,000 question: How do you tell whether the figure the employer first offers you is only their starting bid or is their final offer? You come prepared, by first doing some research on the field and that organization, before you ever go in for an interview. Careful research about the salaries in your field (combined with the knowledge of what you need from the Flower Exercise) could have a significantly positive effect on the amount of money you end up being paid.

It doesn't always happen, but I know many job hunters and career changers to whom it has. It's certainly worth a shot. Remember, you can't negotiate once you accept an offer; you must negotiate *before* you agree. After that, you are usually limited to whatever typical raises the organization offers each year.

Okay, then, how do you do this research? Well, there are two ways to go: online, and off. Let's look at each, in turn.

Salary Research Online

Thanks to the internet, a lot of your research has already been done for you. If you want to research salaries for particular geographical regions, positions, occupations, or industries, or even (sometimes) specific organizations, here are some free sites that may give you just what you're looking for:

- **www.glassdoor.com**: This site allows you to search job titles and their corresponding average salaries in your area. It also features employee reviews from over six hundred thousand companies.
- **www.payscale.com**: Answer a few questions about your field of interest, experience, and preferred geographic location, and you will get an expected salary range. (Note: You don't have to answer every question—only the required ones. But answering more will give you a more accurate result.)
- **www.salary.com**: The most visited of all the salary-specific job sites, with a wide variety of information about salaries.
- **www.indeed.com**: While not specifically a salary site, Indeed posts salaries for specific openings when available and also sorts job listings by salary range. Enter a job title and geographic location to see what is available and the approximate pay range.

- **www.bls.gov/ooh:** The Bureau of Labor Statistics' survey of salaries in individual occupations, from the *Occupational Outlook Handbook 2018–2019*. Available listings include jobs that are highest paying, fastest growing, and offering the highest number of openings.
- **www.MyPlan.com:** This site has several lists of the highest-paying jobs in America, including a list for those without a college degree (under Careers, choose Top Ten Lists).
- **www.salaryexpert.com:** When you need a salary expert, it makes sense to go to "the Salary Expert." Lots of stuff on the subject of salaries here, including a free Salary Report for hundreds of job titles, varying by area, skill level, and experience. It also has some salary calculators.

If you strike out on all the above sites, then you're going to have to get a little more clever and see if you can get individuals in the field to tell you.

Salary Research Offline

Okay, so how do you do salary research offline? Well, there's a simple rule: *generally speaking, abandon books, and go talk to people.* Here are some ideas:

- Talk to people at a nearby university or college who train workers in your field, whatever their department may be. Teachers and professors will usually know what their graduates are making, and some university career centers will post salary data for their alumni. You can also go visit actual workplaces.

- Contact a temp agency or employment agency that hires individuals with your specialty. Ask about the typical salaries (or hourly wages) for position titles you are considering.

- When conducting informational interviews to research your field of interest, ask the individuals you're interviewing what salaries you can expect. Most people will not tell you what they are earning, but they might be willing to give you general salary ranges for that field.

- If you call their office, some human resources staff will provide general salary ranges for position titles in their organization.

- Keep in mind that when you ask people about salaries for positions, you will generally have more success if you inquire about ranges rather than a specific number.

THE SECOND SECRET OF SALARY NEGOTIATION

Never Discuss Salary Until the End of the Whole Interviewing Process at That Organization, When (and If) They Have Definitely Said They Want You

By the end of the interviewing process I mean the point when the employer says, or thinks, "We've got to get this person!" That may be at the end of the first (and therefore the last) interview, or it may be at the end of a whole series of interviews, often with different people within the same company or organization, or with a whole bunch of them all at once. Remember that throughout the interview and negotiating process you are always being evaluated, so use the same positive demeanor in the negotiating process as you did in the interview.

But assuming things are going favorably for you—whether after the first, or second, or third, or fourth interview—*if you like them* and they increasingly like you, a job offer will be made. Then, and only then, is it time to deal with the question that is inevitably on any employer's mind: *How much is this person going to cost me?* And the question that is on your mind: *How much does this job pay?* By now you should have completed any research on salaries for this field or job title.

If the employer raises the salary question earlier—say, by asking (innocently), near the beginning of the interview, "What kind of salary are you looking for?"—you should have three responses ready.

Response #1: Your best and most tactful reply might be, "Until you've decided you definitely want me, and I've decided I definitely could help you with your tasks or projects here, I feel any discussion of salary is premature."

That will work in most cases. There are instances, however, where that doesn't work. Then you need:

Response #2: You may be face to face with an employer who asks within the first two minutes of the interview what salary you are looking for. Here you may need a backup response, such as, "I'll gladly answer that, but could you first help me understand what this job involves?"

That is a good response in most cases. But what if *that* doesn't work? Then you'll need to fall back on:

Response #3: The employer says, "I really want to know what salary you're looking for." Okay, that's that. You have to come clean. But you don't have to mention a single figure; instead you can answer in terms of *a range*. For example, "Based on my research into this field, I'm looking for a salary in the range of $55,000 to $65,000 a year, but I am also open to hearing what the complete package would be in terms of benefits."

You'll just have to see what happens at this point. If they balk at your range, you may decide this isn't the kind of place you want to work at, for if they're inflexible in this, what else will they be inflexible about, once you take the job? You can always ask at that point what salary they have in mind, then make your decision. (Of course, you can always try postponing your decision a day or so, saying "I need a little time to think about this.")

However, all the foregoing is merely the worst-case scenario. Usually, things won't go this badly, where you feel so powerless.

In most interviews these days, the employer, alone or in a group, *will* be willing to save salary negotiation until they've finally decided they want you (and you've decided you want them). And at that point, the salary will be negotiable.

In general, it is in your best interest to *not* discuss salary until all of the following conditions have been fulfilled:

- They've gotten to know you, at your best, so they can see how you stand out above the other applicants, and therefore how you're worth more than they would pay *them*.
- You've gotten to know them, as completely as you can, so you can tell if this really is a place where you want to work.
- You've found out exactly what the job entails.
- They've had a chance to find out how well you match their job requirements.
- You're in the final interview at that place, for that job.
- You've decided *I really would like to work here.*
- They've conveyed to you their feelings, such as, "Well, that's good, because we want you." Or better yet:
- They've conveyed the feeling *We've got to have you.*
- If you'd prefer this be put in the form of a diagram, here it is:

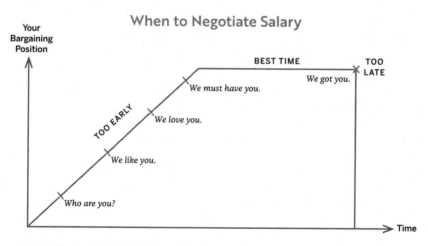

When to Negotiate Salary

Reprinted by permission of Paul Hellman, author of *Ready, Aim, You're Hired!* and president of Express Potential (www.expresspotential.com). All rights reserved.

It all boils down to this: if you really shine during the hiring interview, they may—at the end—offer you a higher salary than they originally had in mind when the interview started. Particularly when the interview has gone so well that they're now *determined* to secure you as an employee.

THE THIRD SECRET OF SALARY NEGOTIATION

During Salary Discussion, Never Be the First One to Mention a Salary Figure

In case you haven't already figured this out, you should not be the first person to mention salary. The employer gets to start this conversation.

Why? Nobody knows. But it has been observed over the years that where the goals are opposite, as in this case—you are trying to get the employer to pay the most they can, and the employer is trying to pay the least they can—whoever mentions the specific point of negotiation first generally loses.

Inexperienced employer/interviewers often don't know this strange rule. But experienced ones are very aware of it. That's why they will try to get you to mention a figure first, by asking you some innocent-sounding question, like: "What kind of salary are you looking for?"

Well, how kind of them to ask me what I want—you may be thinking. No, no, no. Kindness has nothing to do with it. They are hoping you will be the first to mention a figure, because they've learned this lesson from ten thousand interviews in the past.

Accordingly, if they ask you to be the first to name a figure, the simple countermove you should have at the ready is "Well, I have researched typical salaries in this field, but I'm sure you have a general figure in mind."

THE FOURTH SECRET OF SALARY NEGOTIATION

Research the Range That the Employer Likely Has in Mind, and Then Define an Interrelated Range for Yourself, Relative to the Employer's Range

Back when you completed the Flower Exercise, you probably established a salary range that fit your needs and the position you're seeking. (You did, didn't you? If not, go back and complete the Salary Petal exercises that begin on page 160.) What you want, in your research, is not just one salary figure. As you may recall, you want *a range*: a range defined by what's the least the employer may offer you, and what's the most the employer may be willing to pay to get you. This is where online research can assist with the general salary ranges in various fields.

One way to think about the position you're seeking is to consider what level of skill or expertise you bring to it. Many employers group their salaries according to whether the person in the role is new (a learner), mid-range (a do-er who can jump into the role with little training) or a leader (someone who can train others). The salary ranges are generally adjusted based on where the individual falls in that range. So, as you interview for a position, what category do you think you're in? If you believe you are at a do-er level, then you should mention your ability to jump right in and therefore qualify for a mid-range salary. On the other hand, if you are a beginner and will need training, you need to keep that in mind when you discuss salaries.

Note: In your salary research, note that most governmental agencies have civil service positions paralleling those in private industry—and government job descriptions and pay ranges are available to the public. You can find most government salary ranges online at USAJobs.gov.

When this is all done, if you want to be a true expert at this game, then you're going to have to do a little bit of math here.

Suppose you guess that the employer's range for the kind of job you're seeking is $36,000 to $47,000. Before you go in for the interview, you figure out an asking range for yourself that you're going to use when and if the interview gets to the salary negotiation part. This asking range is clever, in that it should hook in just below that employer's maximum and go up from there. This diagram shows you how this works:

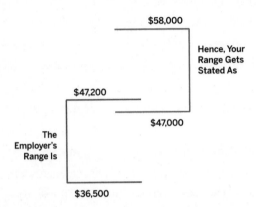

$58,000

Hence, Your
Range Gets
Stated As

$47,200

$47,000

The
Employer's
Range Is

$36,500

So when the employer has stated a figure (probably around their lowest—in this case $36,000), you will be ready to respond with something along these lines: "I understand, of course, the constraints under which all organizations are operating these days, but I am confident that my productivity is going to be such that it will justify a salary"—and here you mention your range, with your bottom figure starting just below the top of their range and going up from there—"in the range of $45,000 to $55,000."

It will help a lot during this discussion if you are prepared to show the ways you will make money or save money for that organization, justifying precisely this higher salary you are asking for. Even if they accept your offer at the bottom of your range, you are still near the top figure they're willing to pay.

Just keep in mind that this is risky. Yes, it takes some work. And confidence in your ability to do the job well.

What if, after all the trouble you've gone to, this just doesn't work? At least, at that place. Say, the employer has a ceiling they have to work with, it's below what you're asking, and you are unwilling to lower your definition of what you're worth.

Daniel Porot, that European jobs expert, suggests that if you're dying to work there but they cannot afford the salary you need and deserve, you might consider offering them part of your time.

If you need, and believe you deserve, say, $50,000 annually, but they can only afford $30,000, you might consider offering them three days a week of your time for that $30,000 (30/50 = 3/5 of a five-day workweek). This leaves you free to take work elsewhere during those other two days. You will, of course, determine to produce so much work during the three days per week you are there that they will be ecstatic about this bargain—won't you?

Of course, the bottom line is: do you want the job even if they can't match your desired salary? You are the only one who knows this, and you will have to decide if the job is worth the potential financial sacrifice. Keep in mind other factors like potential promotions in the future, the benefits you'll receive, and the security of having a job when the economy might be volatile.

THE FIFTH SECRET OF SALARY NEGOTIATION
Consider the Benefits and Know How to Bring the Salary Negotiation to a Close; Don't Leave It Hanging

Salary negotiation with this employer is not finished until you've addressed more than salary. Unless you're an independent contractor, you want to talk about so-called fringe benefits. All those benefits mentioned earlier—such as life insurance, health benefits or health plans, vacation or holiday time, and retirement programs—typically add anywhere from 15 to 28 percent to many workers' salaries. That is to say, if an employee receives a $4,000 salary per month, the fringe benefits are worth another $600 to $1,120 per month.

So before you walk into an interview you should decide what benefits are particularly important to you. The good news, of course, is that you already figured this out when you did the Flower Exercise and included your needed benefits on your Salary Petal. (Oh, you didn't? Well go back again.) Then, after the basic salary discussion is settled, you can go on to ask them what benefits they offer there. If you've given this any thought beforehand, you should have already decided which benefits are most important to you and be ready to fight for *those*.

And when all this is done—the discussion of the job, the finding out if they like you and if you like them, the salary negotiation, and the concluding discussion of benefits—then you want to get everything they're offering summarized, *in writing*. Believe me, you do. In writing, or typed, and *signed*.

Many executives unfortunately "forget" what they told you during the hiring interview, or even deny they ever said such a thing. This shouldn't happen, but it does.

Sometimes they honestly forget what they said. Other times, of course, they're playing a game. Or their successor is, who may disown any *unwritten* promises you claim were made to you at the time of hiring. They may respond, "I don't know what caused them to say that to you, but they clearly exceeded their authority, and of course we can't be held to that."

I repeat: get it all in writing. And signed. It's called a letter of agreement—or an employment contract. If it is a small employer (ten or fewer employees), they may not know how to draw one up. Just put the search term "sample letter of agreement between employer and employee" into your favorite search engine, and you'll get lots of free examples. I particularly like the one from Inc.com. You or the employer can write this up. Then they can sign it.

You have every right to ask for this. If they refuse to give it to you, *beware*.

Remember, job hunting always involves luck, to some degree. But with a little bit of luck, a lot of hard work, and determination on your part, the instructions and advice in this book should work for you.

I do not think there is any thrill
that can go through the human heart
like that felt by the inventor
as he sees some creation of the brain
unfolding to success . . .
Such emotions make a man forget
food, sleep, friends, love, everything.

—NIKOLA TESLA

CHAPTER 11

HOW TO START YOUR OWN BUSINESS

If your job hunt isn't going well, the idea may occur to you in some moment of desperation: *maybe I should stop trying to find jobs where I work for someone else. Maybe I should start my own business.*

Some people have always wished they didn't have to work for someone else but could be their own boss. According to some surveys, up to 80 percent of all workers toy with this idea at some point in their lives. People dream. Maybe your dream is: *I want to create a website where I can teach people how to "go green," and help preserve the environment.* Or maybe your dream is: *I want to create and sell jewelry.* Or maybe: *I want to start my own security service.* Or maybe: *I want to run my own bake shop, where I can sell my own homemade bread and pies.* Or: *run a bed-and-breakfast place.* Or: *grow lavender, and sell soap and perfume made from it.* Or: *be a consultant to people who need my expertise, gathered in the business world over many years.* Or: *sell real estate.* Stuff like that.

Or maybe you don't have a dream. All you know is you don't want to work for someone else; you want to be your own boss. And you're open to any and all suggestions.

Is It as Difficult as We Are So Often Told?

Sometimes taking this step is easy. Sometimes it is super difficult. Let's consider a couple of real case histories.

Case History #1

Alan was trained as a physical therapist and had no difficulty finding employment at local hospitals. But he didn't like being indoors all the time; he longed for a way to work outside. He considered his assets: he was a skilled photographer and a good furniture refinisher, and he loved thrift shops and flea markets. He also liked working with his hands. He particularly liked a certain period of furniture and quickly taught himself to become an expert. He learned how much fans of that furniture would pay for pieces from that period. He began scouring local thrift shops, flea markets, estate sales, and the internet, looking for pieces that were for sale at a price below their true worth. He bought the pieces, took them to his garage, which he had converted into a workshop, and refinished them so they looked beautiful. He then took attractive photos of them and posted the photos on eBay, Etsy, Nextdoor, and other sites. He became known for his expertise, and people soon bought up anything he posted online. He kept a list of his repeat customers, often sending them a notice of a new offering before publicly announcing it. He is making a great profit from his work—and he is outdoors most of the time.

Case History #2

Beth was a stay-at-home parent and former librarian who liked to keep her research skills fresh by volunteering at a local library. She enjoyed helping the patrons find resources for their various projects. When her mother became seriously ill, she no longer had time to volunteer, but watching an episode of the TV show *Finding Your Roots* inspired her to start a new project: researching her mother's family tree. She set up accounts with several genealogy sites and quickly found the process of uncovering family information fascinating. She created an extensive and attractive family tree scrapbook with legal records, photos, newspaper clippings, and other items she found online, tracing her mother's family back to the 1700s. She left the scrapbook in her mother's room at the medical facility and a few days later one of the nurses approached her and inquired about the scrapbook. The nurse wanted to know if she would create a similar project for her mother and father. Word spread, and soon Beth had a new part-time "job" she could blend in with her family responsibilities. She purchased some ancestry software, joined the National Genealogical Society, and started taking online courses in genealogy. She hopes to become a certified genealogist at some point and is marketing her business through presentations at her library and elsewhere. She likes that she can control the pace and timing of her work, and that she will be able to grow her business when her family responsibilities are reduced.

Case History #3

Maria worked in a corporate human resources office for ten years, interviewing candidates for jobs, managing benefits packages, and ensuring that all the paperwork in the hiring process was properly managed and recorded. She found that her energy would rise when she was interviewing candidates for opportunities in the company; her energy fell when she filled out all the forms and paperwork connected with the hiring process. Her company offered training courses, and when she found one on career coaching, she signed up. Throughout the course, she found herself thinking, "I could do this," but she was reluctant to give up her income and benefits. So she started small: she created a website and offered coaching sessions on Saturday mornings. She ran a few coaching groups at her church, and from those groups she started working with just a client or two. In the meantime, she created a name for her new business and wrote a guide to resume writing, which she offered for free to anyone who gave her their email address through her website. She started a blog on her website and began accepting speaking opportunities in her community. As she developed her business, she decided to focus exclusively on helping clients craft their "marketing package" for the job search. When she started getting more clients than she could handle, she raised her rates, thinking that would discourage people. But it didn't, and with the new higher rates she was receiving she could seriously consider leaving her full-time job. After two years, she took the plunge and now works with clients from all over the world, helping them shape their marketing packages, including their resumes and online presence. She doesn't make the same income she did in her corporate job, but she loves the freedom and flexibility, and because she doesn't have to go to an office every day, she is saving money on gas mileage, professional clothing, lunches, and child care.

These are real-life stories; I changed only the names to protect their privacy.

You will notice, right away, some things that are common to these case histories:

- These people didn't need a whole lot of **money** to launch their own business.
- They did have to do **research**, sometimes plenty of it, to make it work.
- All three of them used the **internet** to make their product, service, or expertise known.
- None of them went down the **traditional paths** that people used to go down when considering self-employment, such as buying a franchise, or being sucked in by one of those heavily advertised "work at home" projects that used to sound appetizing to the unwary. Being self-employed wears quite a different face these days, compared to what it used to.

So, now you're reading this chapter, and you're weighing the idea of going out on your own, starting your own business, being your own boss. Where do you start?

When You Have No Idea What Business You Want to Go Into

Let's assume you want to be your own boss, but you have no idea what kind of business you want to have. How do you start? There are four steps that any thorough, intelligent person should faithfully follow: Write. Read. Explore. Get feedback.

Write

1. Begin with the Flower Exercise in this book. Don't just read it. *Do it!* As I repeat throughout this book, Who precedes What. First get a clearer picture of **who** you are, before you try to decide **what** you want to do. Ultimately, **what** you decide to do should flow from **who** you are. When done, look at your whole Flower Diagram and see if any or all of the petals give you an idea for your own business.

2. On a blank sheet of paper, make a list of your ideas. Use this same piece of paper for any ideas that come to you as you do the rest of these steps. You want it all on one page. (Something to do with the right side of your brain, and intuition.)

3. Then write your resume, if you haven't already, and run it through the resume rubric on pages 235–236 to make sure you've created the best resume for your field. When you're done, read through it and see if anything there gives you an idea for a business of your own. It may be that you have been doing it for years—but in the employ of someone else. But now you're thinking about doing this kind of work for yourself, whether it be as an independent accountant, massage therapist, business consultant, repair person,

dance instructor, home decorator, home care nurse, craftsperson, or producer or seller of some kind of product or service. If so, add your great idea to that piece of paper.

4. If nothing inspires you, try Daniel Pink's prescription:
   - Make a list of five things you are good at.
   - Then make a second list of five things you love to do.
   - Then make a third list of where the first two lists overlap.
   - Read that list. Ask yourself, "Will anyone pay me to do these things?"[30]

5. If you're dying to be your own boss, but still have no idea what business to go into, try this: go to O*NET (www.onetonline.org). Click Find Occupations and in the drop-down menu, Career Cluster. Click that drop-down and see if any cluster title appeals to you. Jot it down on that piece of paper. Then click Advanced Search and in that drop-down, Browse by O*NET Data. You will see ten subheadings: Abilities, Interests, Knowledge, Skills, Work Activities, Work Context, Work Styles, Work Values, Skills Search, and Tools and Technology. Click each in turn and jot down anything attractive or interesting on that piece of paper.

Read

Hopefully, from all this thinking and writing, you will have some new ideas. It will be nice if you see the possibilities of three different business ventures. But if there's one of the three that you would really enjoy doing, and you feel passionate about it, then explore that one first. Second. And third!

Next, read up on all the virtues and perils of running your own business. Look before you leap! The internet has tons of stuff about this. For example:

Free Agent Nation

Dan Pink Interview: "Free Nation" Evolves

www.workforce.com/articles dan-pink-interview-free-agent
-nation-evolves

Daniel Pink, before he became famous for such books as *Drive* and *To Sell Is Human*, was the first to call attention to how many people were refusing to work for any employer. He defined them as free agents. His classic book was *Free Agent Nation*. His basic thesis: Self-employment has become a broader concept than it was in another age. The concept now includes not only those who own their own business but also free agents: independent contractors who work for several clients; temps and contract employees who work each day through temporary agencies; limited-time-frame workers who work for only a set time, as on a project, then move on to another company; consultants; and so on. This is a fascinating article to help you decide whether you want to be a "free agent."

Small Business Administration

www.sba.gov
The SBA is a federal program that was established to help start, manage, and grow small businesses. Lots of useful articles and advice are online here.

Business Owner's Toolkit

www.bizfilings.com/toolkit
Yikes, there is a lot of information here for the small business owner. Everything about your business: starting, planning, financing, marketing, hiring, managing, getting government contracts, taxes— all that stuff, including any forms you will need to fill out.

The Business Owners' Idea Café

www.businessownersideacafe.com/starting_business/index.php
Great, fun site for the small business owner. Lots of practical advice, and they have a Facebook site as well.

Nolo's Running Your Small Business

www.nolo.com/legal-encyclopedia/business-llcs-corporations
Lots of practical nitty-gritty stuff here: laws, forms, contracts, and resources needed if you start your own business.

Home Businesses

A Home-Based Business Online (AHBBO) Ezine—Archives
www.ahbbo.com/archives.html
To help you make your own home business succeed, this is a great site, with lots of information for you. There are hundreds of articles here. Just be careful: "home business" opportunities are filled with scams. Always do your research first: start with the Better Business Bureau's scam tracker (www.bbb.org/scamtracker/us) and use Google to further investigate before you invest any money.

Explore

Let's hope that now you have some idea for starting your own business. You likely know that a lot of start-ups, online and off, don't make it. You want to avoid this happening to you. You want to interview others who have started the same kind of business so you don't make the same mistakes they did. Your exploring, then, should have three steps, summarized by this simple formula:

$$A - B = C$$

To explain:

You must find out what skills, knowledge, or experience it takes to make this kind of business idea work, by interviewing several business owners. This is List **A**.

You prepare this list by first writing out in as much detail as you can just exactly what kind of business you are thinking about starting. Do you want to be a freelance writer, or a craftsperson, or a consultant, independent screenwriter, copywriter, digital artist, songwriter, photographer, illustrator, interior designer, videographer, filmmaker, counselor, therapist, plumber, electrician, agent, soap maker, bicycle repairer, public speaker, or something else?

Then you interview people already doing the kind of work you'd like to do. You should approach this exploration after finding at least three names. Find them through your favorite internet search engine or from LinkedIn, Yelp, the chamber of commerce, or various smartphone apps. When you talk to these people, you explain that you're exploring the possibility of starting your own business, similar to theirs, and ask if they would be willing to share something of their own history. You ask them what skills, knowledge, or experience they think are necessary to making this kind of business successful.

These days, everyone's preference is to do such interviewing by email or Zoom. I think this is a big mistake. Face to face is preferable, in every case. Try businesspeople in a city that's an hour's drive away. They are not as likely to see you as a potential competitor, unless you're going to compete with each other head-to-head on the internet. You want them first of all to tell you something about:

- The history of their business
- What they enjoy most about it
- How they got started
- What kinds of challenges they encountered
- What kinds of mistakes they made

- What they would do differently if they were starting again
- What they wish someone had told them when they were starting

Face-to-face, they are more likely to tell you more about the challenges they ran into, the obstacles and pitfalls they encountered, than they ever would in an email; and you want this information—believe me, you do—so that you can avoid making the same missteps if you decide to start a similar business. (No need for you to step on the same land mines that they did.)

You also want them to help you compile a list of the necessary skills, knowledge, and experience they think are essential for the type of business they're doing and you're thinking of doing.

You can also watch YouTube interviews of entrepreneurs where they tell how they began their businesses or read the biographies of famous entrepreneurs to learn more about the challenges they faced in the process of creating their businesses. Sometimes those stories can be very educational—and inspiring.

Keep in mind that most small businesses will require certain skills, such as:

- A talent, product, or service to sell
- A marketing or sales plan
- A website or other online presence
- An analysis of potential customers or clients
- An accounting system
- A payroll or employment plan if you plan to hire other people

When you have a list you're satisfied with, name it List **A**.

Now you're going to make List **B**. Back at home, sit down and inventory your own skills, knowledge, and experience, doing the inventory of who you are described in chapter 6, the Flower Exercise. Take a look at all the skills others have told you are needed for the work you want to do and what skills you currently have. On List **A**, cross off the items that you can do yourself. Anything you will need help with becomes List **C**.

"C" is by definition a list of the skills or knowledge that you don't have, but must find—either by taking courses yourself, or by hiring someone with those skills, or by getting a friend or family member who has those skills to volunteer to help you for a while.

For example, if your investigation revealed that it takes good accounting practices in order to turn a profit, and you don't know a thing about accounting, you now know enough to go out and hire a part-time accountant immediately—or, if you absolutely have no money, maybe you can talk an accountant friend of yours into giving you some volunteer time for a while.

Let's look at a start-up example.

After working in higher education administration for over a decade, Julia decided to switch to teaching gifted high school students. While she enjoyed her work, she became frustrated with the bureaucracy of the public school system and wanted an escape from the daily grind. She realized that one of the activities she enjoyed most was helping her gifted students decide which college to attend. Her background in higher education made her particularly qualified to understand the differences between the many colleges and universities her students were exploring. She decided to create her own college counseling business. She quickly learned that she couldn't do it as a side business and needed to take the leap into a full-time endeavor. But to do this successfully, she had to develop new skills and knowledge as well as learn a lot about business management and the college counseling business. Julia made several decisions as she developed her business. She chose to learn as much as she could about everything so that she didn't need to spend money on "experts." For instance, she manages her billing and accounting on an accounting software package for home businesses, using an accountant only for her taxes. She also decided to market her business primarily through word of mouth and her website, saving money on hiring a publicist or paying for flyers or online advertisements. Finally, she even learned how to set up her own website. Here's how her chart looks:

A − B = C

Skills, Knowledge, and Traits Needed to Run This Kind of Business Successfully	Skills, Knowledge, and Traits That I Have	Skills, Knowledge, and Traits Needed That I Need to Acquire or Hire Someone Else to Do
Thorough knowledge of higher education and the college admissions process	YES	
Thorough knowledge of financial aid systems	YES	
Strong relationships with college admissions officers and other representatives	YES	
Coaching and counseling skills with adolescents, including understanding of family dynamics in the college selection process	YES	
Entrepreneurial traits: hardworking, self-promoting, social, and so on	ACQUIRED	Already a hard worker, but as an introvert had to develop more self-promotion skills and learn to be more social at events to meet more people.
Certification as an Education Planner	ACQUIRED	Studied and trained before taking certification exam.
Ability to travel to at least fifteen colleges a year to maintain certification	YES	
Accounting: bookkeeping, billing, and taxes	SOME	Taught self to use an accounting software program for home businesses, but sends taxes to accountant.
Website design and upkeep	ACQUIRED	Taught self to design a website.
Ability to use Skype and other online communication systems	ACQUIRED	Majority of appointments are through internet, so taught self to use most common systems, including an online scheduling calendar system.
Computer research skills, including purchasing and using databases and Excel programs	ACQUIRED	Learned which research databases are needed to run business. Purchased and learned to use them effectively.

As you can see, by taking the time to learn a lot about her business, Julia is able to run it almost independently. However, all of her do-it-yourself expertise means that she invested a lot of time in setting up everything she needed for her business. It could be that as her business grows and she earns more income she will want to hire others to help with the tasks related to managing the business, so that she can devote more time to client services.

You might choose to hire someone to do many of those tasks for your business from the beginning. It's a matter of knowing what your strengths are, whether you have the time or ability to learn a lot of new tasks (like website design), and how you want to focus your attention when you develop your business.

Get Feedback

So: are you cut out for this sort of thing? Only you can answer that, in your innermost thoughts. But you can get some help.

Take seriously the feedback you received when speaking to other business owners. Don't gloss over negative observations you received; examine them and decide whether they apply to you.

Read as much as you can about entrepreneurship. If you like traditional business planning, there are a ton of books on the market about starting and managing your business. One worth checking out, if you're planning to sell a service, is Michael Port's *Book Yourself Solid* (https://www.bookyourselfsolid.com/). If you're a creative type, and traditional business planning wears you out, check out The Right-Brain Business Plan by Jennifer Lee (https://www.rightbrainbusinessplan.com/).

If you have a spouse or partner, tell them what you're up to, ask their opinion, explore whether this is going to require sacrifices from them (not just you), and find out how they feel about that. If your life is shared with them, and vice versa, you have no right to make this decision unilaterally, all by yourself. They should be part of the whole journey, not just at the end when your mind is already made up. You have a responsibility to make them full partners in any decision you're facing. Love demands it!

If, after all this exploration and feedback, you decide you still want to create your own job by starting this kind of business, go ahead and try—no matter what your well-meaning but cautious friends or family may say. They love you, they're concerned for you, and you should thank them for that; but come on, you have only one life here on this Earth, and that life is yours to say how it will be spent, or not spent. Parents, children, well-meaning friends, and the rest can give loving advice, but in the end they get no vote. Only you and your partner do.

Just remember, it takes a lot of guts to try ANYTHING new (to you) in today's roller coaster economy. It's easier, however, if you keep these things in mind:

- There is always some risk in trying something new. Your goal, I hope, is not to avoid risk—there is no way to do that—but to make sure ahead of time that the risks are manageable.

- As we have seen, you find this out before you start, by first talking to others who have already done what you are thinking of doing; then you evaluate whether you still want to go ahead and try it.

- Before you start, have a plan B laid out for what you will do if it doesn't work out; that is, know where you are going to go next. Don't wait! Write it out, now: *This is what I'm going to do, if this doesn't work out.*

The decision to run your own business is not one to be made lightly. It can involve many more hours, greater risks, and much harder work than working for someone else, but it also can provide a greater chance for personal fulfillment and monetary gain. Knowing yourself—your skills, knowledge, interests, and values—is imperative for success in your own business, so the Parachute system will work just as well whether you are self-employed or not.

CONCLUSION
YOU DID IT!

It's hard to argue with success, and the millions of copies sold of this book are a testament to its value in the job search process. A system like this only works, though, if you do the work and follow it. As I hope you have learned, this is not a book you can just read: it's really a workbook disguised as a book. The Parachute System requires a commitment of both time and energy, but there's also a spark of magic involved. And that magic is you and what you bring to the process.

- Were you able to create your Flower Exercise, and did you gain new insights or receive more clarity on yourself and your plans?
- Did you discover new career fields to pursue, put the internet to work in your search, or create new or better stories for your interviews or conversations?
- Even better, did using this system lead you to a new job, a better job, or whatever you were seeking?

My favorite hobby, aside from writing, is playing the guitar. A friend of mine wrote a wonderful song, and I had the occasion to play it for him. I was nervous playing it in front of him: afraid I wouldn't play it well or do it justice. I started playing the opening chords, apologizing for not performing it exactly the way he would. He stopped me cold, put his hand on my shoulder and said, "It's yours now, Kate. Make it your own."

Well, friends, that's how I feel about this Parachute System. It needs to become a part of you that you can adjust and use in whatever way is helpful. That's where the magic comes in: where you "make it your own." Then you can truly succeed in the job market and the job search. You will have made your career your own and succeeded on your own terms.

Safe journeys and safe landings.

—Katharine "Kate" Brooks

THE ORANGE PAGES
FINDING YOUR
MISSION IN LIFE

———

From the Original Writings of Richard N. Bolles

There are those who think that belief in God is just some fairy tale that humankind invented, to fortify themselves against the darkness. Naturally, therefore, they think that anyone who says they believe in God these days is demonstrably feebleminded, or a pathetic child who has never grown up intellectually.

Given this view, they are horrified to find a section on faith or religion in a job-hunting book. They have written to me and said so.

Well, here it is, anyway.

That's because the percentage of the world's population that says they don't believe there is a God averages less than 18 percent (it varies from country to country: here in the US the figure is 11 percent, while in Canada that figure is 19 to 30 percent). Still, that leaves us with an overwhelming percentage of the US population (89 percent) believing in God.[31] And my more than ten million readers are a pretty typical cross section of this country.

A comprehensive demographic study of more than 230 countries and territories conducted by the Pew Research Center's Forum on Religion & Public Life estimated that there are 6.1 billion religiously affiliated adults and children around the globe, representing 84 percent of the 2015 world population of 7.3 billion.

That demographic study—based on analysis of more than 2,500 censuses, surveys, and population registers—found there are 2.3 billion Christians (31 percent of the world's population) in the world, 1.8 billion Muslims (24 percent), 1.1 billion Hindus (15 percent), nearly 500 million Buddhists (7 percent), and 14.6 million Jews (0.2 percent) as of 2015. (The most recent year for which we have figures.)

This book is used by ten million readers in twenty-six countries around the world. So, leaving out a section that 84 percent of my readers worldwide might be interested in, and helped by, in order to please just 16 percent of my readers, seems to me insane.

Indeed, according to the Pew Research Center, over 75 percent of the world's population lives in areas with severe religious restrictions. That's restrictions against Muslims, Jews, Christians, and other religions. According to the United States Department of State, Christians in more than sixty countries face persecution from their governments or surrounding neighbors simply because of their belief in Jesus Christ.

"Christians . . . have now experienced the full impact of the world's hostility and indifference. We are staggered and alarmed by the extent of it, and dumb-founded by its partial success. Numerically we are drastically reduced, proportion-ately to the enormously increased population, and we shall probably continue in that way; perhaps with even greater numerical reductions. . . . No doubt we survive as a minority but by no means as a pitiful or contemptible minority. We die daily because of our own weakness and unworthiness, yet we live, nevertheless because God is with us. . . . Modern man relies on nothing that will not some day be taken away from him. Those who are utterly committed to the Christian faith rely in the last resort on nothing that could possibly be taken away. That is why the Church, contrary to all appearances, is stronger than the world. And that is why it is the duty of Christians to be sympathetic, compassionate, and merciful in their dealings with their estranged brethren."[32]

I do not want to add to that feeling by keeping silent. Faith is welcome in this book.

As I started writing this section, I toyed at first with the idea of following what might be described as an "all-paths" approach to religion: trying to stay as gen-eral and nonspecific as I could. But, after much thought, I decided not to try that. This, because I have read many other writers who tried, and I felt the approach failed miserably. An "all-paths" approach to religion ends up being a "no-paths" approach, just as a woman or man who tries to please everyone ends up pleasing no one. It is the old story of the "universal" versus the "particular."

Those of us who do career counseling could predict, ahead of time, that trying to stay universal is not likely to be helpful, in writing about faith. We know well from our own field that truly helpful career counseling depends upon defining the particularity or uniqueness of each person we try to help. No employer wants to know what you have in common with everyone else. He or she wants to know what makes you unique and individual. As I have argued throughout this book, the inventory of your uniqueness or *particularity* is crucial if you are ever to find meaningful work.

This particularity invades *everything* a person does; it is not suddenly "jetti-sonable" when he or she turns to matters of faith. Therefore, when I or anyone else writes about faith I believe we must write out of our own particularity— which *starts*, in my case, with the fact that I write, and think, and breathe as a Christian—as you might expect from the fact that I was an ordained Episcopalian minister for many years. Understandably, then, this chapter speaks from a Christian perspective. I want you to be aware of that, at the outset. Balanced against this is the fact that I have always been acutely sensitive to the fact that this is a pluralistic society in which we live, and that I in particular owe a great deal to my readers who have religious convictions quite different from my own. It has turned out that the people who work or have worked here in my office with me, over the years, have been predominantly of other faiths.

Furthermore, *Parachute*'s more than ten million readers have included not only Christians of every variety and persuasion, Christian Scientists, Jews, Hindus, Buddhists, and adherents of Islam, but also believers in "new age" religions, secularists, humanists, agnostics, atheists, and many others. I have therefore tried to be very courteous toward the feelings of all my readers, *while at the same time* counting on them to translate my Christian thought-forms into their own. This ability to thus translate is the indispensable sine qua non of anyone who wants to communicate helpfully with others in this pluralistic society of ours.

In the Judeo-Christian tradition from which I come, one of the indignant biblical questions was, "Has God forgotten to be gracious?" The answer was a clear "No." I think it is important *for all of us* also to seek the same goal. I have therefore labored to make this chapter gracious as well as thought provoking.

Turning Point

For many of us, the job hunt offers a chance to make some fundamental changes in our whole life. It marks a turning point in how we live our life.

It gives us a chance to ponder and reflect, to extend our mental horizons, to go deeper into the subsoil of our soul.

It gives us a chance to wrestle with the question, "Why am I here on Earth?" We don't want to feel that we are just another grain of sand lying on the beach called humanity, unnumbered and lost in the billions of other human beings.

We want to do more than plod through life, going to work, coming home from work. We want to find that special joy "that no one can take from us," which comes from having a sense of Mission in our life.

We want to feel we were put here on Earth for some special purpose, to do some unique work that only we can accomplish.

We want to know what our Mission is.

The Meaning of the Word *Mission*

When used with respect to our life and work, *Mission* has always been a religious concept, from beginning to end. It is defined by *Webster's* as "a continuing task or responsibility that one is destined or fitted to do or specially called upon to undertake," and historically has had two major synonyms: *Calling* and *Vocation*. These, of course, are the same word in two different languages, English and Latin. Both imply God. To be given a Vocation or Calling implies *Someone who calls*. To have a Destiny implies *Someone who determined the destination for us*. Thus, the concept of Mission lands us inevitably in the lap of God, before we have hardly begun.

I emphasize this, because there is an increasing trend in our culture to try to speak about religious subjects without reference to God. This is true of "spirituality," "soul," and "Mission," in particular. More and more books talk about Mission as though it were simply "a purpose you choose for your own life, by identifying your enthusiasms."

This attempt to obliterate all reference to God from the originally religious concept of Mission is particularly ironic because the proposed substitute word—enthusiasms—is derived from two Greek words, *en theos*, and means "God in us."

In the midst of this increasingly secular culture, we find an oasis that—along with athletics—is very hospitable toward belief in God. That oasis is *job hunting*. Most of the leaders who have evolved creative job-hunting ideas were—from the beginning—people who believed firmly in God, and said so: Sidney Fine, Bernard Haldane, John Crystal, Arthur and Marie Kirn, Arthur Miller, Tom and Ellie Jackson, Ralph Matson, and of course myself.

I mentioned at the beginning of this appendix that 89 percent of us in the US believe in God. According to the Gallup Organization, 90 percent of us pray, 88 percent of us believe God loves us, and 33 percent of us report that we have had a life-changing religious experience.

However, it is not clear that we have made much connection between our belief in God and our work. Often our spiritual beliefs and our attitude toward our work live in separate mental ghettos, within our mind.

A dialogue between these two *is* opened up inside our head, and heart, when we are out of work. Unemployment gives us a chance to contemplate why we are here on Earth, and what our Calling, Vocation, or Mission is, uniquely, for each of us.

Unemployment becomes *life transition*, when we can't find a job doing the same work we've always done. Since we have to rethink one thing, many of us elect to rethink *everything*.

Something awakens within us. Call it *yearning*. Call it *hope*. We come to realize the dream we dreamed has never died. And we go back to get it. We decide to resume our search . . . for the life we know within our heart that we were meant to live.

Now we have a chance to marry our work and our religious beliefs, to talk about Calling, and Vocation, and Mission in life—to think out why we are here, and what plans God has for us.

That's why a period of unemployment can absolutely change our life.

The Secret to Finding Your Mission in Life: Taking It in Stages

I will explain the steps toward finding your Mission in life that I have learned in all my years on Earth. Just remember two things. First, I speak from a lifelong Christian perspective, and trust you to translate this into your own thought-forms.

Second, I know that these steps are not the only Way. Many people have discovered their Mission by taking other paths. And you may, too. But hopefully what I have to say may shed some light upon whatever path you take.

I have learned that if you want to figure out what your Mission in life is, it will likely take some time. It is not a *problem* to be solved in a day and a night. It is a *learning process* that has steps to it, much like the process by which we all learned to eat. As a baby, we did not tackle adult food right off. As we all recall, there were three stages: first there had to be the mother's milk or bottle, then strained baby foods, and finally—after teeth and time—the stuff that grown-ups chew. Three stages—and the two earlier stages were not to be disparaged. It was all eating, just different forms of eating—appropriate to our development at the time. But each stage had to be mastered, in turn, before the next could be approached.

There are usually three stages also to learning what your Mission in life is, and the two earlier stages are likewise not to be disparaged. It is all "Mission"—just different forms of Mission, appropriate to your development at the time. But each stage has to be mastered, in turn, before the next can be approached.

Of course, there is a sense in which you never master any of these stages, but are always growing in understanding and mastery of them, throughout your whole life here on Earth.

As it has been impressed on me by observing many people over the years (admittedly through *Christian spectacles*), it appears that the three parts to your Mission here on Earth can be defined generally as follows:

1. *Your first Mission here on Earth* is one that you share with the rest of the human race, but it is no less your individual Mission for the fact that it is shared: and it is, **to seek to stand hour by hour in the conscious presence of God, the One from whom your Mission is derived.** *The Missioner before the Mission,* is the rule. In religious language, your Mission here is: *to know God, and enjoy Him forever, and to see His hand in all His works.*

2. Second, once you have begun doing that in an earnest way, *your second Mission here on Earth* is also one that you share with the rest of the human race, but it is no less your individual Mission for the fact that it is shared: and that is, **to do what you can, moment by moment, day by day, step by step, to make this world a better place, following the leading and guidance of God's Spirit within you and around you.**

3. Third, once you have begun doing that in a serious way, *your third Mission here on Earth* is one that is uniquely yours, and that is:
   - to exercise the Talent that you particularly came to Earth to use—your greatest gift, which you most delight to use,
   - in the place(s) or setting(s) that God has caused to appeal to you the most,
   - and for those purposes that God most needs to have done in the world.

When fleshed out, and spelled out, I think you will find that there you have the definition of your Mission in life. Or, to put it another way, these are the three Missions that you have in life.

The Two Rhythms of the Dance of Mission: Unlearning, Learning, Unlearning, Learning

The distinctive characteristic of these three stages is that in each we are forced to *let* go of some fundamental assumptions that our culture has taught us about the nature of Mission. In other words, throughout this quest and at each stage we find ourselves engaged not merely in a process of *Learning*. We are also engaged in a process of *Unlearning*. Thus, we can restate the three Learnings, in terms of what we also need to *unlearn* at each stage:

- We need in the first stage to *unlearn* the idea that our Mission is primarily to keep busy *doing* something (here on Earth), and learn instead that our Mission is first of all to keep busy *being* something (here on Earth). In Christian language (and others as well), we might say that we were sent here to learn how to *be* sons of God, and daughters of God, before anything else. *"Our Father, who art in heaven. . . ."*
- In the second stage, "Being" issues into "Doing." At this stage, we need to *unlearn* the idea that everything about our Mission must be *unique* to us, and learn instead that some parts of our Mission here on Earth are *shared* by all human beings: that is, we were all sent here to bring more gratitude, more kindness, more forgiveness, and more love into the world. We share this Mission because the task is too large to be accomplished by just one individual.
- We need in the third stage to *unlearn* the idea that the part of our Mission that is truly unique, and most truly ours, is something Our Creator just *orders* us to do, without any agreement from our spirit, mind, and heart. (On the other hand, neither is it something that each of us chooses and then merely asks God to bless.) We need to learn that God so honors our free will, that He has ordained that our unique Mission be something that we have some part in choosing.

In this third stage we need also to *un*learn the idea that our unique Mission must consist of some achievement for all the world to see—and learn instead that as the stone does not always know what ripples it has caused in the pond whose surface it impacts, so neither we nor those who watch our life will always know *what we have achieved* by our life and by our Mission. *It may be* that by the grace of God we helped bring about a profound change for the better in the lives of other souls around us, but it also may be that this takes place beyond our sight, or after we have gone on. And we may never know what we have accomplished, until we see Him face to face after this life is past.

Most finally, we need to *un*learn the idea that what we have accomplished is our doing, and ours alone. It is God's Spirit breathing in us and through us that helps us do whatever we do, and so the singular first-person pronoun is never appropriate, but only the plural. Not "I accomplished this" but "*We* accomplished this, God and I, working together. . . ."

That should give you a general overview. But I would like to add some random comments on my part about each of these three Missions of ours here on Earth.

Some Random Comments About Your First Mission in Life

Your first Mission here on Earth is one that you share with the rest of the human race, but it is no less your individual Mission for the fact that it is shared: and that is, **to seek to stand hour by hour in the conscious presence of God, the One from whom your Mission is derived.** The Missioner before the Mission, is the rule. In religious language, your Mission is: to know God, and enjoy Him forever, and to see His hand in all His works.

Comment 1: How We Might Think of God

Each of us has to go about this primary Mission according to the tenets of our own particular religion. But I will speak what I know out of the context of my own particular faith, and you may perhaps translate and apply it to yours. I will speak as a Christian, who believes (passionately) that Christ is the Way and the Truth and the Life. But I also believe, with St. Peter, "that God shows no partiality, but in every nation anyone who fears Him and does what is right is acceptable to Him" (Acts 10:34–35).

Now, Jesus claimed many unique things about Himself and His Mission; but He also spoke of Himself as the great prototype for us all. He called Himself "the Son of Man," and He said, "I assure you that the man who believes in me will do the same things that I have done, yes, and he will do even greater things than these . . ." (John 14:12).

Emboldened by His identification of us with His Life and His Mission, we might want to remember how He spoke about His Life here on Earth. He put it in this context: **"I came from the Father and have come into the world; again, I am leaving the world and going to the Father"** (John 16:28).

If there is a sense in which this is, in even the faintest way, true also of our lives (and I shall say in a moment in what sense I think it is true), then instead of calling our great Creator "God" or "Father" right off, we might begin our approach to the subject of religion by referring to the One Who gave us our Mission and sent us to this planet not as "God" or "Father" but—*just to help our thinking*—as **"The One From Whom We Came and The One To Whom We Shall Return,"** when this life is done.

If our life here on Earth is to be at all like Christ's, then this is a true way to think about the One Who gave us our Mission. We are not some kind of eternal, preexistent *being*. We are creatures, who once did not exist, and then came into Being, and continue to have our Being, only at the will of our great Creator. But as creatures we are both body and soul; although we know our body was created in our mother's womb, our soul's origin is a great mystery. Where it came from, at what moment the Lord created it, is something we cannot know. It is not unreasonable to suppose, however, that the great God created our *soul* before it entered our body, and in that sense we did indeed stand before God before we were born; and He is indeed **"The One From Whom We Came and The One To Whom We Shall Return."**

Therefore, before we go searching for "what work was I sent here to do?" we need to establish—or in a truer sense *reestablish*—contact with **"The One From Whom We Came and The One To Whom We Shall Return."** Without this reaching out of the creature to the great Creator, without this reaching out of *the creature with a Mission to the One Who Gave Us That Mission*, the question, "*What is my Mission in life?*" is void and null. The *what* is rooted in the *Who*; absent the Personal, one cannot meaningfully discuss The Thing. It is like the adult who cries, "I want to get married," without giving any consideration to *who* it is they want to marry.

Comment 2: How We Might Think of Religion or Faith

In light of this larger view of our creatureliness, we can see that *religion* or *faith* is not a question of whether or not we choose to (*as it is so commonly put*) "have a relationship with God." Looking at our life in a larger context than just our life here on Earth, it becomes apparent that some sort of relationship with God is a given for us, about which we have absolutely no choice. God and we **were** and **are** related, during the time of our soul's existence before our birth and in the time of our soul's continued existence after our death. The only choice we have is what to do about

The Time in Between; that is, what we want the nature of our relationship with God to be during our time here on Earth and how that will affect the *nature* of the relationship, then, after death.

One of the corollaries of all this is that by the very act of being born into a human body, it is inevitable that we undergo a kind of *amnesia*—an amnesia that typically embraces not only our nine months in the womb, our baby years, and almost one-third of each day (sleeping), but more important any memory of our origin or our destiny. We wander on Earth as an amnesia victim. To seek after Faith, therefore, is to seek to climb back out of that amnesia. Religion or Faith is **the hard reclaiming of knowledge we once knew as a certainty**.

Comment 3: The First Obstacle to Executing This Mission

This first Mission of ours here on Earth is not the easiest of Missions, simply because it is the first. Indeed, in many ways, it is the most difficult. All we can see is that our life here on Earth is a very physical life. We eat, we drink, we sleep, we long to be held, and to hold. We inherit a physical body, with very physical appetites, we walk on the physical earth, and we acquire physical possessions. It is the most alluring of temptations, *in our amnesia*, to come up with just a *Physical* interpretation of this life: to think that the Universe is merely interested in the survival of species. Given this interpretation, the story of our individual life could be simply told: we are born, grow up, procreate, and die.

But we are ever recalled to do what we came here to do: that without rejecting the joy of the Physicalness of this life, such as the love of the blue sky and the green grass, we are to reach out beyond all this to recall and recover a *Spiritual* interpretation of our life. *Beyond* the physical and *within* the physicalness of this life, to detect a Spirit and a Person from beyond this Earth who is with us and in us—the very real and loving and awesome Presence of the great Creator from whom we came—and the One to whom we once again shall go.

Comment 4: The Second Obstacle to Executing This Mission

It is one of the conditions of our earthly amnesia and our creatureliness that, sadly enough, some very *human* and very *rebellious* part of us *likes* the idea of living in a world where we can be our own god—and therefore loves the purely Physical interpretation of life, and finds it *anguish* to relinquish it. Traditional Christian vocabulary calls this "sin" and has a lot to say about the difficulty it poses for this first part of our Mission. All who live a thoughtful life know that it is true: our greatest enemy in carrying out this first Mission of ours is indeed *our own* heart and our own rebellion.

Comment 5: Further Thoughts About What Makes Us Special and Unique

As I said earlier, many of us come to this issue of our Mission in life because we want to feel that we are unique. And what we mean by that is that we hope to discover some "specialness" intrinsic to us, which is our birthright, and which no one can take from us. What we, however, discover from a thorough exploration of this topic, is that we are indeed special—but only because God thinks us so. Our specialness and uniqueness reside in Him, and His love, rather than in anything intrinsic to our own *being*. The proper appreciation of this distinction causes our feet to carry us in the end not to the City called Pride, but to the Temple called Gratitude.

> What is religion? Religion is the service of God out of grateful love for
> what God has done for us. The Christian religion, more particularly,
> is the service of God out of grateful love for what God has done for
> us in Christ.
> —*Phillips Brooks, author of O Little Town of Bethlehem*

Comment 6: The Unconscious Doing of the Work We Came to Do

You may have *already* wrestled with this first part of your Mission here on Earth. You may not have called it that. You may have called it simply "learning to believe in God." But if you ask what your Mission is in life, this one was and is the precondition of all else that you came here to do. Absent this Mission, it is folly to talk about the rest. So, if you have been seeking faith, or seeking to strengthen your faith, you have—willy-nilly—already been about *the doing of the Mission you were given*. Born into **This Time in Between**, you have found His hand again, and reclasped it. You are therefore ready to go on with His Spirit to tackle together what you came here to do—the other parts of your Mission.

Some Random Comments About Your Second Mission in Life

Your second Mission here on Earth is also one that you share with the rest of the human race, but it is no less your individual Mission for the fact that it is shared: and that is, **to do what you can moment by moment, day by day, step by step, to make this world a better place—following the leading and guidance of God's Spirit within you and around you.**

Comment 1: The Uncomfortableness of One Step at a Time

Imagine yourself out walking in your neighborhood one night, and suddenly you find yourself surrounded by such a dense fog that you have lost your bearings and cannot find your way. Suddenly, a friend appears out of the fog, and asks you to put your hand in theirs, and they will lead you home. And you, not being able to tell where you are going, trustingly follow them, even though you can only see one step at a time. Eventually, you arrive safely home, filled with gratitude. But as you reflect upon the experience the next day, you realize how unsettling it was to have to keep walking when you could see only one step at a time, even though you had guidance you knew you could trust.

Now I have asked you to imagine all of this, because this is the essence of the second Mission to which *you* are called—and *I* am called—in this life. It is all very different than we had imagined. When the question, *"What is your Mission in life?"* is first broached, and we have put our hand in God's, as it were, we imagine that we will be taken up to *some mountaintop*, from which we can see far into the distance. And that we will hear a voice in our ear, saying, "Look, look, see that distant city? That is the goal of your Mission; that is where everything is leading, every step of your way."

But instead of the mountaintop, we find ourselves in *the valley*—wandering often in a fog. And the voice in our ear says something quite different from what we thought we would hear. It says, "Your Mission is to take one step at a time, even when you don't yet see where it all is leading, or what the Grand Plan is, or what your overall Mission in life is. Trust Me; I will lead you."

Comment 2: The Nature of This Step-by-Step Mission

As I said, in every situation in which you find yourself, you have been sent here to do whatever you can—moment by moment—that will bring more gratitude, more kindness, more forgiveness, more honesty, and more love into this world.

There are dozens of such moments every day. Moments when you stand—as it were—at a spiritual crossroads, with two ways lying before you. Such moments are typically called **"moments of decision."** It does not matter what the frame or content of each particular decision is. It all devolves, in the end, into just two roads before you, *every time*. **The one** will lead to *less* gratitude, *less* kindness, *less* forgiveness, *less* honesty, or *less* love in the world. **The other** will lead to *more* gratitude, *more* kindness, *more* forgiveness, *more* honesty, or *more* love in the world. Your Mission, each moment, is to seek to choose the latter spiritual road, rather than the former, *every time*.

Comment 3: Some Examples of This Step-by-Step Mission

I will give a few examples, so that the nature of this part of your Mission may be unmistakably clear.

You are out on the freeway in your car. Someone has gotten into the wrong lane, to the right of *your* lane, and needs to move over into the lane you are in. You *see* their need to cut in, ahead of you. **Decision time.** In your mind's eye you see two spiritual roads lying before you: the one leading to less kindness in the world (you speed up, to shut this driver out, and don't let them move over), the other leading to more kindness in the world (you let the driver cut in). **Since you know this is part of your Mission, part of the reason why you came to Earth, your calling is clear. You know which road to take, which decision to make.**

You are hard at work at your desk, when suddenly an interruption comes. The phone rings, or someone is at the door. They need something from you, a question of some of your time and attention. **Decision time.** In your mind's eye you see two spiritual roads lying before you: the one leading to less love in the world (you tell them you're just too busy to be bothered), the other leading to more love in the world (you put aside your work, decide that God may have sent this person to you, and say, "Yes, what can I do to help you?"). **Since you know this is part of your Mission, part of the reason why you came to Earth, your calling is clear. You know which road to take, which decision to make.**

Your mate does something that hurts your feelings. **Decision time.** In your mind's eye you see two spiritual roads lying before you: the one leading to less forgiveness in the world (you institute an icy silence between the two of you, and think of how you can punish them or otherwise get even), the other leading to more forgiveness in the world (you go over and take them in your arms, speak the truth about your hurt feelings, and assure them of your love). **Since you know this is part of your Mission, part of the reason why you came to Earth, your calling is clear. You know which road to take, which decision to make.**

You have not behaved at your most noble recently. And now you are face to face with someone who asks you a question about what happened. **Decision time.** In your mind's eye you see two spiritual roads lying before you: the one leading to less honesty in the world (you lie about what happened, or what you were feeling, because you fear losing their respect or their love), the other leading to more honesty in the world (you tell the truth, together with how you feel about it, in retrospect). **Since you know this is part of your Mission, part of the reason why you came to Earth, your calling is clear. You know which road to take, which decision to make.**

Comment 4: The Spectacle That Makes the Angels Laugh

It is necessary to explain this part of our Mission in some detail, because so many times you will see people wringing their hands and saying, "*I want to know what my Mission in life is,*" all the while they are cutting people off on the highway, refusing to give time to people, punishing their mate for having hurt their feelings, and lying about what they did. And it will seem to you that the angels must laugh to see this spectacle. *For these people wringing their hands*, their Mission was right there, on the freeway, in the interruption, in the hurt, and at the confrontation.

Comment 5: The Valley Versus the Mountaintop

At some point in your life your Mission may involve some grand *mountaintop experience*, where you say to yourself, "This, this, is why I came into the world. I know it. I know it." *But until then*, your Mission is here in *the valley*, and the fog, and the little callings moment by moment, day by day. More to the point, it is likely you cannot ever get to your mountaintop Mission unless you have first exercised your stewardship faithfully in the valley.

It is an ancient principle, to which Jesus alluded often, that if you don't use the information the Universe has already given you, you cannot expect it will give you any more. If you aren't being faithful in small things, how can you expect to be given charge over larger things? (Luke 16:10–12, 19:11–24). If you aren't trying to bring more gratitude, kindness, forgiveness, honesty, and love into the world each day, you can hardly expect that you will be entrusted with the Mission to help bring peace into the world or anything else large and important. If we do not live out our day-by-day Mission in the valley, we cannot expect we are yet ready for a larger *mountaintop* Mission.

Comment 6: The Importance of Not Thinking of This Mission as "Just a Training Camp"

The valley is not just a kind of "training camp." There is in your imagination even now an invisible *spiritual* mountaintop to which you may go, if you wish to see where all this is leading. And what will you see there, in the imagination of your heart, but the goal toward which all this is pointed: **that Earth might be more like heaven. That human life might be more like God's.** That is the large achievement toward which all our day-by-day Missions *in the valley* are moving. This is a *large* order, but it is accomplished by faithful attention to the doing of our great Creator's will in little things as well as in large. It is much like the building of the pyramids in Egypt, which was accomplished by the dragging of a lot of individual pieces of stone by a lot of individual men.

The valley, the fog, the going step by step, is no mere training camp. The goal is real, however large. **"Thy Kingdom come, Thy will be done, on Earth, as it is in heaven."**

Some Random Comments About Your Third Mission in Life

Your third Mission here on Earth is one that is uniquely yours, and that is:

1. To exercise the Talent that you particularly came to Earth to use—your greatest gift that you most delight to use,
2. In those place(s) or setting(s) that God has caused to appeal to you the most,
3. And for those purposes that God most needs to have done in the world.

Comment 1: Our Mission Is Already Written, "in Our Members"

It is customary, in trying to identify this part of our Mission, to advise that we should ask God, in prayer, to speak to us—and tell us plainly what our Mission is. We look for a voice in the air, a thought in our head, a dream in the night, a sign in the events of the day, to reveal this thing that is otherwise (*it is said*) completely hidden. Sometimes, from just such answered prayer, people do indeed discover what their Mission is, beyond all doubt and uncertainty.

But having to wait for the voice of God to reveal what our Mission is, is not the truest picture of our situation. St. Paul, in Romans, speaks of a law "written in our members"—and this phrase has a telling application to the question of how God reveals to each of us our unique Mission in life. Read again the definition of our third Mission (above) and you will see: the clear implication of the definition is that God has **already** revealed His will to us concerning our vocation and Mission, by causing it to be **"written in our members."** We are to begin deciphering our unique Mission by studying our Talents and skills, and more particularly which ones (or one) we most rejoice to use.

God actually has written His will *twice* in our members: *first in the Talents* that He lodged there, and second *in His guidance of our heart*, as to which Talent gives us the greatest pleasure from its exercise (**it is usually the one that, when we use it, causes us to lose all sense of time**).

Even as the anthropologist can examine ancient inscriptions, and divine from them the daily life of a long-lost people, so we by examining **our Talents** and **our heart** can *more often than we dream* divine the Will of the Living God. For true it is, our Mission is not something He will reveal; it is something He **has already** revealed. It is not to be found written in the sky; it is to be found written in our members.

Comment 2: Career Counseling—We Need You

Arguably, our first two Missions in life could be learned from religion alone—without any reference whatsoever to career counseling, the subject of this book. Why, then, should career counseling claim that this question about our Mission in life is its proper concern, *in any way*?

It is when we come to this third Mission, which hinges so crucially on the question of our Talents, skills, and gifts, that we see the answer. If you've read the body of this book, before turning to this section, then you know without my even saying it, how much the identification of Talents, gifts, or skills is the province of career counseling. Its expertise, indeed its *raison d'être*, lies precisely in the identification, classification, and (forgive me) "prioritization" of Talents, skills, and gifts. To put the matter quite simply, career counseling knows how to do this better than any other discipline—**including** traditional religion. This is not a defect of religion, but the fulfillment of something Jesus promised: "When the Spirit of truth comes, He will guide you into all truth" (John 16:13). Career counseling is part (we may hope) of that promised late-coming truth. It can therefore be of inestimable help to the pilgrim who is trying to figure out what their greatest, and most enjoyable, Talent is, as a step toward identifying their unique Mission in life.

If career counseling needs religion as its helpmate in the first two stages of identifying our Mission in life, then religion repays the compliment by clearly needing career counseling as its helpmate here in the third stage.

And this place where you are in your life right now—facing the job hunt and all its anxiety—is the perfect time to seek the union within your own mind and heart of both career counseling (as in the pages of this book) and your faith in God.

Comment 3: How Our Mission Got Chosen— A Scenario for the Romantic

It is a mystery that we cannot fathom, in this life at least, as to why one of us has this Talent, and the other one has that; why God chose to give one gift—and Mission—to one person, and a different gift—and Mission—to another. Since we do not know, and in some degree cannot know, we are certainly left free to speculate, and imagine.

We may imagine that before we came to Earth, our souls, *our Breath, our Light*, stood before the great Creator and volunteered for this Mission. And God and we, together, chose what that Mission would be and what particular gifts would be needed, which He then agreed to give us, after our birth. Thus, our Mission was not a command given peremptorily by an unloving Creator to a reluctant slave without a vote, but was a task jointly designed by us both, in which as fast as the great Creator said, "I wish" our hearts responded, **"Oh, yes."** As mentioned in an earlier comment, it may be helpful to think of the condition of our becoming human as that we became amnesiac about any consciousness our soul had before birth—and therefore amnesiac about the nature or manner in which our Mission was designed.

Our searching for our Mission now is therefore a searching to recover the memory of something we ourselves had a part in designing.

I am admittedly a hopeless romantic, so of course I like this picture. If you also are a hopeless romantic, you may like it, too. There's also the chance that it just may be true. We will not know until we see Him face to face.

Comment 4: Mission as Intersection

There are all different kinds of voices calling you to all different kinds of work, and the problem is to find out which is the voice of God rather than that of society, say, or the superego, or self-interest. By

and large a good rule for finding out is this: the kind of work God usually calls you to is the kind of work a) that you need most to do and b) the world most needs to have done. If you really get a kick out of your work, you've presumably met requirement a), but if your work is writing TV deodorant commercials, the chances are you've missed requirement b). On the other hand, if your work is being a doctor in a leper colony, you have probably met b), but if most of the time you're bored and depressed by it, the chances are you haven't only bypassed a) but probably aren't helping your patients much either. Neither the hair shirt nor the soft will do. The place God calls you to is the place where your deep gladness and the world's deep hunger meet.
—Fred Buechner, *Wishful Thinking—A Theological ABC*[33]

Comment 5: Examples of Mission as Intersection

Your unique and individual Mission will most likely turn out to be a mission of Love, acted out in one or all of three arenas: either in the Kingdom of the Mind, whose goal is to bring more Truth into the world; or in the Kingdom of the Heart, whose goal is to bring more Beauty into the world; or in the Kingdom of the Will, whose goal is to bring more Perfection into the world, through Service.

Here are some examples:

"My mission is, out of the rich reservoir of love that God seems to have given me, to nurture and show love to others—most particularly to those who are suffering from incurable diseases."

"My mission is to draw maps for people to show them how to get to God."

"My mission is to create the purest foods I can, to help people's bodies not get in the way of their spiritual growth."

"My mission is to make the finest harps I can so that people can hear the voice of God in the wind."

"My mission is to make people laugh, so that the travail of this earthly life doesn't seem quite so hard to them."

"My mission is to help people know the truth, in love, about what is happening out in the world, so that there will be more honesty in the world."

"My mission is to weep with those who weep, so that in my arms they may feel themselves in the arms of that Eternal Love that sent me and that created them."

"My mission is to create beautiful gardens, so that in the lilies of the field people may behold the Beauty of God and be reminded of the Beauty of Holiness."

Comment 6: Life as Long as Your Mission Requires

Knowing that you came to Earth for a reason, and knowing what that Mission is, throws an entirely different light upon your life from now on. You are, generally speaking, delivered from any further fear about how long you have to live. You may settle it in your heart that you are here until God chooses to think that you have accomplished your Mission, or until God has a greater Mission for you in another Realm. You need to be a good steward of what He has given you, while you are here; but you do not need to be an anxious steward or stewardess.

You need to attend to your health, *but you do not need to constantly worry about it.* You need to meditate on your death, *but you do not need to be constantly preoccupied with it.* To paraphrase the glorious words of G. K. Chesterton: **We now have a strong desire for living combined with a strange carelessness about dying. We desire life like water and yet are ready to drink death like wine.** We know that we are here to do what we came to do, and we need not worry about anything else.

Comment 7: Using Internet Resources

There is a website that deals with news etc. about all faiths, which you may want to look at: www.beliefnet.com.

Then there is a Jesuit site that leads you in a daily meditation for ten or more minutes (in more than twenty languages with a visual, but otherwise no sound or distraction): http://sacredspace.ie.

There is also a site that gives you a daily podcast of church bells, music, Scripture reading, and meditations or homily, with no visuals, but with sound, and an audio MP3 file that can be sent to your phone, computer, etc.: www.pray-as-you-go.org.

There is a site dedicated to helping you keep a divine consciousness 24/7, by helping you link up to other people of faith, through prayer circles, sharing of personal stories of faith, etc., aimed especially, but not exclusively, toward young adults. Its ultimate message: you are not alone: www.24-7prayer.com/communities.

Lastly, there is a site dedicated to helping you find a spiritual counselor (or "spiritual director"), as well as retreat centers, in the Christian, Islamic, Buddhist, Jewish, or Interfaith faiths: www.sdiworld.org.

Final Comment: A Job Hunt Done Well

If you approach your job hunt as an opportunity to work on this issue as well as the issue of how you will keep body and soul together, then hopefully your job hunt will end with your being able to say: "Life has deep meaning to me now. I have discovered more than my ideal job; I have found my Mission, and the reason why I am here on Earth."

THE FINAL WORDS

FROM RICHARD N. BOLLES

The focus of this book is not on me. It's on You. You are the heroes and heroines of this book. You are the ones who struggle to make life work, who tell me of your victories (and defeats). You are the inventive ones. You are the ones who tell me solutions to job-hunting or career-changing problems that puzzle me.

I know that this book demands a lot of every reader, just as life demands a lot of all of us, and I am amazed at how many of the over ten million people who have bought this book (in one of its annual editions) are willing to sit down and do the hard work of the Self-Inventory in chapters 5 and 6.

It takes more than one person to create a book. My particular thanks go to Lisa Westmoreland and Marci M. Bolles. Lisa was an executive editor at Ten Speed Press and has helped greatly with the form and updating of many editions. And Marci has helped greatly with the typing of this manuscript.

My gratitude also to George Young for his help with updating my veterans handout.

This is a book about jobs, but more importantly it is a book about life and hope. I have learned that the secret of living is not to set as our goal a happy life, nor even a successful life (as the world measures "success"), but a victorious life, meeting the obstacles and challenges that life naturally throws into our path, and by grit, determination, and Grace, overcoming them all. And lucky those who find love on their journey. I quote from what a woman dying of ALS once said: "Throughout all this I have learned that the *only* thing that matters is love. When you live in love, everything else just falls into place." May you find such love in your life. I have, with my wonderful wife, Marci.

But there are others, too. Were it not for this book, and social media sites such as Facebook, I would never have met you, never have known many valiant and courageous souls, as you have faced and faced down so many difficulties that might have defeated me. I don't just appreciate my readers; I admire my readers. You are such an inspiration to me.

I am a grateful man, and this is the place, each year, where I recite my litany of love and gratitude, for all the people in my life, past and present.

First of all, I am enchanted by every moment of my life that I get to spend with such a wondrous woman as my wife, Marci. I treasure her love, brains, wit, and caring. For example, back in 2014 I badly injured my back, while vacationing (*and tossing heavy luggage around*) over in Paris and the UK. Always in excellent health (until then), my recovery has been slow but steady. Marci (*coincidentally a licensed nurse*) has created the most loving, beautiful healing environment all around me, for which I shall ever be grateful. I'm grateful, too, for Marci's grown children from a previous marriage, Janice (Marcel) and Adlai (Aimee), and their kids, Logan and Aiden. They are wonderful to me.

I am grateful beyond measure for the family that brought me into this world. I had a really wonderful Mom and Dad, and I loved the brother I grew up with (the famous reporter/martyr Don Bolles), and my one sister (Ann).

I am so grateful for my children—Stephen, Mark, Gary, and Sharon— and my grandchildren—all ten of them. We lost Mark in 2012 to a massive cerebral hemorrhage, at age fifty-eight. I wept over that, a lot. He lived with me for six out of the last twelve years of his life and was the author of our book *Job-Hunting Online*. He was a treasure.

I am so grateful for my three remaining children and their families, plus their most loving mother, my first wife, Jan, who shares in all our family gatherings.

As for friends—what would any of us do without our friends?—I want to express my gratitude for my dearest friend (*besides Marci*), Daniel Porot of Geneva, Switzerland—we taught together for two weeks every summer, for nineteen years; also for Dave Swanson, plus my international friends, Brian McIvor of Ireland; John Webb and Madeleine Leitner of Germany; Yves Lermusi, of Checkster fame, who came from Belgium; Pete Hawkins of Liverpool, England; Debra Angel MacDougall of Scotland; Byung Ju Cho of South Korea; Tom O'Neil of New Zealand;

and, in this country, the late Howard Figler, beloved friend and coauthor of our manual for career counselors; Marty Nemko; Joel Garfinkle; Dick Knowdell; Rich Feller; Dick Gaither; Warren Farrell; Chuck Young; Susan Joyce; and the folks over at Ten Speed Press in Berkeley, California.

Of course, with the passage of time, friends do die. I think it is important to remember them, with deep gratitude for their lives well-lived. I still think of Howard Figler, whom we lost in February 2015. He was the coauthor with me of *The Career Counselor's Handbook* (second edition, 2007). He and I had years of fun writing together. We also lost Judi Grutter, expert on testing and assessments. She died in December of 2014. Prior to that, we lost Jay Conrad Levinson in October of 2013. He was the popular author of many books on *Guerrilla Marketing*. And prior to him, we lost my longtime publisher, Phil Wood, in December, 2010. He was my publisher from the day I first wrote *Parachute*; he was a dear man, and I owe him more than I can ever say for helping *Parachute* find its audience, and for letting me have great control over the annual editions. *Parachute* would never have sold over ten million copies, as it has, if it were not for him.

I much appreciate the staff over at Ten Speed, whom I know best there: that includes Aaron Wehner (Publisher), Lisa Westmoreland (*my best editor ever*), Ashley Pierce, Mari Gill, Chris Barnes, and George Young. And again, my especial thanks to my readers for buying my books, trusting my counsel, and following your dream.

In concluding my litany of gratitude, I must be sure to include our Creator. It is not fashionable these days to talk about one's faith, but I'm going to do it anyway. I am very quiet about my faith; it's just . . . there. But I want to quietly acknowledge that it is the source of whatever grace, wisdom, or compassion I have ever found, or shared with others. I have all my life been a committed Christian, a devoted follower of Jesus Christ, and an Episcopalian/Anglican. (I was an ordained priest in that Church for fifty years.) I thank my Creator every night for such a life, such a wonderful mission, as He has given me: to help millions of people make their lives really count for something, as we all go spinning through space, here on Spaceship Earth.

FROM KATHARINE BROOKS

First and foremost, I want to thank Richard Bolles for writing a ground-breaking career book that I first read in college, and then again in graduate school, and then used in my practice as a career counselor. And I am not alone. Mr. Bolles singlehandedly influenced career planning and development for many generations of readers and career counselors. It was an honor to be asked to work on this edition.

Thank you to my agent, Bonnie Solow, who never fails to guide me brilliantly through the publishing process. And I could not have had a better editorial experience than working with Lisa Westmoreland and Ashley Pierce at Ten Speed Press. Thank you for your careful and insightful edits.

Many thanks to my colleagues and friends who provided stories and examples throughout the book.

Peggy Jennings, your career has taken many turns and you have always found a way to grow where you are planted. Congratulations on your successful work in your college counseling business.

Heidi Robinson, you are a teacher extraordinaire and one of the most caring and conscientious student advocates I know. I have always appreciated your kindness and support.

Allison McWilliams, you have transformed the alumni career programs at Wake Forest University into a thriving, vital service, and I am thrilled with your growing writing career.

Tricia Rose Burt, you were one of the first alumni I met at Vanderbilt University, and your storytelling, creativity, and engaging personality won me over instantly. Thank you for your willingness to share your story and advice. Watching your one-woman show at the home of Vince Gill and Amy Grant was the ultimate Nashville experience!

I would be remiss if I didn't thank my staff at the career center at Vanderbilt University. You provide such spirit and talent and genuine compassion for our students and alumni. You keep me engaged and energized.

Finally, I would like to thank my supervisors at Vanderbilt University: Dr. John Geer, Dr. Dawn Turton, and Dr. Vanessa Beasley. I have such respect and admiration for the work you do, and I greatly appreciate the support you have provided for my work at Vanderbilt and my writing projects.

DICK BOLLES—more formally known as Richard Nelson Bolles—led the career development field for more than four decades. He was featured in *Time*, the *New York Times, BusinessWeek, Fortune, Money, Fast Company*, the *Economist*, and *Publishers Weekly*, and appeared on the *Today* show, CNN, CBS, ABC, PBS, and other popular media. Bolles keynoted hundreds of conferences, including the American Society for Training & Development and the National Career Development Association. A member of Mensa, the Society for Human Resource Management, and the National Resume Writers Association, he was considered "the most recognized job-hunting authority on the planet" (*San Francisco Chronicle*) and "America's top career expert" (*AARP*).

Time magazine chose *What Color Is Your Parachute?* as one of the hundred best nonfiction books written since 1923. The Library of Congress chose it as one of twenty-five books down through history that have shaped people's lives. It appeared on the *New York Times* bestseller list for more than five years. The book has sold ten million copies, to date, and has been translated into twenty languages and used in twenty-six countries.

Bolles was trained in chemical engineering at Massachusetts Institute of Technology, and earned a bachelor's degree cum laude in physics from Harvard University, a master's in sacred theology from General Theological (Episcopal) Seminary in New York City, and three honorary doctorates. He passed away in 2017 at age ninety after a lifetime of service to job hunters across the world.

Website: **www.jobhuntersbible.com**
Online tools: **www.eparachute.com**

KATHARINE BROOKS, EdD—is an award-winning career counselor and coach who is currently the Evans Family Executive Director of the Career Center for Vanderbilt University. She is a licensed professional counselor, a nationally certified counselor, and a board-certified coach. Previously, she had been the Executive Director of the Office of Personal and Career Development at Wake Forest University and Director of Career Services for the College of Liberal Arts at the University of Texas in Austin. She is the author of *You Majored in What? Designing Your Path from College to Career* and writes a blog "Career Transitions" for *Psychology Today*.

1. Bureau of Labor Statistics, US Department of Labor, Job Opportunities and Labor Turnover Survey, July 9, 2019, https://www.bls.gov/news.release/jolts.htm.

2. Aaron Smith and Janna Anderson, "AI, Robotics, and the Future of Jobs," Pew Research Center, August 6, 2014, www.pewinternet.org/2014/08/06 /future-of-jobs.

3. S. Liu, J. L. Huang, and M. Wang, "Effectiveness of Job Search Interventions: A Meta-Analytic Review, *Psychological Bulletin*, 140, no. 4 (2014), 1009–1041, http://dx.doi.org/10. 1037/a0035923.

4. Brett McIntyre, "How Much Does a Bad Hire Really Cost?" Business 2 Community, August 21, 2018, www.business2community.com/human-resources /how-much-does-a-bad-hire-really-cost-02108605.

5. Bureau of Labor Statistics, US Department of Labor, Table A-12, "Unemployed Persons by Duration of Unemployment," November 2018.

6. Bureau of Labor Statistics, US Department of Labor, Table A-16, "Persons Not in the Labor Force and Multiple Jobholders by Sex, Not Seasonally Adjusted," November 2018.

7. Bureau of Labor Statistics, US Department of Labor, Economic News Release, "Number of Jobs Held, Labor Market Activity, and Earnings Growth Among the Youngest Baby Boomers: Results from a Longitudinal Survey Summary," March 31, 2017, www.bls.gov/news.release/nlsoy.nr0.htm.

8. Richard Fry, "Millennials Are the Largest Generation in the US Labor Force," https://www.pewresearch.org/fact-tank/2018/04/11/millennials-largest -generation-us-labor-force/.

9. Bureau of Labor Statistics, US Department of Labor, Table A-16, "Persons Not in the Labor Force and Multiple Jobholders by Sex, Not Seasonally Adjusted," November 2018.

10. D. H. Pink, *Free Agent Nation: The Future of Working for Yourself* (New York: Warner Books, 2002).

11. Jim Tankersley, "The 21st Century Has Been Terrible for Working Americans," *Washington Post*, March 6, 2015, www.washingtonpost.com/blogs/wonkblo g/wp/2015/03/06/the-21st-century-has-been-terrible-for-working-americans.

12. Bureau of Labor Statistics, US Department of Labor, Economic News Release, "Number of Jobs Held, Labor Market Activity, and Earnings Growth Among the Youngest Baby Boomers: Results from a Longitudinal Survey Summary," August 24, 2017, www.bls.gov/news.release/nlsoy.nr0.htm.

13. Michelle Fox, "58% of Young Workers Plan to Change Jobs This Year to Get More of This—and It's Not Compensation," Make It, April 8, 2019, https://www.cnbc.com/2019/04/08/58percent-of-millennials-plan-to-change-jobs-for-more-learning-opportunities.html.

14. Alan B. Krueger and Andreas Mueller, "Job Search, Emotional Well-Being and Job Finding in a Period of Mass Unemployment: Evidence from High-Frequency Longitudinal Data," *Brookings Papers on Economic Activity*, March 8, 2011.

15. S. Schnall, K. D. Harber, J. K. Stefanucci, and D. R. Proffitt, "Social Support and the Perception of Geographical Slant," *Journal of Experimental Social Psychology*, 44, no. 5 (2008), 1246–1255.

16. Daniel has summarized his system in his book *The PIE Method for Career Success: A Unique Way to Find Your Ideal Job* (JIST Works, 1996). It is now basically out of print but can be found used on Amazon.com, BarnesandNoble.com, or Alibris.com for as little as $5.65 plus shipping. Daniel has a *wonderful* website at www.porot.com/en.

17. Robin Pogrebin, "Pritzker Prize for Frei Otto, German Architect, Is Announced After His Death," *New York Times*, March 10, 2015.

18. Daniel Kahneman and Angus Deaton, *Proceedings of the National Academy of Sciences*, Early Edition, September 6, 2010.

19. Erin Osterhaus, "Half of All Job Seekers Consult Glassdoor Reviews," *ERE*, January 23, 2014, www.eremedia.com/ere/half-of-all-job-seekers-consult-glassdoor-reviews.

20. Gina Belli, "How Many Jobs Are Found Through Networking, Really," Payscale.com, April 6, 2017, www.payscale.com/career-news/2017/04/many-jobs-found-networking.

21. Julia Hobsbawm, "Fully Connected," *EY*, http://ukcareers.ey.com/beingconnected.

22. Mark Granovetter, *Getting a Job: A Study of Contacts and Careers*, 2nd ed. (Chicago: University of Chicago Press, 1995), 52–53.

23. Cision PR Newswire, "More Than Half of Employers Have Found Content on Social Media That Caused Them NOT to Hire a Candidate, According to Recent CareerBuilder Survey," PR Newswire, August 9, 2018, https://www.prnewswire.com/news-releases/more-than-half-of-employers-have-found-content-on-social-media-that-caused-them-not-to-hire-a-candidate-according-to-recent-careerbuilder-survey-300694437. html.

24. https://www.squawkfox.com/8-keywords-that-set-your-resume-on-fire/.

25. Novoresume, "How to Write a Cover Letter in 2020—Beginner's Guide," https://novoresume.com/career-blog/how-to-write-a-cover-letter-guide.

26. For additional reading and guidance: *What Color Is Your Parachute? Guide to Rethinking Resumes* (Berkeley, CA: Ten Speed Press, 2014).

27. Tom Jackson, *The Perfect Resume: Today's Ultimate Job Search Tool* (New York: Broadway Books, 2004).

28. Bain & Company provides a helpful video and article called "What Is a Case Interview?" for preparing for case interviews. at https://www.bain.com/careers /interview-prep/case-interview/.

29. Workforce website, "31 Core Competencies Explained," https://www.workforce .com/2002/09/03/31-core-competencies-explained/.

30. Pink, *Free Agent Nation.*

31. Frank Newport, "Most Americans Still Believe in God," Gallup, September 29, 2016, www.gallup.com/poll/193271/americans-believe-god.aspx.

32. Julian Victor Langmead Casserley, *The Church To-day and To-morrow: The Prospect for Post-Christianity* (London: SPCK, 1965), 102, 113f.

33. Excerpted from *Wishful Thinking—A Theological ABC* by Frederick Buechner, revised edition published by HarperOne. Copyright © 1973, 1993 by Frederick Buechner.

Skype, interviews via, 47, 244, 258–59
Sleep, importance of, 25
Small organizations
  definition of, 91
  targeting, 236–37
Social media
  editing, 212–13
  hashtags and, 220–21
Spiritual counselors, 325
Storytelling, during hiring interviews,
  246–48
Strengths, focusing on, 67–68
Subjects, favorite, 158–59
Success
  defining, 9
  envisioning, 29
  increasing chances of, 9
  stories, 99, 181, 184–85

T
Tattoos, 51, 263
Technology, impact of, 8
TED Talks, 224–25
Temp agencies/temporary work, 15,
  90, 197, 204, 282
Tests
  of traits, 147, 149
  vocational, 76–78
Thank-you notes, 63, 205–6, 264,
  274–75
"That One Piece of Paper" exercise.
  See Flower Exercise
Things, skills dealing with, 142
Traits, 131, 132, 147–50
Twitter, 218, 223–24

U
Unemployment
  employer bias and, 47
  feelings during, 23–35
  length of, 13–14
  national statistics on, 7
  as opportunity, 100–101, 312

Unions, 89–90
Uniqueness, identifying your, 67–68,
  255–56, 317–18

V
Vacancies
  existence of, 6–7
  preferred methods for filling,
    employers' vs. job hunters', 9–12
Values, importance of, 265
Veterans, 50
Videos, 224–25
Vision boards, 29
Vocation, 312. *See also* Mission in life
Vocational tests, 76–78
Volunteer work, 197, 204–5

W
Websites
  with employee reviews, 203
  with forums and groups, 221–22
  on gig economy, 90
  of organizations, 203
  on religious beliefs, 325
  with resume examples, 232
  on salaries, 281–82
  on self-employment, 299–300
  See also Internet
"Working conditions petal" on
  Flower Diagram, 124–29

Y
YouTube, 224–25

Z
Zoom, interviews via, 47, 244,
  258–59, 301

THE COMPLETE PARACHUTE LIBRARY

A quick guide to the job search, for when time is of the essence.

A slender guide to writing a winning resume and cover letter that will help you land interviews.

A slender guide to help you ace the interview and land your dream job.

A guide to help students zero in on the perfect major or career.

How to choose a major, create a four-year plan, and make the most of your college experience.

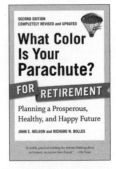

Practical tools and exercises for a prosperous retirement.

A fill-in edition of the famous Flower Exercise.

Learn to use the internet effectively for all aspects of your job-hunt.

A complete guide for practicing or aspiring career counselors.

Visit parachutebook.com and JobHuntersBible.com

Available from Ten Speed Press wherever books are sold.
www.tenspeed.com